21世纪高等学校专业英语系列教材

经济学

专业英语教程（第2版）

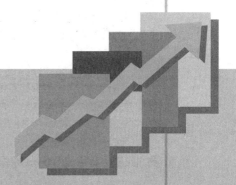

主　编　易　舫　帅力戈　帅建林
副主编　张　青　邓利娜

扫码获取相关教学资源

清　华　大　学　出　版　社
北京交通大学出版社
·北京·

内容简介

本书是以经济学专业知识为主线，厘定微观经济学、宏观经济学和国际经济学的重要内容，以经济学各知识点为平台创建的案例做支撑，以英语为工作语言而打造的一本特色鲜明的专业英语教材。本书各章知识点自成体系，选材严谨，涉及西方经济学中最为根本的概念和理论，既有供需、效用、生产、价格、增长、宏观经济政策等经济学理论概念，又有全球化背景下必须了解的国际经济学基础知识，如世界贸易、国际投资、跨国公司、国际金融市场、外汇市场、经济一体化等。本书所选材料语言地道，行文自然流畅，使读者在学习经济学知识的同时，强化英语应用能力，提高经济学专业英语水平。

本书适合的对象是经济学及相关专业的学生及试图将自己历练为"经济学+英语"或"英语+经济学"复合型人才的读者。

本书封面贴有清华大学出版社防伪标签，无标签者不得销售。
版权所有，侵权必究。侵权举报电话：010-62782989　13501256678　13801310933

图书在版编目（CIP）数据

经济学专业英语教程／易舫，帅力戈，帅建林主编. —2版. —北京：北京交通大学出版社：清华大学出版社，2023.8
ISBN 978-7-5121-5037-9

Ⅰ.经… Ⅱ.①易… ②帅… ③帅… Ⅲ.经济学-英语-高等学校-教材　Ⅳ.F0

中国国家版本馆 CIP 数据核字（2023）第 129955 号

经济学专业英语教程
JINGJIXUE ZHUANYE YINGYU JIAOCHENG

责任编辑：	张利军
出版发行：	清华大学出版社　邮编：100084　电话：010-62776969　http://www.tup.com.cn
	北京交通大学出版社　邮编：100044　电话：010-51686414　http://www.bjtup.com.cn
印　刷　者：	北京时代华都印刷有限公司
经　　　销：	全国新华书店
开　　　本：	185 mm×260 mm　印张：16.25　字数：406千字
版　印　次：	2008年10月第1版　2023年8月第2版　2023年8月第1次印刷
定　　　价：	49.00元

本书如有质量问题，请向北京交通大学出版社质监组反映。对您的意见和批评，我们表示欢迎和感谢。
投诉电话：010-51686043，51686008；传真：010-62225406；E-mail：press@bjtu.edu.cn。

第2版前言

这本备受期待的《经济学专业英语教程》(第2版)终于跟大家见面了。它承载着全国200多所使用该教材的高等院校的期盼,承载着学界专家学者的鼓励和鞭策,承载着广大读者的厚爱。因此,编者倍感责任重大。

构思编写这本《经济学专业英语教程》始于2003年。第1版,于2008年10月出版;第1版修订本,于2020年1月出版,2021年8月进行了第6次印刷。市场的响应热度、读者的选择和需求,证实了读者对该书的认可,肯定了该书的价值。

多年以来,我们这个编写团队所经历的"经济学/金融学+英语"及"英语+经济学/国际贸易学/金融学等学科"艰辛的复合型知识构建学习过程,让我们感受到通过英语学习经济学专业知识的重要性,以及在经济学背景下历练专业英语能力的迫切性。因此,我们的编写动机始于一丝焦虑,源于一份责任。每当目睹经贸专业的高年级大学生对经济学专业英文文献诚惶诚恐,而英语专业的高年级本科生及研究生在翻译现场为经济术语和经济理论吞吞吐吐、尴尬万分时,我们焦虑,我们责无旁贷。

我们深知,我们的编写工作不是孤军奋战。我们看到了同行的行动,感受到了同行的努力。一本本类似教材和著作如雨后春笋般涌现,我们欣赏同行的视角和智慧。这本书的编写,我们承认是站在他们的肩膀上,但也许看得更远。我们承诺将竭力终身维护、精心打磨这本教材。

本书的主要特点如下。

(1) 体系合理,结构紧凑。全书共分20个单元,共20个主题,各单元知识点自成体系,涉及西方经济学中最为根本的理论和概念,既有供需、效用、生产、价格、增长、宏观经济政策等宏、微观经济学理论和概念,又有全球化背景下必须了解的国际经济学基础知识,如世界贸易、国际投资、跨国公司、国际金融市场、外汇市场、经济一体化等。

(2) 理论平台,案例支撑。每单元由Text(课文)和Case Study(案例分析)两部分构成。课文清晰地阐述了该主题所涉及的经济学理论和概念。案例分析则用课文中的经济学理论解读经济现象,尤其中国经济现象,或指导经济实践,或用案例进一步阐释经济理论,从而增强理论的实践性、操作性、针对性和本书的可读性、趣味性,进一步扩大读者的视野,培养读者分析实际问题的能力。

(3) 语言地道,原汁原味。课文均选自英美经典原版经济学著作,原汁原味,精髓地道。案例分析则选材于 Financial Times、The Wall Street Journal、Economics 等英美著名报刊和网站,其视角独特、思想深邃、解读透彻、评论权威、语言精练。

I

（4）解困释惑，拓展技能。每篇课文后配有词汇表、课文注释和专项语言技能训练。词汇表按词汇在文中出现的先后顺序排列，易于检索，便于自学。课文注释简明扼要、综合全面、突出重点，将读者之困惑一扫而光。专项语言技能训练以提高读者运用英语直接进行专业交流的能力为宗旨，通过英汉互译、多项选择等专项训练拓展读者在经济实践背景下的英语语言技能，注重表达，着眼实用。案例分析后面所设计的开放式讨论题目旨在培养学生的批判性阅读习惯，激发思考，探索未知。

总之，本书的编写既着眼于高等院校财经专业学生、财经类院校学生及广大财经工作者的专业知识结构和语言技能现状，又关注中国经济发展对经济学理论提出的现实课题和前瞻性要求。本书以提高高等院校财经专业和财经类院校学生用英语作为语言工具进行专业学术和实践交流的技能为出发点，以经济学的基本概念和基础理论为编排核心，强调课文内容具有实用性、练习具有针对性、讨论具有互动性，高度关注全书课文、案例分析与练习之间的协调性。

通读本书，读者可以了解经济学理论的基本理论框架，掌握经济学基本概念和理论，了解经济学的思想和精髓，学习研究经济问题的视角，把握经济学理论的发展方向，从而丰富自身的智慧，在新的经济发展浪潮中提出新的问题，探索新的答案。

本书内容以经济学专业知识为主线，同时注重培养学生的英语语言技能。因此，学生在学习经济学知识的同时，又可锤炼其英语应用能力。作为兼具经济学专业知识培养与语言训练功能的教程，本书的内容深入浅出但又具有系统性，对于已经具有一定英语基础同时又想运用英语研修经济学相关知识的读者来说，本书是相当适合的。它既是较为理想的"英语+经济学"的专业英语教材，也是引导读者进入经济学殿堂的导读教材。

本书由成都理工大学外国语学院易舫副教授、西南财经大学帅建林博士、成都树桐出入境服务有限公司副总经理帅力戈先生担任主编，由成都树桐出入境服务有限公司教学校长张青女士、成都树桐出入境服务有限公司项目总监邓利娜老师担任副主编。其中，具体的编写分工为：易舫负责编写第1、2、3、4、5、8单元，承担编务工作并审读、总撰全部书稿；帅力戈负责编写第6、7、9、11、12单元，承担部分编务工作并审读书稿；张青负责编写第10、13、14单元，并承担部分编务工作；邓利娜负责编写第15、16单元，并承担部分编务工作；帅建林负责编写第17、18、19、20单元，承担全书的总策划、编写体例的确定及部分编务工作，厘定各单元的主题，并总撰和审读全部书稿。

我们在此对本书所选材料的原刊出单位和机构及相关的著作者表示诚挚的谢意。同时，本书能够顺利出版，要感谢清华大学出版社和北京交通大学出版社的大力支持，尤其要感谢一直呵护本书的张利军编辑，如果没有他的鼓励和支持，这本书早就搁浅了。

由于编写仓促，书中不足之处在所难免，敬请广大读者指正赐教。

编　者
2023年6月于成都

第1版前言

构思编写这本《经济学专业英语教材》至少是我们六年前的想法了。多年以来，我们这个编写团队所经历的"经济学/金融学＋英语"及"英语＋经济学/国际贸易学/金融学等学科"艰辛的复合型知识构建学习过程，让我们感受到通过英语学习经济学专业知识的重要性，以及在经济学背景下历练专业英语能力的迫切性。因此，我们的编写动机始于一丝焦虑，源于一份责任。每当目睹经贸专业的高年级大学生对经济学专业英文文献诚惶诚恐，英语专业的高年级本科生和研究生在翻译现场为经济术语和经济理论吞吞吐吐、尴尬万分时，我们焦虑，我们责无旁贷。

我们深知，六年以来我们错过了很多机会。但是，我们看到了同行的行动，感受到了同行的努力。一本本类似教材和著作如雨后春笋般涌现，我们欣赏同行的视角和智慧。这本书的编写，我们承认是站在他们的肩膀上，但也许看得更远。

本书的主要特点如下。

（1）体系合理，结构紧凑。全书共分 15 个单元，共 15 个主题，各单元知识点自成体系，涉及西方经济学中最为根本的概念和理论，既有供需、效用、生产、价格、增长、宏观经济政策等经济学理论概念，又有全球化背景下必须了解的国际经济学基础知识，如世界贸易、国际投资、跨国公司、国际金融市场、外汇市场、经济一体化等。

（2）理论平台，案例支撑。每单元由 Text（课文）和 Case Study（案例分析）两部分构成。课文清晰地阐述了该主题所涉及的经济学理论和概念。案例分析则用课文中的经济学理论解读经济现象，尤其中国经济现象，或指导经济实践，或用案例进一步阐释经济理论，从而增强了理论的实践性、操作性、针对性和本书的可读性、趣味性，进一步扩大了读者的视野，培养读者分析实际问题的能力。

（3）语言地道，原汁原味。课文均选自英美经典原版经济学著作，原汁原味，精髓地道。案例分析则选材于 *Financial Times*、*The Wall Street Journal*、*Economics* 等英美著名报纸杂志和网站，其视角独特、思想深邃、解读透彻、评论权威、语言精练。

（4）解困释惑，拓展技能。每篇课文后配有词汇表、课文注释和专项语言技能训练。词汇表按词汇在文中出现的先后顺序排列，易于检索，便于自学。课文注释简明扼要、综合全面、突出重点，将读者困惑一扫而光。专项语言技能训练以提高读者运用英语直接进行专业交流的能力为宗旨，通过英汉互译、多项选择等专项训练拓展读者在经济实践背景下的英语语言技能，注重表达，着眼实用。案例分析后面所设计的开放式讨论题目旨在培养学生的批判性阅读习惯，激发思考，探索未知。

总之，本书的编写既着眼于目前财经院校学生和广大财经工作者的专业知识结构和语言技能现状，又关注中国经济发展对经济学理论提出的现实课题和前瞻性要求。本书以提高财经院校学生用英语作为语言工具进行专业学术和实践交流的技能为出发点，以经济学的基本概念和基础理论为编排核心，强调课文内容具有实用性、练习具有针对性、讨论具有互动性，高度关注全书课文、案例分析与练习之间的协调性。

通读本书，读者可以了解经济学理论的基本理论框架，掌握经济学基本概念和理论，了解经济学的思想和精髓，学习研究经济问题的视角，把握经济学理论的发展方向，从而丰富自身的智慧，在新的经济发展浪潮中提出新的问题，探索新的答案。

本书内容以经济学专业知识为主线，同时注重培养学生的英语语言技能。因此，学生在学习经济学知识的同时，又可锤炼其英语应用能力。作为兼具经济学专业知识培养与语言训练功能的教程，本书的课文内容深入浅出但又具有系统性，对于已经具有一定英语基础同时又想运用英语研修经济学相关知识的读者来说，本书是相当适合的。它既是较为理想的"英语+经济学"的专业英语教材，也是引导读者进入经济学殿堂的导读教材。

本书由西南财经大学帅建林、曾志远担任主编，西南财经大学何莉娟、黄银东、吉松涛、栾宏琼及乐山师范学院易俗担任副主编。其中，具体的编写分工为：黄银东编写第1、3、4单元；栾宏琼编写第5、6、7单元；何莉娟编写第8、9、13单元；吉松涛编写第14单元，并审读全部书稿；易俗编写第2、10、11单元的练习题；曾志远编写第2、10单元，厘定各单元的主题，并审读全部书稿；帅建林编写第11、12、15单元，负责全书的总策划、编写体例及所有编务工作，并总撰和审读全部书稿。

我们在此对本书所选材料的原刊出单位和机构及相关的著作者表示诚挚的谢意。同时，本书能够顺利出版，要感谢北京交通大学出版社的大力支持，尤其要感谢一直呵护本书的责任编辑张利军，如果没有他的鼓励和支持，这本书早就搁浅了。

由于编写仓促，书中不足之处在所难免，敬请广大读者指正赐教。

编　者
2008年10月于成都光华园

目 录

Unit 1	Definition of Economics	1
Unit 2	Supply and Demand	13
Unit 3	Utility	24
Unit 4	Production	33
Unit 5	Price System	47
Unit 6	Enterprises in the Competitive Market	58
Unit 7	Monopoly Market	70
Unit 8	GDP and GNP	83
Unit 9	Unemployment and Inflation	95
Unit 10	Macro-economic Policy	109
Unit 11	Monetary Policy	120
Unit 12	Saving, Investment and the Financial System	133
Unit 13	Economic Growth	150
Unit 14	An Overview of International Economics	163
Unit 15	World Trade and National Economy	175
Unit 16	Import and Export Practices	186
Unit 17	Economic Integration	200
Unit 18	Investment and Multinational Corporation	214
Unit 19	International Financial Market	226
Unit 20	Foreign Exchange Market	238
References		249

Unit 1
Definition of Economics

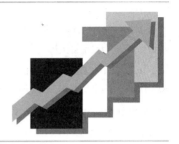

Introduction

Economics is a social science concerned with the production, distribution, exchange, and consumption of goods and services. Economists focus on the way in which individuals, groups, business enterprises, and governments seek to achieve efficiently any economic objective they select. Other fields of study also contribute to this knowledge: psychology and ethics try to explain how objectives are formed; history records changes in human objectives; sociology interprets human behavior in social contexts.

Part One Text

Economics Basics: Introduction

Economics may appear to be the study of complicated tables and charts, statistics and numbers, but, more specifically, it is the study of what constitutes rational human behavior in the endeavor to fulfill needs and wants.

As an individual, for example, you face the problem of having only limited resources with which to fulfill your wants and needs, and as a result, you must make certain choices with your money. You'll probably spend part of your money on rent, electricity and food. Then you might use the rest to go to the movies and/or buy a new pair of jeans. Economists are interested in the choices you make, and inquire into why, for instance, you might choose to spend your money on a new DVD player instead of replacing your old TV. They would want to know whether you would still buy a carton of cigarettes if prices increased by $2 per pack. The underlying essence of economics is trying to understand how both individuals and nations behave in response to certain material constraints.

We can say, therefore, that economics, often referred to as the "dismal science", is a study of certain aspects of society. Adam Smith (1723-1790), the "father of modern economics" and author of the famous book *An Inquiry into the Nature and Causes of the Wealth of Nations*, spawned the discipline of economics by trying to understand why some nations prospered while others lagged behind in poverty. Others after him also explored how a nation's allocation of resources affects its wealth.

To study these things, economics makes the assumption that human beings will aim to fulfill their self-interests. It also assumes that individuals are rational in their efforts to fulfill their unlimited wants and needs. Economics, therefore, is a social science, which examines people behaving according to their self-interests. The definition set out at the turn of the twentieth century by Alfred Marshall, author of *Principles of Economics* (1890), reflects the complexity underlying economics: "Thus it is on one side the study of wealth; and on the other, and more important side, a part of the study of man."

What Is Economics?

In order to begin our discussion of economics, we first need to understand the concept of scarcity and the two branches of study within economics: microeconomics and macroeconomics.

1. Scarcity

Scarcity refers to the tension between our limited resources and our unlimited wants and needs. For an individual, resources include time, money and skill. For a country, limited resources include natural resources, capital, labor force and technology.

Because all of our resources are limited in comparison to all of our wants and needs, individuals and nations have to make decisions regarding what goods and services they can buy and which ones they must forgo. For example, if you choose to buy one DVD as opposed to two video tapes, you must give up owning a second movie of inferior technology in exchange for the higher quality of the one DVD. Of course, each individual and nation will have different values, but by having different levels of (scarce) resources, people and nations each form some of these values as a result of the particular scarcities with which they are faced.

So, because of scarcity, people and economies must make decisions over how to allocate their resources. Economics, in turn, aims to study why we make these decisions and how we allocate our resources most efficiently.

2. Macroeconomics and Microeconomics

Macro and microeconomics are the two vantage points from which the economy is observed. Macroeconomics looks at the total output of a nation and the way the nation allocates its limited resources of land, labor and capital in an attempt to maximize production levels and promote trade and growth for future generations. After observing the society as a whole, Adam Smith noted that there was an "invisible hand" turning the wheels of the economy: a market force that keeps the economy functioning.

Microeconomics looks into similar issues, but on the level of the individual people and firms within the economy. It tends to be more scientific in its approach, and studies the parts that make up the whole economy. Analyzing certain aspects of human behavior, microeconomics shows us how individuals and firms respond to changes in price and why they demand what they do at particular price levels.

Micro and macroeconomics are intertwined; as economists gain understanding of certain phenomena, they can help nations and individuals make more informed decisions when allocating resources. The systems by which nations allocate their resources can be placed on a spectrum where the command economy is on the one end and the market economy is on the other. The market economy advocates forces within a competitive market, which constitute the "invisible hand", to determine how resources should be allocated. The command economic system relies on the government to decide how the country's resources would best be allocated. In both systems, however, scarcity and unlimited wants force governments and individuals to decide how best to manage resources and allocate them in the most efficient way possible. Nevertheless, there are always limits to what the economy and government can do.

Words and Expressions

spawn	v.	引起，缔造，酿成
underlie	v.	构成……的潜在原因，成为……的基础
forgo	v.	放弃，弃绝
allocate	v.	分配，配置
intertwine	v.	缠结，交织
informed	a.	见闻广的，有根据的
spectrum	n.	范围，幅度

advocate	v.	倡导
constitute	v.	构成
vantage point		有利位置；观点，看法

1. **Adam Smith** 亚当·斯密（1723—1790）

   Adam Smith is a Scottish economist who strongly believed in free enterprise（自由企业制度，an economic system in which private businesses are free to make money, and there is not much government control）. He developed his ideas in his book *The Wealth of Nations*, which has had an important influence on modern economic and political ideas.

2. **An Inquiry into the Nature and Causes of the Wealth of Nations** 《国民财富的性质和原因研究》（简称《国富论》）

   In his famous treatise, *The Wealth of Nations*, Adam Smith argued that private competition free from regulation produces and distributes wealth better than government-regulated markets. Since 1776, when Smith produced his work, his argument has been used to justify capitalism and discourage government intervention（政府干预）in trade and exchange. Smith believed that private businesses seeking their own interests organize the economy most efficiently, "as if by an invisible hand".

3. **allocation of resources** 资源配置

   It refers to apportionment of productive assets among different uses. Resource allocation arises as an issue because the resources of a society are in limited supply, whereas human wants are usually unlimited, and because any given resource can have many alternative uses. In free-enterprise systems, the price system is the primary mechanism through which resources are distributed.

4. **Alfred Marshall** 阿尔弗雷德·马歇尔（1842—1924）

   British economist, born in Bermondsey, London, England, and educated at Saint John's College, University of Cambridge. Marshall was the foremost British economist of his time. He was also an outstanding teacher and exerted a strong influence on the following generation of European and American economists. His principal contribution to economics lay in systematizing classical economic theories and in developing a concept of marginal utility. He emphasized the importance of detailed analysis and adjustment of theory to emerging facts. Marshall's writings include *Principles of Economics*（1890） *and Industry* and *Trade* (1919).

5. **Principles of Economics** 《经济学原理》
Marshall's most important book was *Principles of Economics*. In it Marshall emphasized that the price and output of a good are determined by both supply and demand: the two curves are like scissor blades that intersect at equilibrium. Modern economists trying to understand why the price of a good changes still start by looking for factors that may have shifted demand or supply. They owe this approach to Marshall.

6. **scarcity** 短缺
In economics, scarcity is defined as a condition of limited resources and unlimited wants and needs, i.e. the society does not have sufficient resources to produce enough to fulfill subjective wants. Alternatively, scarcity implies that not all of society's goals can be attained at the same time, so that trade-offs(贸易，交换) are made of one good against others. Neoclassical economics(新古典经济学派), the dominant school of economics today, defines its field as involving scarcity: following Lionel Robbins'(利奥尼尔·罗宾斯, 1898—1984, 英国经济学家, 伦敦学派主要代表人物) definition, economics is a science which studies human behavior as a relationship between ends and scarce means which have alternative uses.

7. **microeconomics** 微观经济学
Microeconomics is a branch of Economics that studies how individuals, households, and firms make decisions to allocate limited resources, typically in markets where goods or services are being bought and sold. Microeconomics examines how these decisions and behaviors affect the supply and demand for goods and services, which determines prices, and how prices, in turn, determine the supply and demand of goods and services. Macroeconomics(宏观经济学), on the other hand, involves the "sum total of economic activity, dealing with the issues of growth, inflation, and unemployment and with national economic policies relating to these issues" and the effects of government actions (e.g., changing taxation levels) on them. Particularly in the wake of the Lucas critique (卢卡斯批判, 指新古典经济学派代表人物、诺贝尔经济学奖得主罗伯特·卢卡斯于1976年对传统大型计量模型所做的政策检测结果提出的质疑), much of modern macroeconomic theory has been built upon "micro-foundations" — i.e. based upon basic assumptions about micro-level behaviour.

8. **command economy** 计划经济
A command economy (also known as a planned economy or centrally planned economy) is an economic system in which the state or government controls the factors of production and makes all decisions about their use and about the distribution of income. In such an economy, the planners decide what should be produced and direct enterprises to produce those goods. Planned economies are in contrast to unplanned economies, i.e. a market

economy(市场经济), where production, distribution, and pricing decisions are made by the private owners of the factors of production based upon their own interests rather than upon furthering some overarching macroeconomic plan.

I Make verb phrases by linking those in Column A and Column B.

Column A	Column B
promote	resources
maximize	assumptions
spawn	trade and growth
make	production levels
manage	discipline

II Match the following words or terms with their definitions.

advocate	spectrum	constitute	resource	want
production	discipline	allocate	economics	scarcity

1. _____ : to use something for a particular purpose
2. _____ : a complete range of opinions, people, situations, etc.
3. _____ : publicly say that something should be done
4. _____ : form, make up
5. _____ : an area of knowledge or teaching
6. _____ : all the money, property, skills, etc. that you have available to use
7. _____ : something that you need
8. _____ : a situation in which there is not enough of something
9. _____ : the process of making or growing things to be sold
10. _____ : the study of the way in which money and goods are produced and used

III Reading comprehension: choose the best answer from the four choices.

1. Why economics is categorized as a social science?
    A. Because it is the study of what constitutes rational human behavior in the endeavor to fulfill needs and wants, a study of certain aspects of society.

B. Because it studies complicated tables and charts, statistics and numbers.

C. Because it is regarded as a "dismal science".

D. Because it studies the economic phenomena of a country.

2. What is the relationship between scarcity and allocation of resources?

A. Natural resources are all exhaustible and that is what scarcity is all about.

B. Because all of our resources are limited in comparison to all of our wants and needs, people and economies must make decisions over how to allocate their resources.

C. They are mutually dependent and mutually inclusive.

D. We have to allocate properly those limited resources.

3. What is the "invisible hand" as noted by Adam Smith?

A. It is the governmental manipulation.

B. It is consumers' consumption habit.

C. It is social moral principles.

D. It is a market force that keeps the economy functioning.

4. Briefly distinguish between macroeconomics and microeconomics.

A. They look into similar issues, but the former at the total output of a nation and the way the nation allocates its limited resources while the latter on the level of the individual people and firms within the economy.

B. They study quite different issues and are 2 branches of a discipline.

C. They study the same issues but employ different study methods.

D. They study similar issues but originated from different times.

Part Two Case Study

TEN YEARS ON

HOW ASIA SHRUGGED OFF ITS ECONOMIC CRISIS

From *The Economist Intelligence Unit ViewsWire*, July 4th, 2007

Ten years ago, on July 2nd 1997, Thailand's central bank floated the baht[①] after failing to protect the currency from speculative attack. The move triggered a financial and economic collapse that quickly spread to other economies in the region,

---

① 铢(泰国的货币名称)

causing GDP growth rates to contract precipitously①, bankrupting companies that had overexposed themselves to foreign-currency risk, and ultimately necessitating costly and politically humiliating IMF-led bailouts② in the worst-affected countries. Thus began the Asian financial crisis of 1997 – 1998. Its effects, and governments' subsequent responses to it, have defined much of the region's economic policies and direction in the past decade. What has been learnt, and how has the region changed in the intervening period?

The financial crisis can be described as having been a "perfect storm": a confluence③ of various conditions that not only created financial and economic turbulence but also greatly magnified its impact. Among the key conditions were the presence of fixed or semi-fixed exchange rates in countries such as Thailand, Indonesia and South Korea; large current-account deficits that created downward pressure on those countries' currencies, encouraging speculative attacks; and high domestic interest rates that had encouraged companies to borrow heavily offshore (at lower interest rates) in order to fund aggressive and poorly supervised investment. Weak oversight of domestic lending and, in some cases, rising public debt also contributed to the crisis and made its effects worse once the problems had begun.

If factors such as exchange-rate policies had helped to precipitate the financial crisis, above all it was excessive and poorly supervised foreign borrowing that made it so disastrous. As it became too expensive to fend off speculators, currencies were forced to float. This resulted in large falls in the baht, the won and the rupiah④ against the US dollar. For instance, from an average of Rp2,342 to the US dollar in 1996, the rupiah fell to an average of Rp10,014 in 1998. As a result, companies that had received large unhedged⑤ foreign-currency loans now faced impossibly high debt repayments in domestic-currency terms. The panicked capital flight that ensued only exacerbated the currency depreciation, leaving indebted companies in even direr straits. The workout of the bad debts and disposal of the distressed assets created by the crisis was one of the major tasks for policymakers for several years thereafter.

The situation now could not be more different. Most Asian economies now enjoy sizeable current-account surpluses and have built up extensive foreign-exchange reserves with which, in theory, they could protect their currencies from speculative attack in future. (Indeed, it is an enduring complaint of economists these days that Asian countries have gone too far in the opposite direction, having built up far greater levels of

---

① 急转直下地，突然而来地
② 应付紧急状况
③ 汇集
④ 印尼盾
⑤ 无保证或没有套期保值的

reserves than they need.) Non-performing loans (NPLs)① in the banking sector have fallen, and extensive financial reforms have taken place. As a result, not only are the region's fundamentals no longer conducive to an exact repeat of the 1997 - 1998 crisis, but regulatory controls have also, by and large, improved substantially. Thus, even were some of the conditions that existed in 1996 and early 1997 to reappear in the region, it would no longer be so easy for companies to get themselves into as much trouble as they did then.

This does not mean, of course, that the region no longer faces substantial economic risks. New imbalances and problems have emerged in the past few years, in part relating to the massive US current-account deficit and Asian central banks' large holdings of US Treasuries. The following paragraphs explore the specific changes that individual "crisis" economies in Asia have undergone in the past decade, and the new challenges and risks they face.

Thailand

A decade on from the financial crisis of 1997, Thailand finds itself in the midst of another crisis, this time a political one. Although the economy has been suffering from a downturn in business confidence in the wake of the September 2006 military coup, Thailand's economic fundamentals are nevertheless generally strong. Indeed, rather than battling the markets to prop up the baht, the Bank of Thailand (BOT, the central bank) has been under pressure to weaken it. In order to do so, in late 2006 the BOT imposed controls on the inflow of capital. The baht now stands at a nine-year high of around Bt34.5:US$1 on the local market, and on the offshore market it has risen to Bt32.3:US$1.

The country's external accounts are far healthier: the current account has been in surplus every year since 1997 except 2005; foreign-exchange reserves have soared to US$71 bn, up from the 1997 low of US$26 bn reached when the BOT gave up its costly efforts to keep the baht fixed to the dollar; and external debt levels have dropped sharply, with most of the private sector's short-term debt taking the form of trade credits rather than loans, a reversal from the pre-1997 situation.

The banking sector has also recovered well, with NPLs dropping to around 4% - 5% of total outstanding loans — a decade ago the ratio was close to 50%. A process of consolidation in the banking sector has also been under way since 2004, and regulatory standards and bank lending practices have improved markedly.

---

① 坏账

South Korea

"The bigger they are, the harder they fall," is a maxim that aptly describes South Korea's experiences — and those of many of the chaebol①, the country's industrial conglomerates② — during the Asian financial crisis. South Korea was one of the countries worst hit by the crisis, and its IMF-led emergency bail-out programme cost around US$ 60 bn.

To its credit, South Korea has also been one of the most diligent countries in implementing post-crisis economic and financial reforms, and it is now reaping the rewards of these efforts. The country's financial sector is one of the region's strongest, combining greater openness with better regulation. It is a measure of the improvement in prudential standards that the crisis among overextended credit-card lenders in 2003 had almost no contagious effect on the broader financial system.

In addition, South Korea's economy is now more transparent and flexible, interest rates are lower, and foreign reserves — which at the height of the crisis in December 1997 were down to US$ 8.9 bn — have risen massively, to US$ 243 bn as of end-March 2007. Indeed, South Korea is typical of post-crisis Asian economies in that it now faces considerable difficulty in preventing further accumulation of foreign reserves and keeping its currency from appreciating. This is a concern for exporters, particularly given the current weakness of the yen, as South Korean industrial exporters compete with Japan in numerous sectors.

Despite the progress on reforms that South Korea has made, unfinished business remains. This is particularly the case with regard to the labour market, which is still rigid and prone to disruptive unrest.

Hong Kong

Hong Kong's small and open economy is inherently vulnerable to events outside its control. As a result, despite not suffering from any of the imbalances that the other crisis-hit economies were showing on the eve of the Asian financial crisis, Hong Kong ended up being one of the worst hit by the turmoil. Real GDP contracted by 5.5% in 1998, and with the territory suffering from six consecutive years of deflation, nominal GDP in Hong Kong did not overtake its pre-crisis level until 2005. Growth in the first five years after the crisis continued to be volatile, with the economy suffering a deep downturn in

---

① 韩国综合企业财团
② 集团,联合大企业

2001, after the collapse of the dotcom bubble① in the US; the economy also wobbled again briefly in 2003, at the height of the SARS crisis.

However, the past three years have seen a return to sustained, strong economic growth, with real GDP growing by an average of 7.7% in the period 2004 – 2006. The main reason for this strong recovery has been the fast-growing economy of Chinese mainland. Booming trade with Chinese mainland has led to a big increase in Hong Kong's re-export trade, and has driven a massive expansion in Hong Kong's container port throughput②, as well as air cargo traffic. Looser travel restrictions on tourists from Chinese mainland have also provided a significant boost to Hong Kong's hotel, restaurant and retail sectors. Finally, the listing③ of a number of major companies from Chinese mainland in the past two years, including three of China's "Big Four" state-owned banks④, has given a significant boost to Hong Kong's important financial-services sector.

Although Hong Kong has recovered strongly from the Asian financial crisis, the openness of the economy means that Hong Kong's prospects will continue to be tied to events elsewhere. Although the territory's closer integration with the mainland economy may have made it less vulnerable to a slowdown in Asian growth, by the same token it has also made Hong Kong more vulnerable to a slowdown in Chinese growth.

Questions for Discussion

1. What is the cause for the Asian financial crisis of 1997 – 1998?

2. How did Asia recover from the crisis?

3. What is special about Hong Kong's economy?

---

① 网络泡沫
② 吞吐量
③ 上市
④ 中国四大国有商业银行

Translation

1. The move triggered a financial and economic collapse that quickly spread to other economies in the region, causing GDP growth rates to contract precipitously, bankrupting companies that had overexposed themselves to foreign-currency risk, and ultimately necessitating costly and politically humiliating IMF-led bailouts in the worst-affected countries.

2. "The bigger they are, the harder they fall," is a maxim that aptly describes South Korea's experiences — and those of many of the chaebol, the country's industrial conglomerates — during the Asian financial crisis.

3. Hong Kong's small and open economy is inherently vulnerable to events outside its control. As a result, despite not suffering from any of the imbalances that the other crisis-hit economies were showing on the eve of the Asian financial crisis, Hong Kong ended up being one of the worst hit by the turmoil.

4. Although Hong Kong has recovered strongly from the Asian financial crisis, the openness of the economy means that Hong Kong's prospects will continue to be tied to events elsewhere. Although the territory's closer integration with the mainland economy may have made it less vulnerable to a slowdown in Asian growth, by the same token it has also made Hong Kong more vulnerable to a slowdown in Chinese growth.

Unit 2
Supply and Demand

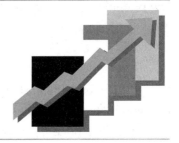

Introduction

Supply and demand is perhaps one of the most fundamental concepts of economics and it is the backbone of a market economy. To put it simple, supply is materials or products that are made available to you and me. Demand is certain materials or products that you and I buy. So, the market price of a good is determined by both the supply and the demand for it. The price level of a good essentially is determined by the point at which quantity supplied equals to quantity demanded.

Part One Text

Supply and demand is perhaps one of the most fundamental concepts of economics and it is the backbone of a market economy. Demand refers to how much (quantity) of a product or service is desired by buyers. The quantity demanded is the amount of a product people are willing to buy at a certain price; the relationship between price and quantity demanded is known as the demand relationship. Supply represents how much the market can offer. The quantity supplied refers to the amount of a certain good producers are willing to supply when receiving a certain price①. The correlation between price and how much of a good or service is supplied to the market is known as the supply relationship. Price, therefore, is a reflection of supply and demand.

The relationship between demand and supply underlie the forces behind the allocation of resources. In market economy theories, demand and supply theory will allocate resources in the most efficient way possible. Now let us take a closer look at the

---

① In 1890, English economist **Alfred Marshall** published his work, ***Principles of Economics***, which was one of the earlier writings on how both supply and demand interacted to determine price.

law of demand and the law of supply.

A. The Law of Demand

The law of demand states that, if all other factors remain equal, the higher the price of a good, the less people will demand that good (See Figure 2 – 1). In other words, the higher the price, the lower the quantity demanded. The amount of a good that buyers purchase at a higher price is less because as the price of a good goes up, so does the opportunity cost of buying that good. As a result, people will naturally avoid buying a product that will force them to forgo the consumption of something else they value more. The chart below shows that the curve is a downward slope.

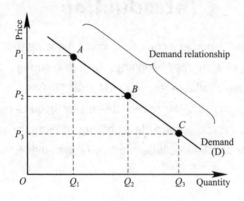

Figure 2 – 1 The law of demand

A, B and C are points on the demand curve. Each point on the curve reflects a direct correlation between quantity demanded (Q) and price (P). So, at point A, the quantity demanded will be Q_1 and the price will be P_1, and so on. The demand relationship curve illustrates the negative relationship between price and quantity demanded. The higher the price of a good the lower the quantity demanded (A), and the lower the price, the more the good will be in demand (C).

B. The Law of Supply

Like the law of demand, the law of supply demonstrates the quantities that will be sold at a certain price. But unlike the law of demand, the supply relationship shows an upward slope (See Figure 2 – 2). This means that the higher the price, the higher the quantity supplied. Producers supply more at a higher price because selling a higher quantity at a higher price increases revenue.

A, B and C are points on the supply curve. Each point on the curve reflects a direct correlation between quantity supplied (Q) and price (P). At point B, the quantity supplied will be Q_2 and the price will be P_2, and so on.

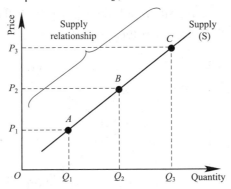

Figure 2-2 The law of supply

C. Supply and Demand Relationship

Now that we know the law of supply and demand, let's turn to an example to show how supply and demand affect price.

Imagine that a special edition CD of your favorite band is released for $20. Because the record company's previous analysis showed that consumers will not demand CDs at a price higher than $20, only ten CDs were released because the opportunity cost is too high for suppliers to produce more. If, however, the ten CDs are demanded by 20 people, the price will subsequently rise because, according to the demand relationship, as demand increases, so does the price. Consequently, the rise in price should prompt more CDs to be supplied as the supply relationship shows that the higher the price, the higher the quantity supplied.

If, however, there are 30 CDs produced and demand is still at 20, the price will not be pushed up because the supply more than accommodates demand. In fact after the 20 consumers have been satisfied with their CD purchases, the price of the leftover CDs may drop as CD producers attempt to sell the remaining ten CDs. The lower price will then make the CD more available to people who had previously decided that the opportunity cost of buying the CD at $20 was too high.

D. Equilibrium

When supply and demand are equal (i.e. when the supply function and demand function intersect) the economy is said to be at equilibrium (See Figure 2-3). At this point, the allocation of goods is at its most efficiency because the amount of goods being supplied is exactly the same as the amount of goods being demanded. Thus, everyone (individuals, firms, or countries) is satisfied with the current economic condition. At the given price, suppliers are selling all the goods that they have produced and consumers are getting all the goods that they are demanding.

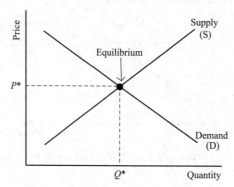

Figure 2-3 Equilibrium

As you can see on the chart, equilibrium occurs at the intersection of the demand and supply curve, which indicates no allocative inefficiency. At this point, the price of the goods will be P^* and the quantity will be Q^*. These figures are referred to as equilibrium price and quantity.

In the real market place equilibrium can only ever be reached in theory, so the prices of goods and services are constantly changing in relation to fluctuations in demand and supply.

E. Shifts in Supply and Demand

To understand how the law of supply and demand functions when there is a shift in demand, consider the case in which there is a shift in demand (See Figure 2-4).

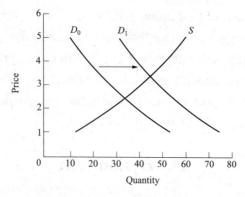

Figure 2-4 Shift in demand

In this example, the positive shift in demand results in a new supply-demand equilibrium point that is higher in both quantity and price. For each possible shift in the supply or demand curve, a similar graph can be constructed showing the effect on equilibrium price and quantity. Table 2 – 1 summarizes the results that would occur from shifts in supply, demand, and combinations of the two.

Table 2 – 1 Result of shifts in supply and demand

Demand	Supply	Equilibrium price	Equilibrium quantity
+		+	+
−		−	−
	+	−	+
	−	+	−
+	+	?	+
−	−	?	−
+	−	+	?
−	+	−	?

In the above table, " + " represents an increase, " − " represents a decrease, a blank represents no change, and a question mark indicates that the net change cannot be determined without knowing the magnitude of the shift in supply and demand. If these results are not immediately obvious, drawing a graph for each will facilitate the analysis.

Words and Expressions

backbone	n.	脊椎，中枢，主力
correlation	n.	相互关联，相互作用
revenue	n.	总收入，收益
release	v.	发行
leftover	a.	剩下的，残余的
Intersection	n.	交叉点，交点
magnitude	n.	大小，量值
allocation of resources		资源配置

1. supply 供应

    The total quantity of a good or service that is available for purchase at a given price.

2. demand 需求

    The amount of a particular economic good or service that a consumer or group of consumers will want to purchase at a given price.

3. the law of demand 需求定律

    If supply is held constant, an increase in demand leads to an increased market price, while a decrease in demand leads to a decreased market price.

4. opportunity cost 机会成本

    In economics, opportunity cost, or economic cost, is the cost of something in terms of an opportunity forgone (and the benefits which could be received from that opportunity), or the most valuable forgone alternative (or highest-valued option forgone), i.e. the second best alternative. An early representation of the concept of opportunity cost is the broken window fallacy(破窗谬论) illustrated by Frédéric Bastiat(法国经济学家巴斯蒂亚) in 1850.

5. demand curve 需求曲线

    The demand curve can be defined as the graph depicting the relationship between the price of a certain commodity, and the amount of it that consumers are willing and able to purchase at that given price (see demand).

6. the law of supply 供应定律

    If demand is held constant, an increase in supply leads to a decreased price, while a decrease in supply leads to an increased price.

7. allocative inefficiency 配置非效率

    Allocative efficiency theory says that the distribution of resources between alternatives does not fit with consumer taste (perceptions of costs and benefits).

8. equilibrium price 均衡价格

    Equilibrium price is the price at which the quantity demanded of a good or service is equal to the quantity supplied.

Unit 2 Supply and Demand

I Make verb phrases by linking those in Column A and Column B.

Column A	Column B
allocate	a graph
release	goods and services
supply	resources
forgo	the consumption of sugar
construct	CDs and books

II Match the following words or terms with their definitions.

| allocation | opportunity cost | equilibrium | shift | consumption |
| supply | correlation | price | demand | product |

1. _____: the desire of a good that the buyers wish to purchase at each conceivable price
2. _____: the total amount of a good or service available for purchase
3. _____: the assigned numerical monetary value of a good, service or asset
4. _____: the cost of something in terms of an opportunity forgone, or the most valuable forgone alternative
5. _____: using a product or service until it has no remaining value
6. _____: balance, for example when demand equals supply
7. _____: change, switch, fluctuation
8. _____: the end result of the manufacturing process
9. _____: a statistical measurement of the relationship between two variables
10. _____: the distribution of a limited quantity of resources over various time periods, products, operations, or investments

III Reading comprehension: choose the best answer from the three choices.

1. The market price of a good is determined by the _____ of it.
   A. supply   B. demand   C. both the supply and demand

2. According to the law of demand, which of the following statements is true?
   A. The higher the price, the higher the quantity demanded.
   B. The higher the price, the lower the quantity demanded.
   C. The lower the price, the lower the quantity demanded.
3. Each point on the demand curve reflects a correlation between _____.
   A. quantity demanded and price
   B. quantity supplied and price
   C. quantity supplied and quantity demanded
4. Which of the following statements is true?
   A. The demand curve illustrates the negative relationship between price and quantity demanded.
   B. The supply curve illustrates the negative relationship between price and quantity supplied.
   C. The demand curve illustrates the positive relationship between price and quantity demanded.
5. What is the result when both the demand and supply of a good increase?
   A. Equilibrium price: increase; equilibrium quantity: increase.
   B. Equilibrium price: not sure; equilibrium quantity: increase.
   C. Equilibrium price: decrease; equilibrium quantity: decrease.

Part Two Case Study

REASONS TO BE CHEERFUL ABOUT COMMODITIES

By **Harry Kat**[①]
From *Financial Times*, November 9, 2006

Commodity prices have more than doubled over the past four years, leading many investors to ask themselves whether commodities are still worth investing in.

To answer this question, we must revisit the main arguments for investment in commodities. The most popular argument is China. China is becoming an economic powerhouse. Given its sheer size, this is said to lead to a virtually insatiable demand for just about every commodity under the sun. The second most popular argument relates to the supply side. After many years of under-investment many commodity producers are in

---

① Harry Kat is a professor of risk management and director of the Alternative Investment Research Centre at Cass Business School, UK.

bad shape. They are unable to meet the recent increase in demand; a situation that is said to continue for many years to come. A third argument is found in a 2005 Yale research paper that shows over the period 1959-2004 a portfolio of 34 different commodities would have generated average returns comparable to stocks, but with negative correlation with stocks and bonds. This combination makes commodities the perfect diversifier for any traditional stock/bond portfolio.

How much truth is there in these arguments? One reason why China is doing well is the global economy has done well over the last couple of years. It is on track to grow 5.1 per cent this year alone. Another reason is the majority of China's population is poor, so labour costs are minimal. As a result, production is moved from the west to China.

Taken together, this means China is a lot more dependent on the global economy than many believe and a significant chunk of the growth in China's demand for commodities reflects a shift in manufacturing location. Having become a superpower in the global commodities markets, it is only a matter of time before China will force its suppliers to lower prices and increase its own production of various commodities as well as shift production from low-priced to higher-priced agricultural commodities. In time, China could well become a net exporter of a variety of commodities.

Finally, China's future growth could easily be short-circuited. Apart from inadequate infrastructure, a poorly functioning equity market, corruption and serious bad loan problems, China's economic expansion has a tremendous impact on the environment — water is in short supply, millions of people are migrating from rural areas to the big cities, inequality is growing. In addition, if inflation in China picks up, the central bank will have to raise interest rates and a hard landing may be unavoidable.

The supply side argument makes more sense, as it is true that production of many commodities is running low relative to demand. High commodity prices will stimulate the development of additional production capacity and the search for alternatives, as well as slowing down demand. However, these processes take time, because commodity producers will need to be convinced that prices will stabilise at a relatively high level before they embark on multi-billion dollar expansion projects. As a result, assuming demand doesn't suddenly stall, prices of at least a number of commodities will remain high.

Finally, contrary to the Yale paper's argument, more recent research has shown that most commodities do not offer a consistent risk premium. It does confirm that commodities are uncorrelated with stocks and bonds, however.

This is an important point as it means that adding commodities to a more traditional portfolio will be highly effective in reducing volatility.

Of course, without a significant risk premium this will also reduce that portfolio's expected return. As long as the expected return on commodities isn't too low, however, volatility will come down a lot more than expected return, making it a worthwhile trade-off.

In fact, due to the zero correlation, commodities are a worthwhile diversifier under a variety of assumptions with respect to their expected return. The only time when it doesn't work is when the risk premium on commodities is highly negative. In that case the reduction in volatility is not worth the loss in expected return.

This takes us back to the prospects for commodities. Although there are serious shortcomings in the main arguments for a further commodity bull market, prices do not have to drop substantially.

Asset managers and banks are rolling out a wide range of commodity-linked investment products: funds, ETFs, trackers, and all kinds of structured products. Given investors' appetite for these products, it is not unlikely that increased investment/speculative demand will keep prices high, leaving the case for commodities intact.

Under this scenario commodities are primarily a bet on the madness of crowds rather than a fundamentally justifiable investment.

Questions for Discussion

1. How does China decide whether it is worthy of investing in commodities? Explain in your own words.

2. By the law of Supply, Demand and Price, please explain the influence the supply side makes on the worthiness of commodity investment.

3. It has been shown by the report that commodities are uncorrelated with stocks and bonds. Is it significant for commodity investment?

4. Why does the author point out in the end of the passage that asset managers and banks are rolling out a wide range of commodity-linked investment products? What are the prospects for commodities?

Translation

1. Having become a superpower in the global commodities markets, it is only a matter of time before China will force its suppliers to lower prices and increase its own production of various commodities as well as shift production from low-priced to higher-priced agricultural commodities.

2. Apart from inadequate infrastructure, a poorly functioning equity market, corruption and serious bad loan problems, China's economic expansion has a tremendous impact on the environment — water is in short supply, millions of people are migrating from rural areas to the big cities, inequality is growing.

3. As long as the expected return on commodities isn't too low, however, volatility will come down a lot more than expected return, making it a worthwhile trade-off.

4. Given investors' appetite for these products, it is not unlikely that increased investment/speculative demand will keep prices high, leaving the case for commodities intact.

Unit 3
Utility

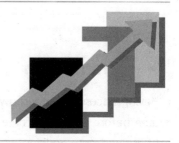

Introduction

In economics, utility is a measure of the relative satisfaction from or desirability of consumption of various goods and services. Given this measure, one may speak meaningfully of increasing or decreasing utility, and thereby explain economic behavior in terms of attempts to increase one's utility. For illustrative purposes, changes in utility are sometimes expressed in units called utils.

Part One Text

We have already seen that the focus of economics is to understand the problem of scarcity: the problem of fulfilling the unlimited wants of humankind with limited and/or scarce resources. Because of scarcity, economies need to allocate their resources efficiently. Underlying the laws of demand and supply is the concept of utility, which represents the advantage or fulfillment a person receives from consuming a good or service. Utility, then, explains how individuals and economies aim to gain optimal satisfaction in dealing with scarcity.

Utility is an abstract concept rather than a concrete, observable quantity. The units to which we assign an "amount" of utility, therefore, are arbitrary, representing a relative value. Total utility is the aggregate sum of satisfaction or benefit that an individual gains from consuming a given amount of goods or services in an economy. The amount of a person's total utility corresponds to the person's level of consumption. Usually, the more the person consumes, the larger his or her total utility will be. Marginal utility is the additional satisfaction, or amount of utility, gained from each extra unit of consumption.

Although total utility usually increases as more of a good is consumed, marginal utility usually decreases with each additional increase in the consumption of a good. This decrease demonstrates the law of diminishing marginal utility. Because there is a certain threshold of satisfaction, the consumer will no longer receive the same pleasure from consumption once that threshold is crossed. In other words, total utility will increase at a slower pace as an individual increases the quantity consumed.

Take, for example, a chocolate bar (See Table 3–1). Let's say that after eating one chocolate bar your sweet tooth has been satisfied. Your marginal utility (and total utility) after eating one chocolate bar will be quite high. But if you eat more chocolate bars, the pleasure of each additional chocolate bar will be less than the pleasure you received from eating the one before — probably because you are starting to feel full or you have had too many sweets for one day.

Table 3–1 Marginal utility and total utility

Chocolate bars eaten	Marginal chocolate utility	Total chocolate utility
0	0	0
1	70	70
2	10	80
3	5	85
4	3	88

This table shows that total utility will increase at a much slower rate as marginal utility diminishes with each additional bar. Notice how the first chocolate bar gives a total utility of 70 but the next three chocolate bars together increase total utility by only 18 additional units.

The law of diminishing marginal utility helps economists understand the law of demand and the negative sloping demand curve. The less of something you have, the more satisfaction you gain from each additional unit you consume; the marginal utility you gain from that product is therefore higher, giving you a higher willingness to pay more for it. Prices are lower at a higher quantity demanded because your additional satisfaction diminishes as you demand more.

In order to determine what a consumer's utility and total utility are, economists turn to Consumer Demand Theory, which studies consumer behavior and satisfaction (See Figure 3–1). Economists assume the consumer is rational and will thus maximize his or her total utility by purchasing a combination of different products rather than more of one particular product. Thus, instead of spending all of your money on three chocolate bars, which has a total utility of 85, you should instead purchase the one chocolate bar, which has a utility of 70, and perhaps a glass of milk, which has a utility of 50. This combination will give you a maximized total utility of 120 but at the same cost as the three chocolate bars.

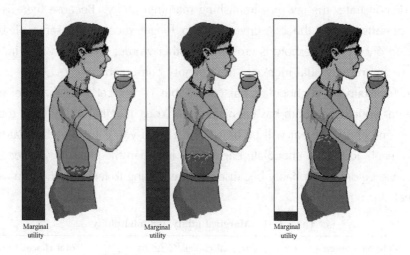

Figure 3-1 Marginal utility

Notes: Marginal utility refers to the change in satisfaction, or utility, resulting from consuming a little more or a little less of a commodity. In this example, the marginal utility of the first glass of water is greater than that of the third glass. As each glass of water is consumed, the marginal utility (desire for one more) diminishes.

Words and Expressions

optimal	a.	最适宜的，最有利的，最优的
arbitrary	a.	随意的，武断的
aggregate	a.	总的，总计，合计
diminish	v.	减少
threshold	n.	起点，下限

1. utility 效用

   In economics, utility is a measure of the relative happiness or satisfaction (gratification) (满足) gained. Given this measure, one may speak meaningfully of increasing or decreasing utility, and thereby explain economic behavior in terms of attempts to increase one's utility. The theoretical unit of measurement for utility is the util(尤特尔).

2. **total utility**　总效用

It refers to the full satisfaction of a consumer's wants or needs through the consumption of specific goods or services. As an example, the total utility of consuming four chocolate bars in a week would be the total or sum satisfaction achieved in consuming all of those four chocolate bars. Total utility, in other words, is the sum of the marginal utility gained from each chocolate bar consumed.

3. **marginal utility**　边际效用

It refers to the additional satisfaction a consumer gains from consuming one more unit of a good or service. For example, if you were really thirsty you'd get a certain amount of satisfaction from a glass of water. This satisfaction would probably decrease with the second glass, and then even more with the third glass. The additional amount of satisfaction that comes with each additional glass of water is marginal utility.

4. **law of diminishing marginal utility**　边际效用递减法则

It is a law of economics stating that as a person increases consumption of a product — while keeping consumption of other products constant — there is a decline in the marginal utility that person derives from consuming each additional unit of that product. This is the premise on which buffet-style restaurants operate. They entice you with "all you can eat", all the while knowing each additional plate of food provides less utility than the one before. And despite their enticement, most people will eat only until the utility they derive from additional food is slightly lower than the original. For example, say you go to a buffet and the first plate of food you eat is very good. On a scale of ten you would give it a ten. Now your hunger has been somewhat tamed, but you get another full plate of food. Since you're not as hungry, your enjoyment rates at a seven at best. Most people would stop before their utility drops even more, but say you go back to eat a third full plate of food and your utility drops even more to a three. If you kept eating, you would eventually reach a point at which your eating makes you sick, providing dissatisfaction, or "dis-utility"(无效用).

5. **Consumer Demand Theory**　消费者需求理论

Consumer Demand Theory is a theory of economics. It relates preferences（偏好）[through indifference curves（无差异曲线）and budget constraints（预算约束）] to consumer demand curves. The models that make up consumer theory are used to represent prospectively observable demand patterns for an individual buyer on the hypothesis of constrained optimization.

I Make verb phrases by linking those in Column A and Column B.

Column A	Column B
maximize	benefit
cross	utility
fulfill	threshold
assign	wants and needs
gain	an amount

II Match the following words or terms with their definitions.

aggregate	satisfaction	maximize	demand	curve
rational	utility	threshold	marginal	consumption

1. _____ : the level at which something starts to happen
2. _____ : the quality of being useful, or the degree to which something is useful
3. _____ : the total after a lot of different figures or points have been added together
4. _____ : a feeling of happiness or pleasure because you have achieved something or got what you wanted
5. _____ : the act of buying and using products
6. _____ : relating to a change in cost, value, etc. when one more thing is produced, one more dollar is earned, etc.
7. _____ : to increase something such as profit or income as much as possible
8. _____ : reasonable, sensible
9. _____ : a line that gradually bends like part of a circle
10. _____ : the need or desire that people have for particular goods and services

III Reading comprehension: choose the best answer from the four choices.

1. What is the relationship between marginal utility and total utility?

A. Total utility usually decreases as more of a good is consumed; marginal utility usually increases with each additional increase in the consumption of a good.

B. Total utility usually increases as more of a good is consumed and so does marginal utility.

C. Total utility usually increases as more of a good is consumed; marginal utility usually decreases with each additional increase in the consumption of a good.

D. Total utility usually decreases as more of a good is consumed and do does marginal utility.

2. Which of the following explanations of the law of diminishing marginal utility is right?

   A. The less of something you have, the less satisfaction you gain from each additional unit you consume; the marginal utility you gain from that product is therefore higher, giving you a higher willingness to pay more for it.

   B. The more of something you have, the more satisfaction you gain from each additional unit you consume; the marginal utility you gain from that product is therefore lower, giving you a lower willingness to pay more for it.

   C. The more of something you have, the more satisfaction you gain from each additional unit you consume; the marginal utility you gain from that product is therefore higher, giving you a higher willingness to pay more for it.

   D. The less of something you have, the more satisfaction you gain from each additional unit you consume; the marginal utility you gain from that product is therefore higher, giving you a higher willingness to pay more for it.

3. What is the relationship between total utility and level of consumption?

   A. The amount of a person's total utility and the person's level of consumption are in inverse proportion. Usually, the more the person consumes, the smaller his or her total utility will be.

   B. The amount of a person's total utility corresponds to the person's level of consumption. Usually, the more the person consumes, the larger his or her total utility will be

   C. The amount of a person's total utility is not necessarily in direct relation to the person's level of consumption.

   D. The amount of a person's total utility sometimes corresponds to the person's level of consumption but sometimes the former is not directly related to the latter.

Part Two Case Study

MORE ISN'T ALWAYS BETTER

By **Barry Schwartz**[①]
From *Harvard Business Review*, June, 2006

Marketers assume that the more choices they offer, the more likely customers will be able to find just the right thing. They assume, for instance, that offering 50 styles of jeans instead of two increases the chances that shoppers will find a pair they really like. Nevertheless, research now shows that there can be too much choice; when there is, consumers are less likely to buy anything at all, and if they do buy, they are less satisfied with their selection.

It all began with jam. In 2000, psychologists Sheena Iyengar and Mark Lepper published a remarkable study. On one day, shoppers at an upscale[②] food market saw a display table with 24 varieties of gourmet[③] jam. Those who sampled the spreads received a coupon for $1 off any jam. On another day, shoppers saw a similar table, except that only six varieties of the jam were on display. The large display attracted more interest than the small one. But when the time came to purchase, people who saw the large display were one-tenth as likely to buy as people who saw the small display.

Other studies have confirmed this result that more choice is not always better. As the variety of snacks, soft drinks, and beers offered at convenience stores increases, for instance, sales volume and customer satisfaction decrease. Moreover, as the number of retirement investment options available to employees increases, the chance that they will choose any decreases. These studies and others have shown not only that excessive choice can produce "choice paralysis", but also that it can reduce people's satisfaction with their decisions, even if they made good ones. My colleagues and I have found that increased choice decreases satisfaction with matters as trivial as ice cream flavors and as significant as jobs.

These results challenge what we think we know about human nature and the determinants[④] of well-being[⑤]. Both psychology and business have operated on the

---

① Barry Schwartz is a professor of psychology at Swarthmore College in Pennsylvania and the author of *The Paradox of Choice: Why More Is Less*.
② 高档的
③ 美食家
④ 决定因素
⑤ 生活幸福

assumption that the relationship between choice and well-being is straight-forward: The more choices people have, the better off they are. In psychology, the benefits of choice have been tied to autonomy and control. In business, the benefits of choice have been tied to the benefits of free markets more generally. Added options make no one worse off, and they are bound to make someone better off.

Choice is good for us, but its relationship to satisfaction appears to be more complicated than we had assumed. <u>There is diminishing marginal utility in having alternatives; each new option subtracts① a little from the feeling of well-being, until the marginal benefits of added choice level off.</u> What's more, psychologists and business academics alike have largely ignored another outcome of choice: More of it requires increased time and effort and can lead to anxiety, regret, excessively high expectations, and self-blame if the choices don't work out. When the number of available options is small, these costs are negligible, but the costs grow with the number of options. Eventually, each new option makes us feel worse off than we did before.

Without a doubt, having more options enables us, most of the time, to achieve better objective outcomes. Again, having 50 styles of jeans as opposed to two increases the likelihood that customers will find a pair that fits. But the subjective outcome may be that shoppers will feel overwhelmed and dissatisfied. <u>This dissociation② between objective and subjective results creates a significant challenge for retailers and marketers that look to choice as a way to enhance the perceived value of their goods and services.</u>

Choice can no longer be used to justify a marketing strategy in and of itself. More isn't always better, either for the customer or for the retailer. Discovering how much assortment is warranted is a considerable empirical③ challenge. But companies that get the balance right will be amply rewarded.

Questions for Discussion

1. Use the law of diminishing marginal utility to explain the relationship between choice and satisfaction.

_____

_____

_____

---

① 减去，扣除
② 分裂，分离
③ 实证的

2. What does the author mean by "choice paralysis"?

Translation

1. These studies and others have shown not only that excessive choice can produce "choice paralysis", but also that it can reduce people's satisfaction with their decisions, even if they made good ones. My colleagues and I have found that increased choice decreases satisfaction with matters as trivial as ice cream flavors and as significant as jobs.

2. There is diminishing marginal utility in having alternatives; each new option subtracts a little from the feeling of well-being, until the marginal benefits of added choice level off.

3. This dissociation between objective and subjective results creates a significant challenge for retailers and marketers that look to choice as a way to enhance the perceived value of their goods and services.

Unit 4
Production

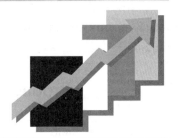

Introduction

In microeconomics, production is the act of making things, in particular the act of making products that will be traded or sold commercially. Production decisions concentrate on what goods to produce, how to produce them, the costs of producing them, and optimizing the mix of resource inputs used in their production. This production information can then be combined with market information (like demand and marginal revenue) to determine the quantity of products to produce and the optimum pricing. In macroeconomics, production is measured by gross domestic product and other measures of national income and output.

Part One Text

Factors of Production

The factors of production are the requirements for production, usually represented as capital, labour, and land. Capital covers all man-made aids to future production; fixed capital stays put, and includes the physical plant, buildings, tools and machinery, while circulating capital includes raw materials and components.

Labour includes all human resources. It may be unskilled, semi-skilled, or skilled, and local labour markets vary in the size and nature of the pool of labour. Cheap, unskilled and semi-skilled labour may be an important locational factor for multinational corporations while skilled labour is significant in high technology industries. Industries may be capital — or labour-intensive. Management skills can be a vital factor of labour or can be seen as a separate factor of production under the heading of entrepreneurship.

Land includes natural resources, as in mining, and is an increasingly important factor as modern factories extend on one level and require space for storage and parking.

Production Possibility Frontier (PPF)

Under the field of macroeconomics, the Production Possibility Frontier (PPF) represents the point at which an economy is most efficiently producing its goods and services and, therefore, allocating its resources in the best way possible. If the economy is not producing the quantities indicated by the PPF, resources are being managed inefficiently and the production of society will dwindle. The production possibility frontier shows there are limits to production, so an economy, to achieve efficiency, must decide what combination of goods and services can be produced.

Let's turn to the chart below (See Figure 4 – 1). Imagine an economy that can produce only wine and cotton. According to the PPF, points A, B and C — all appearing on the curve — represent the most efficient use of resources by the economy. Point X represents an inefficient use of resources, while point Y represents the goals that the economy cannot attain with its present levels of resources.

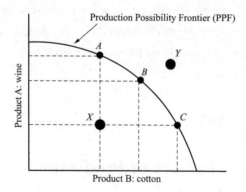

Figure 4 – 1   Production possibilities curve (I)

As we can see, in order for this economy to produce more wine, it must give up some of the resources it uses to produce cotton (point A). If the economy starts producing more cotton (represented by points B and C), it would have to divert resources from making wine and, consequently, it will produce less wine than it is producing at point A. As the chart shows, by moving production from point A to B, the economy must decrease wine production by a small amount in comparison to the increase in cotton output. However, if the economy moves from point B to C, wine output will be significantly reduced while the increase in cotton will be quite small. Keep in mind that A, B, and C all represent the most efficient allocation of resources for the economy; the nation must decide how to achieve the PPF and which combination to use. If more wine is in demand, the cost of increasing its output is proportional to the cost of decreasing cotton production.

Point X means that the country's resources are not being used efficiently or, more specifically, that the country is not producing enough cotton or wine given the potential of its resources. Point Y, as we mentioned above, represents an output level that is currently unreachable by this economy. However, if there was a change in technology while the level of land, labor and capital remained the same, the time required to pick cotton and grapes would be reduced. Output would increase, and the PPF would be pushed outwards. A new curve, on which Y would appear, would represent the new efficient allocation of resources (See Figure 4 – 2).

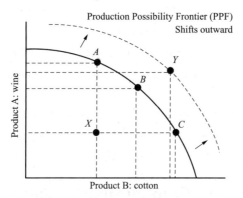

Figure 4 – 2   Production possibilities curve (Ⅱ)

When the PPF shifts outwards, we know there is growth in an economy. Alternatively, when the PPF shifts inwards it indicates that the economy is shrinking as a result of a decline in its most efficient allocation of resources and optimal production capability. A shrinking economy could be a result of a decrease in supplies or a deficiency in technology.

An economy can be producing on the PPF curve only in theory. In reality, economies constantly struggle to reach an optimal production capacity. And because scarcity forces an economy to forgo one choice for another, the slope of the PPF will always be negative; if production of product A increases then production of product B will have to decrease accordingly.

Opportunity Cost

Opportunity cost is the value of what is foregone in order to have something else. This value is unique for each individual. You may, for instance, forgo ice cream in order to have an extra helping of mashed potatoes. For you, the mashed potatoes have a greater value than dessert. But you can always change your mind in the future because there may be some instances when the mashed potatoes are just not as attractive as the ice cream. The opportunity cost of an individual's decisions, therefore, is determined by his or her needs, wants, time and resources (income).

This is important to the PPF because a country will decide how to best allocate its resources according to its opportunity cost. Therefore, the previous wine/cotton example shows that if the country chooses to produce more wine than cotton, the opportunity cost is equivalent to the cost of giving up the required cotton production.

Let's look at another example to demonstrate how opportunity cost ensures that an individual will buy the least expensive of two similar goods when given the choice. For example, assume that an individual has a choice between two telephone services. If he or she were to buy the most expensive service, that individual may have to reduce the number of times he or she goes to the movies each month. Giving up these opportunities to go to the movies may be a cost that is too high for this person, leading him or her to choose the less expensive service.

Remember that opportunity cost is different for each individual and nation. Thus, what is valued more than something else will vary among people and countries when decisions are made about how to allocate resources.

Trade, Comparative Advantage and Absolute Advantage

1. Specialization and Comparative Advantage

An economy can focus on producing all of the goods and services it needs to function, but this may lead to an inefficient allocation of resources and hinder future growth. By using specialization, a country can concentrate on the production of one thing that it can do best, rather than dividing up its resources.

For example, let's look at a hypothetical world that has only two countries (Country A and Country B) and two products (cars and cotton). Each country can make cars and/or cotton. Now suppose that Country A has very little fertile land and an abundance of steel for car production. Country B, on the other hand, has an abundance of fertile land but very little steel. If Country A were to try to produce both cars and cotton, it would need to divide up its resources. Because it requires a lot of effort to produce cotton by irrigating the land, Country A would have to sacrifice producing cars. The opportunity cost of producing both cars and cotton is high for Country A, which will have to give up a lot of capital in order to produce both. Similarly, for Country B, the opportunity cost of producing both products is high because the effort required to produce cars is greater than that of producing cotton.

Each country can produce one of the products more efficiently (at a lower cost) than the other. Country A, which has an abundance of steel, would need to give up more cars than Country B would to produce the same amount of cotton. Country B would need to give up more cotton than Country A to produce the same amount of cars. Therefore, County A has a comparative advantage over Country B in the production of cars, and Country B has a comparative advantage over Country A in the production of cotton.

Now let's say that both countries (A and B) specialize in producing the goods with which they have a comparative advantage. If they trade the goods that they produce for other goods in which they don't have a comparative advantage, both countries will be able to enjoy both products at a lower opportunity cost. Furthermore, each country will be exchanging the best product it can make for another good or service that is the best that the other country can produce. Specialization and trade also works when several different countries are involved. For example, if Country C specializes in the production of corn, it can trade its corn for cars from Country A and cotton from Country B.

Determining how countries exchange goods produced by a comparative advantage ("the best for the best") is the backbone of international trade theory. This method of exchange is considered an optimal allocation of resources, whereby economies, in theory, will no longer be lacking anything that they need. Like opportunity cost, specialization and comparative advantage also apply to the way in which individuals interact within an economy.

2. Absolute Advantage

Sometimes a country or an individual can produce more than another country, even though countries both have the same amount of inputs. For example, Country A may have a technological advantage that, with the same amount of inputs (arable land, steel, labor), enables the country to manufacture more of both cars and cotton than Country B. A country that can produce more of both goods is said to have an Absolute Advantage. Better quality resources can give a country an absolute advantage as can a higher level of education and overall technological advancement. It is not possible, however, for a country to have a comparative advantage in everything that it produces, so it will always be able to benefit from trade.

Words and Expressions

dwindle	v.	减少，变小，缩小，变瘦
divert	v.	转换，转移
proportional	a.	成比例的，相称的，平衡的，调和的
deficiency	n.	缺乏，不足，短缺
hypothetical	a.	假设的
arable	a.	适于耕种的，可耕的

Notes

1. **Production Possibility Frontier (PPF)** 生产可能性边界

    Production possibilities frontier is a graph that shows the different quantities of two goods that an economy could efficiently produce with limited productive resources. In economics, we have a Production Possibilities Curve (PPC)(生产可能性曲线) or "transformation curve". Points along the curve describe the trade-off between the two goods. The curve illustrates that increasing production of one good reduces production of the other good. Transferring resources away from the other good reduces production of that good.

2. **comparative advantage** 比较优势

    In economics, the theory of Comparative Advantage explains why it can be beneficial for two parties (countries, regions, individuals and so on) to trade if one has a lower relative cost of producing some good. What matters is not the absolute cost of production but the opportunity cost, which measures how much production of one good is reduced to produce one more unit of the other good. Comparative Advantage is critical to understanding modern international trade theory.

3. **absolute advantage** 绝对优势

    A country has an absolute advantage economically over another, in a particular good, when it can produce that good at a lower cost. Using the same input of resources a country with an absolute advantage will have greater output. Assuming this one good is the only item in the market, beneficial trade is impossible.

Unit 4　Production

I Make verb phrases by linking those in Column A and Column B.

Column A	Column B
increase	choices
forgo	resources
expand	mind
change	goods
trade	outputs

II Match the following words or terms with their definitions.

| efficiency | deficiency | specialization | cost | opportunity |
| absolute | advantage | pricing | PPF | hypothetical |

1. _____: the practice of limiting your interests or activities to one particular subject
2. _____: the money that you must regularly spend in order to run a business, a home, a car, etc.
3. _____: a lack of something that is necessary
4. _____: complete or total
5. _____: a graph that shows the different quantities of two goods that an economy could efficiently produce with limited productive resources
6. _____: based on a situation that is not real, but that might happen
7. _____: the act of deciding the price of something that you sell
8. _____: a good or useful quality or condition that something has
9. _____: the quality of doing something well and effectively
10. _____: a chance to do something or an occasion when it is easy for you to do something

III Reading comprehension: choose the best answer from the four choices.

1. How does the production possibilities frontier illustrate production efficiency?
   A. The production possibility frontier only shows there are limits to production and that's only theoretical.

B. The production possibility frontier represents the point at which an economy is most efficiently producing its goods and services and, therefore, allocating its resources in the best way possible.

C. The production possibilities frontier is a curve depicting the efficiency of production.

D. The production possibilities frontier is a set of curves depicting the efficiency of production.

2. How does the production possibilities frontier show that every choice involves a tradeoff?

A. The production possibility frontier shows there are limits to production, so an economy, to achieve efficiency, must decide what combination of goods and services can be produced.

B. An economy can be producing on the PPF curve only in theory. In reality, economies constantly struggle to reach an optimal production capacity.

C. When the PPF shifts outwards, we know there is growth in an economy. Alternatively, when the PPF shifts inwards it indicates that the economy is shrinking as a result of a decline in its most efficient allocation of resources and optimal production capability.

D. If the economy starts producing more cotton, it would have to divert resources from making wine and, consequently, it will produce less wine than it is producing at another point.

3. How does the production possibilities frontier illustrate opportunity cost?

A. The PPF shows that if the country chooses to produce more A than B, the opportunity cost is equivalent to the cost of giving up the required B production.

B. The opportunity cost of an individual's decisions is determined by his or her needs, wants, time and resources (income).

C. The PPF shows that if the country chooses to produce more A than B, the opportunity cost is not equivalent to the cost of giving up the required B production.

D. The PPF shows that if the country chooses to produce more A than B, the opportunity cost is equivalent to the cost of the production of A and giving up of the required B production.

4. Why do people specialize and trade?

A. Because people have different tastes and needs so they need to specialize the production and trade products with others.

B. Because different countries have different advantages in different productions.

C. By using specialization, a country can concentrate on the production of one thing that it can do best. If two or more countries specializing in producing the goods with which they have a comparative advantage trade the goods that they produce for other goods in which they don't have a comparative advantage, all countries will be able to enjoy both products at a lower opportunity cost.

D. Because economic globalization requires people and countries to do so.

Part Two   Case Study

THE PROBLEM WITH MADE IN CHINA

CHINA IS CHOKING ON ITS SUCCESS AT ATTRACTING THE WORLD'S FACTORIES. THAT HAS HANDED ITS ASIAN NEIGHBOURS A BIG OPPORTUNITY.

From *The Economist*, Jan. 11th, 2007

As a vote of confidence in Vietnam, the decision by Intel early in 2006 to spend $350 m building a new factory in the emerging South-East Asian economy was hard to beat. And yet, before the year was out, the American chipmaker went further and raised its investment to $1 billion. In eight months Intel had committed as much money to Vietnam as it had to China in the previous ten years.

In the Johor region of Malaysia, another global firm, Flextronics①, has fired up the production lines of a new M$400 m ($110 m) factory to make computer printers for another American firm, Hewlett-Packard②. One of the largest contract electronics manufacturers, Flextronics already has vast facilities in China. But it chose Malaysia as the site for its latest investment.

Further east, in Indonesia, Yue Yuen③, a Hong Kong-based shoemaker, has been ramping up its output of trainers and casual footwear for brands like Nike and Adidas. Production is increasing at the firm's factories in China and Vietnam too, but output in Indonesia is growing the fastest.

Although all three companies had different reasons for their decisions, the outcome was the same: they chose to avoid China's thundering economy in order to put their factories elsewhere in Asia. These companies are not alone. In the calculus④ of costs, risks, customers and logistics⑤ that goes into building global operations, an increasing

---

① 伟创力集团, 成立于1969年, 是一家总部设在美国, 并在 NASDAQ 上市的跨国公司。
② 美国惠普公司
③ 香港裕元工业 (集团) 有限公司, 是全球最大的体育用品生产商。
④ 运算, 演算
⑤ 后勤, 物流

number of firms are coming to the conclusion that China is not necessarily the best place to make things.

With its seemingly limitless supply of cheap labour and the rapid acquisition of technological prowess①, China appears to be unstoppable. Indeed, the perception is that every factory closing in America or Europe is destined to reopen in China. Many have, helping China's share of the world's exported goods to triple to 7.3% between 1993 and 2005. In comparison, every member of the G8 group② of rich nations, with the exception of Russia, saw its share fall. It is a similar story with manufacturing output. Whereas China doubled its share of global production to almost 7% in the decade to 2003, most of the G8 saw their shares fall. Interestingly, only the United States and Canada saw their shares rise — with just over a quarter between them. Most things nowadays might seem to be made in China, but North America remains the true workshop of the world.

Yet it is not only China that is booming as a base for low-cost production. Manufacturing and exports are growing rapidly in other parts of Asia (See Figure 4-3). Taken together, South Korea, India and the Association of South-East Asian Nations (ASEAN)③ increased their share of global manufacturing from less than 5% to more than 7% in the decade to 2003. Exports also rose across the board. China is the emerging giant, but the investments that are being diverted away from the Middle Kingdom④ present the rest of Asia with a huge opportunity to become manufacturing hubs in their own right. The question is whether they can seize it.

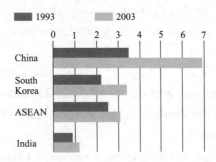

Figure 4-3 Share of world manufacturing output (%)

---

① 本领，本事
② 八国集团
③ 东盟
④ 中国（这是"中国"二字的意译）

Too Far, Too Expensive

Scott Brixen, an analyst at CLSA Asia-Pacific Markets①, a Hong Kong-based investment bank, gives two big reasons why China has not found itself at the top of the list for some new factories: "Rising costs and a natural desire by companies for diversification."

So far, most industrial development in China has taken place in the country's eastern coastal regions, particularly around Shanghai and the Pearl River Delta near Hong Kong. But costs in these centres are now rising sharply. Office rents are soaring, industrial land is in short supply and utility costs are climbing. Most significant of all are rocketing wages. In spite of the mass migration of workers from China's vast interior to the coast, pay for factory workers has been rising at double-digit rates for several years. For managers, the situation is worse still.

"China has become a victim of its own success," sighs Peter Tan, president and managing director of Flextronics in Asia. He finds it especially hard to hire and retain technical staff, ranging from finance directors to managers versed in international production techniques such as "six sigma②" and "lean manufacturing③". There are not enough qualified workers to go around, causing rampant poaching and extremely fast wage inflation. "China is definitely not the cheapest place to produce any more," he says.

An analysis of labour rates across Asia by CLSA's Mr. Brixen supports that view. Average wages for a factory worker, combined with social security costs, came to almost $350 a month in Shanghai in 2005 and almost $250 a month in Shenzhen. By comparison, monthly wages were less than $200 in Manila, around $150 in Bangkok and just over $100 in Batam in Indonesia. Although the productivity of Chinese workers is rising, in many industries it is not keeping pace with wages.

One solution is for companies to move inland where many costs are much lower than on China's heavily developed coastline. Indeed, the government has been promoting such a policy since 2000, to spread the benefits of development to China's poor interior. Domestic Chinese companies have led the charge into the hinterland and a small, but growing, number of foreign firms have followed them.

Intel is one. In 2004 it decided to invest $525 m in a new plant in Chengdu, the capital of Sichuan province, to complement its existing factories on the coast in

---

① 里昂证券亚太市场公司
② 六西格玛管理的核心理念实际上不仅是一个质量上的标准，它更代表着一种全新的管理理念，即要企业改变过去那种"我一直都这样做，而且做得很好"的思想，因为尽管过去确实已经做得很好，但是离六西格玛管理的目标还差得很远。
③ 精益生产

Shanghai, 1,600 km (994 miles) away. Brian Krzanich, general manager of Intel's test and assembly business, says the company's decision was based on cost. The government was keen to promote its "go west" policy①, so it offered Intel generous incentives. Needless to say, being so far inland raises transport costs for exporters. But Mr. Krzanich reckons there are compensations, because labour and utilities are much cheaper than on the coast.

But not everyone is convinced. At Flextronics, Mr. Tan's China factories are all located in eastern coastal provinces. "We have no interest in going west," he says, because it is too expensive to get products to America and Europe from there. Other observers add that the shortage of management talent inland is even greater than on the coast. And it is not easy persuading expatriate workers to take their families to places like Chongqing and Chengdu, where foreign companions and international schools are thin on the ground. So many firms decide they would rather invest elsewhere in Asia.

Costs are only part of the equation. Just as important is diversification. Having already moved a big chunk of their production to China, many firms are reluctant to put any more of their eggs in the same basket. A research report written last year by the Japan External Trade Organisation concluded: "Due to the country's increasing business risks and rising labour costs … Japanese firms employing a 'China-plus-one' strategy — in which they invest in China and another country, namely in ASEAN — should consider placing more emphasis on the 'plus one' country."

Equally important are concerns about growing protectionism. The United States and the European Union are becoming more assertive in holding China to account over its World Trade Organisation obligations. Companies worry that this could lead to sudden interruptions to trade.

Ask Yue Yuen, the world's largest contract shoe manufacturer. The company produces more than 180 m shoes a year from factories in China, Vietnam and Indonesia, most of them bound for America and Europe. So when the European Union imposed anti-dumping duties in October 2006 on leather shoes imported from China and Vietnam, the firm was quick to raise its production in Indonesia. "Trade relations with other nations and the tariff and quota situation are vital considerations for where we invest," says Terry Ip, a spokesman for the company.

So too are wage rates. With each shoe passing through up to 200 pairs of hands on the production line, Yue Yuen's operations are highly labour-intensive. In China the firm is experiencing rapid wage inflation. Although this is partly offset by productivity improvements which mean that overall unit labour costs are rising by 8% a year. Pay for

---

① 西部大开发政策

factory workers is rising in Vietnam and Indonesia too, notes Mr. Ip, but labour costs there are as much as 35% lower than in coastal China.

Another company with a China-plus-one strategy is Uniqlo①, a Japanese clothing retailer. Last year it decided to reduce the share of clothes it sources in China from 90% to 60% as a hedging strategy against future trade disputes. New factories in Cambodia and Vietnam will make up the shortfall. Intel, with facilities in Vietnam, the Philippines, Malaysia and China, is creating a diversified portfolio also.

Questions for Discussion

1. Why did many foreign companies decide to establish factories in China and why do many companies now begin to move their business elsewhere?

2. Why do many firms decide they would rather invest elsewhere in Asia than in inland China? Explain in your own words.

Translation

1. In the calculus of costs, risks, customers and logistics that goes into building global operations, an increasing number of firms are coming to the conclusion that China is not necessarily the best place to make things.

2. Exports also rose across the board. China is the emerging giant, but the investments that are being diverted away from the Middle Kingdom present the rest of Asia with a huge opportunity to become manufacturing hubs in their own right.

---

① Uniqlo 的全名是 Unique Clothing Warehouse，为日本著名服装品牌。

3. Office rents are soaring, industrial land is in short supply and utility costs are climbing. Most significant of all are rocketing wages. In spite of the mass migration of workers from China's vast interior to the coast, pay for factory workers has been rising at double-digit rates for several years. For managers, the situation is worse still.

4. So too are wage rates. With each shoe passing through up to 200 pairs of hands on the production line, Yue Yuen's operations are highly labour-intensive. In China the firm is experiencing rapid wage inflation. Although this is partly offset by productivity improvements which mean that overall unit labour costs are rising by 8% a year.

Unit 5
Price System

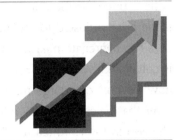

Introduction

Price is another key concept of microeconomics. All the trade-offs are based on the prices faced by consumers, workers and firms. A consumer trades off beef for chicken partly on his preferences but also partly on their prices. Likewise, workers trade off labor for leisure based in part on wage, the price they get for their labor. Firms decide whether to hire a worker or purchase more machines based in part on wage rates and machine prices. Price is determined by a whole collection of buyers and sellers who keep changing and thus is subject to changes and fluctuations.

Then can we compare prices in different stages on a constant basis?

Part One Text

Real vs Nominal Prices

We often want to compare the price of a good today with what it was in the past or is likely to be in the future. To make such a comparison meaningful, we need to measure prices relative to an overall price level. In absolute terms, the price of a dozen eggs is many times higher today than it was 50 years ago. Relative to prices overall, however, it is actually lower. Therefore, we must be careful to correct for inflation when comparing prices across time. This means measuring prices in real rather than nominal terms.

The nominal price of a good (sometimes called the "current-dollar" price) is its absolute price. For example, the nominal price of a pound of butter was about $0.87 in 1970, $1.88 in 1980, about 1.99 in 2001. These are the prices you would have seen in supermarkets in those years. The real price of a good (sometimes called its "constant-dollar" price) is the price relative to an aggregate measure of prices. In other words, it is the price adjusted for inflation.

The aggregate measure most often used is the consumer price index (CPI). The CPI is calculated by the US Bureau of Labor Statistics and is published monthly. It records how the cost of a large market basket of goods purchased by a "typical" consumer in some base year changes over time. (Currently the base year is 1983.) Percentage changes in the CPI measure the rate of inflation in the economy.

After correcting for inflation, do we find that butter was more expensive in 2001 than in 1970? To find out, let's calculate the 2001 price of butter in terms of 1970 dollars. The CPI was 38.8 in 1970 and rose to about 177 in 2001. (There was considerable inflation in the United States during the 1970s and early 1980s.) In 1970 dollars, the price of butter was

$$\frac{38.8}{177} \times \$3.30 = \$0.72$$

In real terms, therefore, the price of butter was lower in 2001 than it was in 1970. Put another way, the nominal price of butter went up by about 280%, while the CPI went up 356%. Relative to the aggregate price level, butter prices fell.

We'll usually be concerned with real rather than nominal prices because consumer choices involve analyses of price comparisons. These relative prices can most easily be evaluated if there is a common basis of comparison. Stating all prices in real terms achieves this objective. Thus, even though we will often measure prices in dollars, we will be thinking in terms of the real purchasing power of these dollars.

Example 1: The Price of Eggs and the Price of a College Education

In 1970, Grade A large eggs cost about 61 cents a dozen. In the same year, the average annual cost of a college education at a private four-year college, including room and board, was about $2 530. By 2002, the price of eggs had risen to $1.03 a dozen, and the average cost of a college education was $18,273. In real terms, were eggs more expensive in 2002 than in 1970? Had a college education become more expensive?

Table 5-1 shows the nominal price of eggs, the nominal cost of a college education, and the CPI for 1970-2002. (The CPI is based on 1983 = 100.) Also shown are the real prices of eggs and a college education in 1970 dollars, calculated as follows:

$$\text{Real price of eggs in 1975} = \frac{\text{CPI 1970}}{\text{CPI 1975}} \times \text{nominal price in 1975}$$

$$\text{Real price of eggs in 1980} = \frac{\text{CPI 1970}}{\text{CPI 1980}} \times \text{nominal price in 1980}$$

and so forth.

Table 5–1 The real prices of eggs and a college education

Year		1970	1975	1980	1985	1990	1995	2002
Consumer Price Index		38.8	53.8	82.4	107.6	130.7	152.4	181.0
Nominal Prices	Grade A Large Eggs	$0.61	$0.77	$0.84	$0.80	$1.01	$0.93	$1.03
	College Education	$2,530	$3,403	$4,912	$8,202	$12,018	$16,207	$18,273
Real Prices	Grade A Large Eggs	$0.61	$0.56	$0.40	$0.29	$0.30	$0.24	$0.22
	College Education	$2,530	$2,454	$2,313	$2,953	$3,568	$4,126	$3,917

This table shows clearly that the cost of a college education rose (by 55%) during this period while the real cost of eggs fell (by 74%). It is these relative changes in prices that are important for choices consumers make, not the fact that both eggs and college cost more in nominal terms today than they did in 1970.

In the table, we calculated real prices in terms of 1970 dollars, but we could have just as easily calculated them in terms of dollars of some other base year. For example, suppose we want to calculate the real price of eggs in 1980 dollars. Then:

$$\text{Real price of eggs in 1975} = \frac{\text{CPI 1980}}{\text{CPI 1975}} \times \text{nominal price in 1975}$$

$$\text{Real price of eggs in 1985} = \frac{\text{CPI 1980}}{\text{CPI 1985}} \times \text{nominal price in 1985}$$

and so forth.

By going through the calculations, you can check to see that in terms of 1980 dollars, the real price of eggs was $1.30 in 1970, $1.18 in 1975, $0.84 in 1980, $0.61 in 1985, $0.64 in 1990, and $0.47 in 2002. You will also see that the percentage declines in real price are the same no matter which base year we use.

Words and Expressions

trade-off	n.	抉择
preference	n.	偏好
fluctuation	n.	波动
aggregate	a.	总的，全部的
good	n.	商品
considerable	a.	一定的，相当的
involve	v.	包含，包括，涉及
analysis	n.	分析
state	v.	表述，表示，申明
decline	v.	下降，减少
real price		实际价格
nominal price		名义价格
absolute price		绝对价格
current-dollar price		现值美元，时价
constant-dollar price		定值美元，不变美元
consumer price index		消费者价格指数
US Bureau of Labor Statistics		美国劳工统计局
in absolute terms		按绝对价格
in real terms		按实际价格
in nominal terms		按名义价格
in terms of 1970 dollars		按 1970 美元价格
overall price level		综合价格水平，价格总水平
relative to		相对于
base year		基年
put another way		换句话说
purchasing power		购买力
room and board		食宿

Notes

1. **nominal price** 名义价格

   It refers to price without adjustment for inflation, the price of a product or financial security in terms of current price levels, not adjusted for the effects of inflation.

2. **real price** 实际价格

   It refers to price with adjustment for inflation, the price of a product or financial security in terms of constant price levels, adjusted for the effects of inflation.

3. **constant dollar** 不变美元, 定值美元

   It refers to dollars at value on previous date, dollars valued at a rate that applied on a particular date in the past.

4. **current dollar** 现值美元, 时价

   It refers to dollar at current replacement cost, dollars valued at a rate that applied on a particular date now.

5. **room and board** 食宿

   It is an offering of lodging and meals (usually in exchange for work).

6. **purchasing power** 购买力

   It refers to the value of a currency expressed in terms of the amount of goods or services that one unit of money can buy. Purchasing power is important because, all else being equal, inflation decreases the amount of goods or services you'd be able to purchase. To measure purchasing power, you'd compare against price index such as CPI. A simple way to think about purchasing power is to imagine if you made the same salary as your grandfather. Clearly you could survive on much less a few generations ago, however, because of inflation, you'd need a greater salary just to maintain the same quality of living.

7. **base year** 基年

   It is the year or date chosen to set an index at 100. Any year can be chosen as a base year, but it is generally desirable to use a fairly recent year. Widely used in the compilation of macro-economic data.

8. **the Bureau of Labor Statistics (BLS)** 劳工统计局

   It is the principal fact-finding agency for the Federal Government in the broad field of labor economics and statistics. The BLS is an independent national statistical agency that collects, processes, analyzes, and disseminates (收集、处理、分析、发布) essential statistical data to the American public, the US Congress, other Federal agencies, State and local governments, business, and labor. The BLS also serves as a statistical resource to the Department of Labor. BLS data must satisfy a number of criteria, including relevance to (相关) current social and economic issues, timeliness (及时) in reflecting today's rapidly changing economic conditions, accuracy and consistently high statistical quality, and impartiality in both subject matter and presentation.

9. **market basket** 市场篮子

   It refers to a collection of consumer goods and services that are tracked in the process of calculating a consumer price index.

Exercises

I Make verb phrases by linking those in Column A and Column B.

Column A	Column B
trade off	prices for inflation
compare	in current dollar price
adjust/correct	the price of a good in nominal prices
rise or decline	pork for beef
express	the price of a good with what it was ten years ago

II Match the following words or terms with their definitions.

real price	nominal price	current dollar
constant dollar	corrected price	overall price
market basket	consumer price index	purchasing power

1. _____: price without adjustment for inflation
2. _____: the value of a currency expressed in terms of the amount of goods and services that one unit of money can buy
3. _____: dollar at value on a previous date
4. _____: price adjusted for inflation
5. _____: a collection of consumer goods and services to be covered when calculating a consumer price index
6. _____: an aggregate measure of prices
7. _____: dollar at current replacement cost
8. _____: across-time changes in the cost of a large market basket of goods a "typical" consumer purchases in some base year
9. _____: price with adjustment for inflation

III Reading comprehension: choose the best answer from the four choices.

1. Correction for inflation means measuring prices _____.
   A. in either real or nominal prices
   B. in both real and nominal prices

C. in neither real nor nominal terms
  D. in real rather than nominal terms
2. Percentage changes in the CPI can measure _____.
  A. the rate of inflation in the economy
  B. the changes in the rate of interest
  C. the overall price levels in some base year
  D. the rate of economic growth and price changes
3. To make a meaningful price comparison across time, it's necessary to measure prices _____.
  A. relative to a particular price level
  B. in absolute terms
  C. relative to an aggregate measure of prices
  D. in relative terms
4. _____ offers a common basis for a convenient comparison of relative prices.
  A. Measuring prices in dollars
  B. Measuring the real purchasing powers
  C. Measuring all prices in real terms
  D. Measuring all prices in absolute terms
5. In 1990 it cost $1 to print a photo. In 2002, it cost $1.2 to print one. The real price of printing a photo in 1990 and 2002 (taking 1995 as the base year) was respectively _____ and _____.
  A. 0.70, 1.17   B. 0.86, 0.70   C. 1.17, 0.86   D. 1.17, 0.70

Part Two Case Study

RISING CPI AND FED RATE CUTS WON'T TIE PBOC'S HANDS

By **Dai Yan** (chinadaily.com.cn)
By **Judy Hua** and **Alison Leung** (Reuters)
From www.chinadaily.com.cn, Sep. 21, 2007

THE CONSUMER PRICE INDEX (CPI), A BAROMETER OF INFLATION, WILL LIKELY CONTINUE TO RISE SLOWLY UNTIL 2009, AND CHINA IS ALSO EXPECTED TO RAISE INTEREST RATES AND THE DEPOSIT RESERVE RATIO[①] AGAIN WITHIN THE YEAR,

---

① 存款准备金率

SAID AN ECONOMIST.

China's CPI has been driven up mainly by rising pork prices, but the situation will not last long because pork prices are expected to stabilize, said Wang Zhihao, an economist with Standard Chartered Bank (China) Limited①.

The CPI rose 6.5 percent year-on-year② in August, the biggest monthly rise since 1996, after a 5.6 percent increase in the previous month.

"Now we are worried about manufacturing prices rising, which may be propelled by increases in raw material prices and labor costs as well as the low efficiency of outdated machines," said Wang.

Price hikes in the manufacturing industry will have a greater impact on the country, especially when the CPI is going up, according to Wang. Enterprises will have to raise salaries, adding to inflationary pressures.

Wang forecasted China to raise the one-year loan interest rate once again this year to 7.65 percent, and the deposit reserve ratio once or twice more to 14 percent.

China has raised the one-year benchmark interest rates③ five times this year in a bid to curb rising inflation and control excessive liquidity④. In its latest move, on September 15, the central bank raised one-year deposit and loan interest rates by 27 basis points to 3.87 percent and 7.29 percent respectively.

The central bank will be in a dilemma, said Wang. On the one hand, deposits are flowing into the stock markets and real estate because of low deposit interest rates. The best solution is to narrow the interest spread⑤.

On the other hand, narrowing the interest spread will affect Chinese banks' second-half profits⑥, as many listed banks'⑦ first-half income from the interest spread accounted for more of their total, Wang added.

Continuous interest rate hikes have increased the burden of housing mortgage loan⑧ borrowers, and banks are loose in inspecting borrowers' qualifications⑨. These create banking industry risks in housing loan business.

But Chinese banks will not be struck with a crisis like the subprime crisis⑩ in the

---

① 标准渣打银行中国有限责任公司
② 与去年同期相比的
③ 一年期基准利率
④ 流动性泛滥
⑤ 利差
⑥ 下半年利润
⑦ 上市银行
⑧ 住房抵押贷款
⑨ 资格
⑩ 次贷危机

United States, because housing loan borrowers do not need to offer down payments① in the US as they do in China, Wang noted.

Wang also urged individual real estate and stock investors to consider interest rate risks besides market prices. Otherwise they will possibly suffer lower life quality due to increasing monthly payments.

China will set monetary policy according to the needs of its economy and will not let itself be boxed in② by a narrowing gap between Chinese and US interest rates or by CPI hikes, central bank governor③ Zhou Xiaochuan said on Friday.

His comments were fresh confirmation that the People's Bank of China (PBOC), in order to curb inflation and get real deposit rates④ back into positive territory, is prepared to run the risk of attracting capital inflows betting on a stronger yuan⑤.

"China has a large-sized economy and we would very much emphasize the domestic economic situation, such as domestic CPI⑥, investment and consumption, in considering our interest rate policy," Zhou told a conference in Hong Kong.

The Federal Reserve⑦ cut interest rates by half a point on Tuesday and is expected to reduce them further.

The PBOC, by contrast, has raised rates five times so far this year — most recently a week ago — and economists confidently expect one more increase before the end of the year.

In the process, the premium⑧ of US rates over Chinese rates has shrunk to about 1.5 percentage points.

After China depegged⑨ the yuan from the US dollar in July 2005, the PBOC maintained a gap of 3 percentage points⑩ or more to make it expensive for speculators⑪ to borrow dollars and bet on a rise in the Chinese currency.

Wu Xiaoling, Zhou's deputy, said this month that the PBOC had given up maintaining a certain rate gap because money kept coming into China in any case, to chase gains in its red-hot asset markets.⑫

---

① 定金,首付
② 被挡住,被束缚
③ 央行行长
④ 实际存款利息
⑤ 人民币升值
⑥ 国内消费者指数
⑦ 美联储
⑧ 溢价
⑨ 脱钩
⑩ 3个百分点的利差
⑪ 投机者
⑫ 资本市场

Although China has been cautiously relaxing its capital controls, Zhou said there was no timetable for making the currency fully convertible①.

❓ Questions for Discussion

1. What does CPI stand for? Why has it attracted so much attention throughout the country since August 2007? What has pushed it to such a steep rise?

2. How will rising CPI influence China's economy in general?

3. How will rising CPI influence China's stock market and real estate market specifically? Will China suffer the same stock market bubbles and the subprime crisis as USA has experienced?

4. Is the rising CPI in the short run a blessing or a curse to Chinese farmers whose produces benefit from the price hikes? And in the long run?

5. How does the ever-increasing CPI challenge the monetary authorities in its efforts to stabilize CPI and economy? What does PBOC have to face if USA continues its interest rate cuts?

6. How can PBOC curb speculative inflows of foreign capital more effectively?

---

① 可兑换的

7. What are the prospects of PBOC's success in its fight against inflation and hot money?

Translation

1. The CPI rose 6.5 percent year-on-year in August, the biggest monthly rise since 1996, after a 5.6 percent increase in the previous month.

2. In its latest move, on September 15, the central bank raised one-year deposit and loan interest rates by 27 basis points to 3.87 percent and 7.29 percent respectively.

3. His comments were fresh confirmation that the People's Bank of China (PBOC), in order to curb inflation and get real deposit rates back into positive territory, is prepared to run the risk of attracting capital inflows betting on a stronger yuan.

4. After China depegged the yuan from the US dollar in July 2005, the PBOC maintained a gap of 3 percentage points or more to make it expensive for speculators to borrow dollars and bet on a rise in the Chinese currency.

5. Although China has been cautiously relaxing its capital controls, Zhou said there was no timetable for making the currency fully convertible.

Unit 6
Enterprises in the Competitive Market

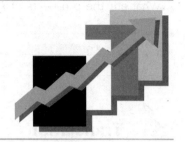

Introduction

If the price of a particular hotel in your city increases by 25% (non-tourist season), you will see its occupancy rate drop dramatically. Customers will probably choose another hotel. However, if you find that the local electric company has raised its prices by 25%, you will find that electricity sales are only slightly reduced. People may not keep their home lights on a constant level and use electricity more sparingly.

Part One Text

In economic theory, perfect competition occurs when all companies sell identical products, market share does not influence price, companies are able to enter or exit without barriers, buyers have perfect or full information, and companies cannot determine prices. In other words, it is a market that is entirely influenced by market forces. It is the opposite of imperfect competition, which is a more accurate reflection of a current market structure.

If each buyer and car buyer is insignificant compared to the size of the market, and thus has no ability to influence market prices, then the market is competitive (hotel, perfectly competitive). In contrast, if a firm can influence the price at which it sells, we say that the firm is imperfect competitive firms (electric company). Imperfect competition can be found in the following types of market structures: monopolies, oligopolies, monopolistic competition, monopsonies, and oligopsonies.

There are five key characteristics of perfect competition, which are:

(1) Many competing firms;

(2) Similar products sold;

(3) Equal market share;
(4) Buyers have full information;
(5) Easy to entry and exit.

When these characteristics are seen in the market, we can consider it perfectly competitive. Let us look at them in more detail below.

A perfectly competitive firm has only one major decision to make—namely, what quantity to produce. To understand why this is so, consider a different way of writing out the basic definition of profit:

$$\text{Profit} = \text{total revenue} - \text{total cost}$$
$$= (\text{price})(\text{quantity produced}) - (\text{average cost})(\text{quantity produced})$$

Since a perfectly competitive firm must accept an output price determined by the market supply and demand for its product, it is not free to determine its price. This means that the firm faces a perfectly elastic demand curve for its product: buyers are willing to buy any quantity of the product from the firm at the market price. When a perfectly competitive firm chooses what quantity to produce, that quantity—along with the prices of output and inputs in the market—will determine the firm's total revenues, total costs, and total profits.

Benefits for Competitive Firms

A perfectly competitive firm can sell as large a quantity as it wishes, as long as it accepts the current market price. Total revenue is going to increase as the firm sells more, depending on the price of the product and the number of units sold. If you increase the number of units sold at a given price, then total revenue will increase. If the price of the product increases for every unit sold, then total revenue also increases.

As an example of how a perfectly competitive firm decides what quantity to produce, consider the case of a small farmer who produces apples and sells them frozen for $4 per pack. Sales of one pack of apples will bring in $4, two packs will be $8, three packs will be $12, and so on. If, for example, the price of frozen apples doubles to $8 per pack, then sales of one pack of apples will be $8, two packs will be $16, three packs will be $24, and so on. Price and marginal revenue of frozen apples are shown in Table 6-1.

Table 6–1 Price and marginal revenue of frozen apples

Quantity (Q)	Price (P)	Total profits (TR = P × Q)	Average revenue (AR = TR/Q)	Marginal revenue (MR = △TR/△Q)
1	$8	$8	$8	
2	$8	$16	$8	$8
3	$8	$24	$8	$8
4	$8	$32	$8	$8
5	$8	$40	$8	$8
6	$8	$48	$8	$8
7	$8	$56	$8	$8
8	$8	$64	$8	$8
9	$8	$72	$8	$8
10	$8	$80	$8	$8
11	$8	$88	$8	$8

Based on the above table, we can draw two conclusions. For non-competitive firms, the average apple's total revenue ($P \times Q$) is divided by the quantity (Q). Thus, for all firms, the average revenue is equal to the price of the item. Moreover, for competing firms, marginal revenue equals the price of the goods, since the price (P) is fixed. It is important to remember that for a competitive firm, the price of the firm's product is equal to both its average revenue and its marginal revenue.

Maximizing the Benefits of Competitive Firms

Let's see how a competitive firm can maximize the benefits of its business. It's still the same farm, and it's still those frozen apples. With a fixed cost of $5, each additional pack of apples sold increases the marginal cost (MC) by $1. For instance, when the farm does not sell apples, it makes a profit of −5 because there are fixed costs. When it sells one pack, its profit is $1. When it sells two packs, its profit is $6. And so on. When it sells 6 and 7 boxes, its profit reaches a maximum of $16. This Equilibrium point (Q_{max}) is the maximum profit of the farm. However, If the farm continues to sell apples, the profits per pack of apples is continuously decreasing. Total revenue, average revenue and marginal efficiency of frozen apples are shown in Table 6–2.

Unit 6 Enterprises in the Competitive Market

Table 6-2 Total revenue, average revenue and marginal efficiency of frozen apples

Quantity (Q)	Total revenue (TR)	Total cost (TC)	Total profits (TR - TC)	Marginal revenue (MR = $\Delta TR/\Delta Q$)	Marginal cost (MC = $\Delta TC/\Delta Q$)	Changes in profits (MR - MC)
0	$0	$5	-5			
1	$8	$7	$1	$8	$2	6
2	$16	$10	$6	$8	$3	5
3	$24	$14	$10	$8	$4	4
4	$32	$19	$13	$8	$5	3
5	$40	$25	$15	$8	$6	2
6	$48	$32	$16	$8	$7	1
7	$56	$40	$16	$8	$8	0
8	$64	$49	$15	$8	$9	-1
9	$72	$59	$13	$8	$10	-2
10	$80	$70	$10	$8	$11	-3

This indicates that when the farm does not reach the equilibrium point (Q_{max}), the marginal revenue (MR) is greater than the marginal cost (MC). Profit is equal to total revenue minus total cost (TR - TC), and profit will increase. When production is greater than the equilibrium point (Qmax), the marginal cost (MC) is greater than the marginal revenue (MR).

The profit-maximizing choice for a perfectly competitive firm will occur where marginal revenue is equal to marginal cost—that is, where MR = MC. A profit-seeking firm should keep expanding production as long as MR > MC. But at the level of output where MR = MC, the firm should recognize that it has achieved the highest possible level of economic profits. (In the example above, the profit maximizing output level is between 6 and 7 units of output, but the firm will not know they've maximized profit until they reach 7, where MR = MC.) Expanding production into the zone where MR < MC will only reduce economic profits. Because the marginal revenue received by a perfectly competitive firm is equal to the price P, so that P = MR, the profit-maximizing rule for a perfectly competitive firm can also be written as a recommendation to produce at the quantity where P = MC.

We can draw this conclusion:

(1) If the marginal benefit is greater than the marginal cost, the firm should increase its output.

(2) If marginal revenue is less than marginal cost, the firm should reduce output.

(3) If the marginal revenue is equal to the marginal cost, the firm maximizes its profit.

Barriers to Entry Prohibit Perfect Competition

Many industries also have significant barriers to entry, such as high startup costs (as seen in the auto manufacturing industry) or strict government regulations (as seen in the utility industry), which limit the ability of firms to enter and exit such industries. And although consumer awareness has increased with the information age, there are still few industries where the buyer remains aware of all available products and prices.

Significant obstacles exist that prevent perfect competition from developing in the economy. The agricultural industry probably comes closest to exhibiting perfect competition because it is characterized by many small producers with virtually no ability to alter the selling price of their products.

The commercial buyers of agricultural commodities are generally very well-informed and, although agricultural production involves some barriers to entry, it is not particularly difficult to enter the marketplace as a producer.

Advantages and Disadvantages of Perfect Competition

Perfect competition is an idealized framework for a market economy. While it provides a convenient model for how an economy works, it is not always accurate and has significant departures from the real-world economy. Like with other models, the value of a perfect competition framework is only accurate to the extent that it reflects actual conditions.

One notable feature of perfect competition is low profit margins. Since all consumers have access to the same products, they naturally gravitate towards the lowest prices. Firms cannot set themselves apart by charging a premium for higher-quality products and services. For instance, it would be impossible for a company like Apple (AAPL) to exist in a perfectly competitive market because its phones are more expensive than those of its competitors.

Another is the absence of innovation. The prospect of greater market share and setting themselves apart from the competition is an incentive for firms to innovate and make better products. But no firm possesses a dominant market share in perfect competition, meaning that the long-term profitability of their operations is zero.

Another disadvantage is the absence of economies of scale. Limited to zero profit margins means that companies will have less cash to invest in expanding their production capabilities. An expansion of production capabilities could potentially bring down costs

Unit 6　Enterprises in the Competitive Market

for consumers and increase business profit margins. But the presence of several small firms cannibalizing the market for the same product prevents this and ensures that the average firm size remains small.

Words and Expressions

gravitate	v.	受引力作用，被吸引
incentive	n.	激励，刺激
monopolies	n.	垄断
oligopolies	n.	寡头
competitive market		竞争市场
perfectly competitive firm		完全竞争企业
maximizing the benefits		利益最大化
expanding the production capabilities		扩大产能
cannibalizing		同类相食，拆台
perfect competition		完全竞争
imperfect competition		不完全竞争
market share		市场份额
monopolistic competition		垄断竞争
utility industry		通用工业，实用工业
consumer awareness		消费者意识
exhibiting perfect competition		展示完全竞争
total revenues		总收入
total costs		总成本
total profits		利润总额，总收益
marginal cost		边际成本
average revenue		平均收益
marginal revenue		边际收益
equilibrium point (Q_{max})		平衡点

1. elastic demand 弹性需求

When a change in the price of something leads to a larger change in the amount of it that is sold or that could be sold if it was available. Elastic demand occurs when the price of a good or service affects consumer demand. If the price goes down just a little, consumers will buy a lot more. If prices rise just a bit, they'll stop buying as much and wait for prices to return to normal.

2. **economic equilibrium 经济平衡**

Economic equilibrium is a condition or state in which economic forces are balanced. In effect, economic variables remain unchanged from their equilibrium values in the absence of external influences. Economic equilibrium is also referred to as market equilibrium.

Economic equilibrium is the combination of economic variables (usually price and quantity) toward which normal economic processes, such as supply and demand, drive the economy. The term economic equilibrium can also be applied to any number of variables such as interest rates or aggregate consumption spending. The point of equilibrium represents a theoretical state of rest where all economic transactions that "should" occur, given the initial state of all relevant economic variables, have taken place.

3. **profit margin 利润率, 利润幅度**

the difference between the price of a product or service and the cost of producing it, or between the cost of producing all of a company's products or services and the total sum they are sold for.

4. **economies of scale 规模经济**

The decrease in unit cost as a result of increasing production so that fixed costs may be spread out over a greater number of units produced.

Exercises

I Make verb phrases by linking those in Column A and Column B.

Column A	Column B
draw	production
maximize	industry
expand	prices
enter	benefits
determine	conclusions

Unit 6 Enterprises in the Competitive Market

II Match the following words or terms with their definitions.

| equilibrium | cannibalize | recommendation | utility | gravitate |
| incentive | marginal cost | oligopoly | monopsony | sparingly |

1. _____ : a situation in which there is a balance between different forces or aspects
2. _____ : a situation in which a small number of organizations or companies has control of an area of business, so that others have no share
3. _____ : a situation in a market in which there is only one buyer for goods or services offered by several sellers
4. _____ : the additional cost of producing one more item for sale
5. _____ : move toward or be attracted to a place, person, or thing
6. _____ : a thing that motivates or encourages one to do something
7. _____ : to cause a reduction in the sales of an existing product or service by starting to sell a new product or service
8. _____ : a service that is used by the public, such as an electricity or gas supply
9. _____ : a suggestion that something is good or suitable for a particular purpose
10. _____ : in a restricted manner; in small quantities

III Reading comprehension: choose the best answer from the four choices.

1. In economic theory, perfect competition occurs in the following situations except _____.
   A. companies don't have a say in determining prices
   B. market is not influenced by market forces
   C. companies sell same products
   D. information is fully accessible for consumers

2. The only major decision for a perfectly competitive firm to make is _____.
   A. to accept the output prices
   B. to accept the input prices
   C. to determine prices
   D. to determine what quantity to produce

3. When will the profit-maximizing choice for a perfectly competitive firm occur?
   A. Expanding production into the zone where MR < MC.
   B. Marginal revenue is equal to marginal cost where MR = MC.

C. Marginal benefit is greater than the marginal cost.

D. Marginal revenue is less than marginal cost.

4. Many industries also have significant barriers to entry, which of the following is not the barrier to entry according to the text?

A. The startup costs are high.

B. There is strict official control.

C. Consumer remains unaware of all products and prices.

D. Small producers have abilities to alter the selling price.

5. According to the text, which of the following statements is not true?

A. A perfect competition framework is only accurate to the extent that it reflects actual conditions.

B. Low profit margins is a remarkable characteristic for perfect competition.

C. Innovation would be advanced in perfect competition.

D. Small firms for the same products help to stabilize the average firm size.

Part Two Case Study

THIS IS THE AGE OF THE MICROSOFT AND AMAZON ECONOMY.

By **Tim Harford**

From *Financial Times*, May 19, 2017

One of my first economics lessons contrasted perfect competition, which was judged to be a good thing, with monopoly, which was not. There are worse places to begin than by being shown the difference between championing the miracle of the free market and favoring the depredations of dominant businesses.

But monopoly power has often seemed like yesterday's issue. Standard Oil was broken up in 1911; AT&T in 1984. To the extent that we economists worried about companies being too big, we were thinking about the systemic risks from banks that were too big to fail. But we are starting to notice again the risks not of corporate failure but of corporate success.

The most obvious examples are the big digital players: Google dominates search; Facebook is the Goliath of social media; Amazon rules online retail. But, as documented in a new working paper by five economists, American business is in general becoming more concentrated.

David Autor and his colleagues looked at 676 industries in the US — from cigarettes to greeting cards, musical instruments to payday lenders. They found that for the typical industry in each of six sectors — manufacturing, retail, finance, services, wholesale and utilities/transportation — the biggest companies are producing a larger share of output.

For example, in the early 1980s the largest four players in any given US manufacturing industry averaged 38 per cent of sales; three decades later the figure was 43 per cent. In utilities and transportation the typical market share of the biggest four companies rose from 29 per cent to 37 per cent. In retail, overshadowed by Walmart and Amazon, the rise was dramatic: 14 per cent to 30 per cent.

This is surprising. As the world economy grows, one might expect markets to become more like the perfectly competitive textbook model, not less. Deregulation should allow more competition; globalization should expose established players to pressure from overseas; transparent prices should make it harder for fat cats to maintain their position. Why hasn't competition chipped away at the market position of the leading companies? The simplest explanation: they are very good at what they do. Competition isn't a threat to them. It's an opportunity.

What Professor Autor and his colleagues call "superstar firms" tend to be more efficient. They sell more at a lower cost, so they enjoy a larger profit margin. Google is the purest example: its search algorithm won market share on merit. Alternatives are easily available, but most people do not use them. But the pattern holds more broadly: superstar firms have grown not by avoiding competitors but by defeating them.

This is not entirely bad news. But it's not entirely good news, either. The superstar firm phenomenon is the best explanation we have of a little-noticed but worrisome trend: since 1980, in the US and many other advanced economies, workers have been getting a steadily smaller slice of the economic pie (the distribution of this labor income also became much more unequal during the 1980s and 1990s).

Workers, from shelf-stackers to chief executives, have seen their total share of economic value-added fall from about 66 per cent to about 60 per cent in the US since 1980. This decline in "labor share" is often blamed on international trade making life harder for workers and easier for footloose capital. Prof Autor and his colleagues find little evidence for this idea.

Superstar firms, instead, seem to be the cause. The story is simple. These businesses are highly productive and achieve more with less. Because of this profitability, more of the value added by the company flows to shareholders and less to workers. And what happens in these groups will tend to be reflected in the economy as a whole, because superstar firms have an increasingly important role.

All this poses a headache for policymakers — assuming policymakers can pay attention to the issue for long enough. The policy response required is subtle: after all, the growth of innovative, productive companies is welcome. It's the unintended consequences of that growth that pose problems.

Those consequences are not easy to predict, but here are two possibilities. Either the US economy ends up like Amazon, or it ends up like Microsoft. The Amazon future is one of relentless competition, a paradise for consumers but a nightmare for workers, and with the ever-present risk that dominant businesses will snuff out competition as the mood takes them.

The Microsoft future epitomizes the economist John Hicks's quip: "the best of all monopoly profits is a quiet life". Microsoft in the 1990s became famous as a once-brilliant company that decided to pull up the drawbridge, locking in consumers and locking out competitors.

In either scenario ordinary people lose out, unless they can enjoy returns from capital as well as returns from working. In the very long run a superstar economy could become a technological utopia, where nobody needs to work for a living. That would require quite a realignment in our economic system; I wouldn't bet on such an outcome happening by chance.

Questions for Discussion

1. Why hasn't competition chipped away at the market position of the leading companies? Why is monopoly not judged to be a good thing compared with perfect competition?

_____
_____

2. What's your opinion of superstar firms? Do you agree that in the very long run a superstar economy could become a technological utopia, where nobody needs to work for a living?

_____
_____

Translation

1. One of my first economics lessons contrasted perfect competition, which was judged to be a good thing, with monopoly, which was not. There are worse places to begin than by being shown the difference between championing the miracle of the free market and favoring the depredations of dominant businesses.

Unit 6 Enterprises in the Competitive Market

2. As the world economy grows, one might expect markets to become more like the perfectly competitive textbook model, not less. Deregulation should allow more competition; globalization should expose established players to pressure from overseas; transparent prices should make it harder for fat cats to maintain their position.

3. All this poses a headache for policymakers—assuming policymakers can pay attention to the issue for long enough. The policy response required is subtle: after all, the growth of innovative, productive companies is welcome. It's the unintended consequences of that growth that pose problems.

4. The Amazon future is one of relentless competition, a paradise for consumers but a nightmare for workers, and with the ever-present risk that dominant businesses will snuff out competition as the mood takes them.

Unit 7
Monopoly Market

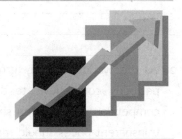

Introduction

A monopoly is a market where one firm (or manufacturer) is the sole supplier of certain goods or services. This firm faces no competition due to which it can set its own prices, thereby exercising full control over the market. The monopolist aims to generate high profits by selling products (or services) that do not have close substitutes.

Monopolies are discouraged in several countries as power and wealth tend to concentrate with a single seller. Moreover, such sellers may offer low-quality products at high prices, thus exploiting the consumer. A monopoly can be broken by imposing government regulations or opening the market to competition.

Part One Text

Monopoly in Economics Explained

Monopoly is derived from the words "monos" (single) and "polein" (to sell) of Greek. Monopoly was first depicted in The Landlord's Game, which was invented by Elizabeth Magie Phillips (or Lizzie Magie) in 1904. This game inspired the monopoly board game that is played by most students today.

In economics, a monopoly exists when the following conditions are satisfied:

(1) A single seller dominates either the entire industry (or market) or a substantial percentage of the industry. This domination makes the monopolist firm a price setter (or price maker) rather than a price taker.

(2) There is a lack of competition in the market. Additionally, there are barriers to the entry of new firms. This implies that it is difficult to enter the market as the

consumers prefer the products of the established firm over those of the new entrants. Moreover, the established firm can produce the products at low prices while the new entrants cannot do this initially.

(3) There is an absence of the availability of close substitutes. This implies that the consumer has no choice but to purchase from the monopolist firm.

Monopolies can often lead to unfair trade practices like charging different prices from different consumers (price discrimination), setting prices far above the costs of manufacturing, selling inferior products and services, etc. Due to these practices, a monopoly may be dissolved sooner or later.

Types of Monopoly

The different types of monopolies are discussed as follows:

(1) Simple monopoly.

A simple monopoly charges uniform prices for its product (or service) from all the buyers. In this, the monopolist firm usually operates in one market and its consumers are price takers.

(2) Pure monopoly.

A pure monopoly is the rarest form wherein the product (or service) being sold has no close substitutes. Moreover, competitors are discouraged from entering the market often due to high initial costs.

(3) Natural monopoly.

A natural monopoly depends on unique raw materials or sophisticated technology to manufacture its products. In this, the monopolist firm utilizes its copyright and patents to prevent competition. In addition, such firms usually provide public utilities (like electricity, gas, etc.), adhere to government regulations, and incur high costs on research and innovation.

(4) Legal monopoly.

A legal monopoly is one wherein the monopolist firm reserves the right to manufacture a product by way of a patent, trademark or copyright. Since the monopolist is the inventor of such a product (or process), it is the exclusive supplier in the market. Patents allow time to firms to recover the high costs of development and research.

(5) Public or industrial monopoly.

A public monopoly is set up by the government to supply important products and services. The government creates such monopolies for the following reasons:

- The costs associated with production and deliveries are too high.
- The presence of a sole supplier is considered to be more reliable and beneficial for the general public.

Public monopolies are created when the government nationalizes certain industries to serve the interest of the people.

Characteristics

The features of a monopoly are listed as follows:

(1) Maximizes profits.

The monopolist firm aims to maximize its profits owing to no rivalry and lack of consumer choices. This is the major reason a monopolist firm wants to continue enjoying its monopoly. The monopolist firms strive to earn abnormal (or supernormal) profits.

(2) Sets prices.

The single manufacturer has the power to set the prices of its products or services. The monopolist firm (price maker) may or may not charge the same price from all its consumers. The consumers (price takers) have to accept the prices set by the firm unless the government intervenes to impose a maximum price.

(3) Poses high entry barriers.

The new entrants have to face several challenges while trying to enter a monopolist market. Such challenges include high startup costs, specialized technologies, high government restrictions, complex business contracts, restricted purchase of raw materials, etc.

(4) Lacks close substitutes.

There are no products (or services) that match the offerings of the monopolist firm. The absence of close substitutes makes the demand for monopolist products relatively inelastic. The demand is inelastic when it does not change much with a change in the price of the product. Inelastic demand makes it easier to make profits in the market.

(5) Becomes the industry.

The single firm, being the sole supplier, becomes synonymous with the industry. This implies that the difference between a firm and an industry ceases to exist in the case of a monopoly.

Top 8 Examples of Monopoly in Real Life

The following are examples of monopolies in real life.

(1) Railways.

The government provides public services like the railways. Hence, they are a monopolist because new partners or privately held companies are not allowed to run railways. However, the price of the tickets is reasonable so that most people can use public transport.

(2) Luxottica.

Luxottica—A company that owns all the major brands of sunglasses. The company has bought almost all the major eyewear brands. However, they are still named differently. It creates an illusion in the customer's mind that they have a variety of sunglasses to choose from, although they are all manufactured by one company. Luxottica produces more than 80% of the eyewear worldwide.

(3) Microsoft.

Microsoft—Microsoft is a Computer and software manufacturing Company. It holds more than 75% market share and is the tech space's market leader and virtual monopolist.

(4) AB InBev.

AB InBev—A company formed by the merger of Anheuser-Busch and InBev distributes over 200 types, including Budweiser, Corona, Beck's, etc. While these beer names are different and have different compositions to give a different taste, they belong to a single company. So, when people consume different Beers, they are paying a single company in a sense.

(5) Google.

Google has become a household name and whenever we don't know any answer, probably googling is the answer. With their secret algorithm, the biggest web searcher controls more than 70% market share. In addition, the company has grown into a web of services interlinked like maps, Gmail, search engines, etc. As a result, the company has left its competitors—Yahoo and Microsoft—behind its innovation and technological advancement.

(6) Patents.

Patents provide a legal monopoly to a company, albeit for a short period. When the patent is in force, no other company can use its invention for its purposes. For example, a casino in Genting Highlands, Malaysia, held an exclusive patent for legalized casino, and it enjoyed the legal monopoly for years in Malaysia.

(7) AT&T.

In 1982, AT&T, a telecommunications firm, was the sole supplier of telephone services across the US, which was violating the antitrust laws. Due to its monopolistic activities for service as essential telecommunication, the company was forced to split into six subsidiaries called "Baby Bells."

(8) Facebook.

Social media is the new market in the current century. While the users are offered free services, the companies earn from the advertising revenue. With its huge portion of the market share, Facebook almost has a monopoly in this business. The company is ahead of all its competitors like Google +, Twitter, etc. It has seen organic growth in users and social media advertisers and acquisition of other companies like Whatsapp,

Oculus Rift, etc. The company is so big that they recently charged it with affecting the users' sentiments on how the elections are fought and inclines them towards a single person or a party.

Words and Expressions

merger	n.	合并，兼并
acquisition	n.	兼并，收购
algorithm	n.	算法，运算法则
subsidiaries	n.	子公司，下属分公司
albeit	conj.	虽然，尽管
simple monopoly (state monopoly)		国家垄断
pure monopoly		纯粹垄断，完全垄断
natural monopoly		自然垄断
public utilities		公共事业类公司
legal monopoly		合法垄断
exclusive supplier		独家供应商
public or industrial monopoly		公共或行业垄断
rivalry abnormal (or supernormal) profits		竞争异常（或超正常）利润
close substitutes		相似替代品
antitrust laws		反托拉斯法，反垄断法
social media		社会媒体，社交媒体
affecting the users' sentiments		影响用户情绪

Notes

1. **price setter (or price maker) 价格制定者**
   Price setters are individuals or firms that influence the whole market and can set prices in the market and have some control over the market price. Only a firm with some degree of monopoly power can be a price-setter.

2. **price taker 价格接受者**
   A company or person that has little influence on the price of something, and has to follow what other companies and people do. Price takers have no control over prices and must accept prevailing market prices. Price takers are competitive firms or individuals

who have to treat the market price as given.

3. **unfair trade practices** 不正当贸易行为,不公平贸易行为

   Unfair trade practices refer to the use of various deceptive, fraudulent, or unethical methods to obtain business. Unfair business practices include misrepresentation, false advertising or representation of a good or service, tied selling, false free prize or gift offers, deceptive pricing, and noncompliance with manufacturing standards. Such acts are considered unlawful by statute through the Consumer Protection Law, which opens up recourse for consumers by way of compensatory or punitive damages. An unfair trade practice is sometimes referred to as "deceptive trade practices" or "unfair business practices."

4. **price discrimination** 价格歧视

   the price of charging different prices for the same product in different markets

5. **organic growth** 有机增长(指企业通过自身业务扩展、提高生产效率和销售额等内部途径实现的增长,而非通过兼并、收购等外部途径)

   Organic growth is the growth a company achieves by increasing output and enhancing sales internally. This does not include profits or growth attributable to mergers and acquisitions but rather an increase in sales and expansion through the company's own resources. Organic growth stands in contrast to inorganic growth, which is growth related to activities outside a business's own operations.

I Make verb phrases by linking those in Column A and Column B.

Column A	Column B
exploit	regulations
impose	consumer
dominate	profits
maximize	laws
violate	market

II Match the following words or terms with their definitions.

monopoly	entry barriers	discourage	exclusive
inelastic demand	price discrimination	intervene	antitrust laws
innovative	substitutes		

1. _____ : to try to prevent or persuade someone not to do something or to lose confidence or enthusiasm for something
2. _____ : to come between two parties or situations in order to prevent or alter a result or course of events
3. _____ : the exclusive possession or control of the supply or trade in a commodity or service
4. _____ : goods or services that can be used in place of each other for a particular purpose or need
5. _____ : a situation in which the demand for a product or service does not significantly change in response to changes in price
6. _____ : restricted or limited to a specific person, group, or category; not available to others
7. _____ : the practice of charging different prices to different customers for the same product or service
8. _____ : obstacles or restrictions that make it difficult for new firms to enter a market and compete with established companies
9. _____ : laws and regulations aimed at promoting fair competition in the marketplace and preventing monopolistic practices
10. _____ : introducing or using new ideas, methods, or technologies; characterized by creativity and originality

III Reading comprehension: choose the best answer from the four choices.

1. What is the main characteristic of a monopoly?
   A. Limited options for consumers.
   B. Fierce competition among multiple firms.
   C. Government regulation of prices.
   D. High-quality products at affordable prices.
2. Why are monopolies often discouraged in many countries?
   A. Monopolies tend to generate excessive profits.
   B. Monopolies promote healthy market competition.
   C. Monopolies offer a wide range of product alternatives.
   D. Monopolies provide affordable prices for consumers.
3. Which example illustrates a monopoly that controls a significant portion of the market?
   A. Railways   B. Luxottica   C. Microsoft   D. AB InBev
4. How do natural monopolies maintain their dominance in the market?
   A. By providing close substitutes to consumers.

B. By constantly innovating and improving their products.
C. By utilizing copyrights and patents to prevent competition.
D. By offering low prices to attract new entrants.
5. What does a natural monopoly rely on to maintain its market dominance?
A. Advanced technology and innovation.
B. Unique raw materials and resources.
C. Government regulations and restrictions.
D. Exclusive patents and copyrights.

Part Two Case Study

US ACCUSES GOOGLE OF ILLEGALLY PROTECTING MONOPOLY

By Cecilia Kang, David McCabe and Daisuke Wakabayashi
From *The New York Times*, Oct. 20, 2020

WASHINGTON — The Justice Department accused Google on Tuesday of illegally protecting its monopoly over search and search advertising, the government's most significant challenge to a tech company's market power in a generation and one that could reshape the way consumers use the internet.

In a much-anticipated lawsuit, the agency accused Google of locking up deals with giant partners like Apple and throttling competition through exclusive business contracts and agreements.

Google's deals with Apple, mobile carriers and other handset makers to make its search engine the default option for users accounted for most of its dominant market share in search, the agency said, a figure that it put at around 80 percent.

"For many years," the agency said in its 57-page complaint, "Google has used anticompetitive tactics to maintain and extend its monopolies in the markets for general search services, search advertising and general search text advertising—the cornerstones of its empire."

The lawsuit, which may stretch on for years, could set off a cascade of other antitrust lawsuits from state attorneys general. About four dozen states and jurisdictions, including New York and Texas, have conducted parallel investigations and some of them are expected to bring separate complaints against the company's grip on technology for online advertising. Eleven state attorneys general, all Republicans, signed on to support the federal lawsuit.

Attorney General William P. Barr had spoken publicly about the investigation for months. He urged the agency to file a case by the end of September, prompting resistance from some of its lawyers who wanted more time and complained of political motivations.

Google called the suit "deeply flawed." But the agency's action signaled a new era for the technology sector. It reflects pent-up and bipartisan frustration toward a handful of companies—Google, Amazon, Apple and Facebook in particular — that have evolved from small and scrappy companies into global powerhouses with outsize influence over commerce, speech, media and advertising. Conservatives like President Trump and liberals like Senator Elizabeth Warren have called for more restraints over Big Tech.

The suit, filed in the US District Court in the District of Columbia, will also be a major test of antitrust law. Many Democrats argue that the laws need to be adjusted to account for the digital era, when many products are free and it can be more difficult to prove the harm to consumers from a company's firm grip on a market.

A victory for the government could remake one of America's most recognizable companies and the internet economy that it has helped define since it was founded by two Stanford University graduate students in 1998. The Justice Department did not immediately put forward remedies, such as selling off parts of the company or unwinding business contracts, in the lawsuit. Such actions are typically pursued in later stages of a case.

Ryan Shores, an associate deputy attorney general, said "nothing is off the table" in terms of remedies.

Google has long denied accusations of antitrust violations, and the company is expected to fight the government's efforts by using its global network of lawyers, economists and lobbyists. Alphabet, valued at $1.04 trillion and with cash reserves of $120 billion, has fought similar antitrust lawsuits in Europe. The company spent $12.7 million lobbying in the United States in 2019, making it one of the top corporate spenders in Washington.

The company says it has strong competition in the search market, with more people finding information on sites like Amazon. It says its services have been a boon for small businesses.

"People use Google because they choose to, not because they're forced to, or because they can't find alternatives," Kent Walker, the company's chief legal officer, said in a blog post.

Mr. Walker said the lawsuit would do "nothing to help consumers. To the contrary, it would artificially prop up lower-quality search alternatives, raise phone prices and make it harder for people to get the search services they want to use."

Democratic lawmakers on the House Judiciary Committee released a sprawling report on the tech giants two weeks ago, also accusing Google of controlling a monopoly over online search and the ads that come up when users enter a query.

"A significant number of entities—spanning major public corporations, small businesses and entrepreneurs—depend on Google for traffic, and no alternate search engine serves as a substitute," the report said. The lawmakers also accused Apple, Amazon and Facebook of abusing their market power. They called for more aggressive enforcement of antitrust laws, and for Congress to consider strengthening them.

The scrutiny reflects how Google has become a dominant player in communications, commerce and media over the last two decades. That business is lucrative: Last year, Google brought in $34.3 billion in search revenue in the United States, according to the research firm eMarketer. That figure is expected to grow to $42.5 billion by 2022, the firm said.

In its complaint, the Justice Department said that Google's actions had hurt consumers by stifling innovation, reducing choice and diminishing the quality of search services, including consumer data privacy. It also said that advertisers that use its products "must pay a toll to Google's search advertising and general search text advertising monopolies."

The lawsuit is the result of an investigation that has stretched for more than a year. Prosecutors have spoken with Google's rivals in technology and media, collecting information and documents that could be used to build a case.

The Justice Department also investigated Google's behavior and acquisitions in the overall market for digital advertising, which includes search, web display and video ads.

But the search case is the most straightforward, giving the government its best chance to win. To prevail, the Justice Department has to show two things: that Google is dominant in search, and that its deals with Apple and other companies hobble competition in the search market.

The Justice Department said Google estimates that almost 50 percent of its search traffic originated on Apple devices in 2019. Because it is such a large portion of its queries, Google pays the iPhone maker an estimated $8 billion to $12 billion a year to remain the default option on its phones, iPads and Mac computers.

That arrangement has made Apple and Google hugely reliant on each other, while edging out other search engines and, according to the government, protecting Google's monopoly. Inside Google, losing its pole position on iPhones is considered a "Code Red" scenario, according to the lawsuit, while at Apple, Google's payments account for roughly 15 to 20 percent of Apple's profits.

Gene Kimmelman, a former senior antitrust official at the agency, said the case focused on how Google's lock on search allowed it to "control a treasure trove of user data and deny access to competitors." He said the focus on contracts was significant because some were made when Microsoft's Bing and Yahoo posed a competitive threat to Google's search.

In its blog post, Google argued that there was nothing wrong with its agreements with Apple, other handset manufacturers and carriers, comparing them to cereal brands paying for prominent placement on store shelves. It also said it was not difficult for consumers to switch default settings from Google to another search engine.

Mr. Barr, a former telecom executive at Verizon who once argued an antitrust case before the Supreme Court, signaled that he would put the tech giants under new scrutiny at his confirmation hearing in early 2019. He said that "a lot of people wonder how such huge behemoths that now exist in Silicon Valley have taken shape under the nose of the antitrust enforcers."

He put the investigation under the control of his deputy, Jeffrey Rosen, who in turn hired Mr. Shores, an aide from a major law firm, to oversee the case and other technology matters. Mr. Barr's grip over the investigation tightened when the head of the Justice Department's antitrust division, Makan Delrahim, recused himself from the investigation because he represented Google in its acquisition of the ad service DoubleClick in 2007.

Mr. Barr wanted prosecutors to wrap up their inquiries—and decide whether to bring a case—before Election Day. While Justice Department officials are usually tight-lipped about their investigations until a case is filed, Mr. Barr publicly declared his intention to make a decision on the Google matter by the end of the summer.

This year, most of the roughly 40 lawyers building the case said they opposed bringing a complaint by Mr. Barr's Sept. 30 deadline. Some said they would not sign the complaint, and several left the case this summer.

Google last faced serious scrutiny from an American antitrust regulator nearly a decade ago, when the Federal Trade Commission investigated whether it had abused its power over the search market. The agency's staff recommended bringing charges against the company, according to a memo reported on by The Wall Street Journal. But the agency's five commissioners voted in 2013 not to bring a case.

Other governments have been more aggressive toward the big tech companies. The European Union has brought three antitrust cases against Google in recent years, focused on its search engine, advertising business and Android mobile operating system. Regulators in Britain and Australia are examining the digital advertising market, in inquiries that could ultimately implicate the company.

"It's the most newsworthy monopolization action brought by the government since the Microsoft case in the late '90s," said Bill Baer, a former chief of the Justice

Department's antitrust division. "It's significant in that the government believes that a highly successful tech platform has engaged in conduct that maintains its monopoly power unlawfully, and as a result injures consumers and competition."

Google and its allies will most likely criticize the suit as politically motivated. The Trump administration has attacked Google, which owns YouTube, and other online platform companies as being slanted against conservative views.

The lawsuit is likely to outlast the Trump administration. The Justice Department spent more than a decade taking on Microsoft.

Google's representatives said they anticipated that it would be at least a year before the case went to trial.

While it is possible that a new Democratic administration would review the strategy behind the case, experts said it was unlikely that it would be withdrawn under new leadership.

Questions for Discussion

1. Should there be stricter regulations on tech giants like Google, Amazon, Apple, and Facebook? Discuss the arguments for and against increased regulatory scrutiny, considering factors such as market power, innovation, consumer protection, and freedom of speech.

_____
_____
_____

2. How can the government strike a balance between promoting competition and innovation, and ensuring a level playing field in the technology industry? Explore potential regulatory approaches or policy measures that could foster competition, protect consumer interests, and encourage technological advancements.

_____
_____
_____

Translation

1. The Justice Department accused Google on Tuesday of illegally protecting its monopoly over search and search advertising, the government's most significant challenge to a tech company's market power in a generation and one that could reshape the way consumers use the internet.

2. A victory for the government could remake one of America's most recognizable companies and the internet economy that it has helped define since it was founded by two Stanford University graduate students in 1998.

3. The lawsuit is the result of an investigation that has stretched for more than a year. Prosecutors have spoken with Google's rivals in technology and media, collecting information and documents that could be used to build a case.

4. The European Union has brought three antitrust cases against Google in recent years, focused on its search engine, advertising business and Android mobile operating system. Regulators in Britain and Australia are examining the digital advertising market, in inquiries that could ultimately implicate the company.

Unit 8
GDP and GNP

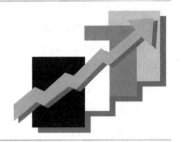

Introduction

GDP and GNP are important data that economists and policymakers use to monitor the performance of the overall economy. These data reflect the economic changes that macroeconomists try to explain. They are among the most closely watched economic statistics because they are thought to be the best measures of a society's economic well-being.

Part One Text

GNP is a little bit different from GDP. A country's Gross National Product (GNP) is the total value, measured in the country's currency, of the final goods and services produced during a certain period, such as a year, or a calendar quarter of a year. Why final goods and services? Final goods are the end-products of the production process and are used by their buyers in finished form rather than incorporated in further stages of production. We count goods sold to final or ultimate users such as households, because it would not make sense to add together the values of an economy's production of iron, steel, and cars. Doing so would involve double-counting; the value of steel includes the value of iron ore that goes into the steel and the value of a car includes the value of the steel that goes into the car. Iron and steel are intermediate goods. Intermediate goods are goods such as materials, parts and the computer-repair services used in the production of other goods.

When the overall economy is growing smoothly — that is, when the GNP is rising steadily — there are ordinarily significant differences in the growth rates of various industries. For example, the steel industry may be growing slowly or even declining, while the computer industry is growing rapidly. Macroeconomic disturbances change the growth of the GNP, and often affect almost all industries in the same direction. When the GNP suffers a sustained decline, the steel industry goes from rapid growth to slow growth or mild decline, and so forth. A central task of macroeconomics is to study, understand, and control if possible these widespread disturbances that affect most industries at the same time. Because so many industries exhibit a common response to macro disturbances, economists often think of the aggregate GNP as if it were a single, generalized good.

Nominal and Real GNP

The US GNP in 1982 was $3,166 billion. Think about this number as being derived from a huge table listing all the quantities and prices of all the goods produced for final users in 1982. Multiply price and quantity for each good to obtain the total 1982 value for each good, and then add together these values. What you get is the nominal GNP.

Now do the same thing for 1989. As compared to 1982, each of the quantities is different unless they happen to be the same by statistical fluke. Multiplying price and quantity for all final products in 1989 and adding up the values yield the nominal GNP for 1989. The number happens to be $5,200.8 billion.

Now consider the following two thought experiments.

(1) Suppose that all the 1989 quantities just happened to be the same as in 1982, but all the prices were higher. Nominal GNP would be higher, but only because prices were higher.

(2) Suppose that all the 1989 prices were the same as in 1982, but all the quantities were higher. Nominal GNP would be higher, but this time because quantities were higher.

The dollar value of the 1989 GNP might be identical in these two cases, but clearly we would want to distinguish between them. The value of GNP obtained in these thought experiments is called nominal or current-dollar GNP. Nominal GNP, or current-dollar GNP, is the value of a year's prices. To distinguish between the two cases, we need to find a way to separate changes in nominal GNP because of changes in prices from those resulting from changes in quantities.

The easiest way to understand how economists distinguish between changes in the GNP resulting from changes in quantities is to consider a simple example. Suppose we value the quantity of peanut butter production in 1989 with its dollar value in 1982, only the quantity is different, because we have standardized the prices for both years by using the 1982 price. We can repeat this calculation for all years of interest, multiplying each year's quantity of peanut butter by the 1982 price of peanut butter. The year 1982 is known as the base year.

We then proceed to treat all the goods the economy produces just as we have peanut butter in the previous paragraph. We multiply the quantities of all the final goods in a particular year by their base-year prices, and add up the values so calculated. The result is called real or constant-dollar GNP. Real GNP, or constant-dollar GNP, for a particular year is the sum of the values of all the final goods produced in that year, where the values are calculated by multiplying the year's quantities by the prices of the goods in a base year. This concept is also sometimes called "GNP corrected for inflation" because the effects of price changes have been removed by using prices held constant to those of a base year.

For any individual product, the 1989 quantity may be larger or smaller than that for 1982, but when we calculate real GNP we obtain a measure showing whether the economy's total output has gone up or down. In fact, US GNP in 1989 in 1982 dollars was 4,117.7 billion. This number is larger than the 1982 GNP of $3,166.0 billion but not as large as the 1989 current-dollar GNP of $5,200.8 billion. These facts indicate that part of the increase in nominal GNP between 1982 and 1989 was because of prices increases and part was because of quantity increases.

We used 1982 as the base year in this illustration because, at the time of this writing, the GNP statistics use that as the base year. The Bureau of Economic Analysis (BEA), which is the government agency responsible for GNP statistics in the United States, changes the base year from time to time to maintain a base year reasonably up to date. For example, the BEA replaced the 1972 base year with 1982 base year in 1985 and, at the time of this writing, expected to adopt a 1987 base year in 1991. The GNP statistics are subject to frequent minor revisions and occasional major ones, including changes in the base year.

Words and Expressions

fluke	n.	侥幸，碰巧
multiply	v.	乘以
yield	v.	产生，得到
identical	a.	相同的，相似的
distinguish	v.	区分
standardize	v.	将……标准化
Gross National Product (GNP)		国民生产总值

Gross Domestic Product (GDP)	国内生产总值
nominal GNP	名义国民生产总值
real GNP	实际国民生产总值
end/finished product	最终产品
intermediate product	中间产品
constant dollar	不变美元
current dollar	现值美元
be subject to	受制于……，一定会遭受……
the Bureau of Economic Analysis, USA	美国经济分析局
double counting	重复计算
sustained decline	持续下降,持续衰退
mild decline	温和下降,温和衰退
minor revision	小修正,小修改
major change	大修正,大修改

1. Gross Domestic Product (GDP) 国内生产总值

GDP is one of the several measures of the size of an economy. The GDP of a country is defined as the market value of all final goods and services produced within a country in a given period of time. It is also considered the sum of value added at every stage of production of all final goods and services produced within a country in a given period of time. Until the 1 980s the term GNP or gross *national* product was used in the United States. The two terms GDP and GNP are almost identical. The most common approach to measuring and understanding GDP is the expenditure method(支出法):

GDP = consumption + investment + government spending + (exports − imports)

"Gross" means depreciation (贬值) of capital stock is not included. With depreciation, with net investment instead of gross investment, it is the net domestic product(国内生产净值). Consumption and investment in this equation (等式) are the expenditure on final goods and services. The exports minus imports part of the equation [often called cumulative exports (累计出口)] then adjusts this by subtracting the part of this expenditure not produced domestically (the imports), and adding back in domestic production not consumed at home (the exports).

2. **Gross National Product (GNP)**　国民生产总值

   GNP is the former measure of the United States economy. It refers to the total market value of goods and services produced by all citizens and capital during a given period (usually 1 year).

3. **real GNP**　实际国民生产总值

   It is a version of the GNP that has been adjusted for the effects of inflation.

4. **nominal GNP**　名义国民生产总值

   It is a version of the GNP that has not been adjusted for the effects of inflation.

5. **final products (also known as finished products, end products)**　最终产品

   When used in measures of national income and output, the term final goods only includes new goods. For instance, the GDP excludes items counted in an earlier year to prevent double counting(重复计算) of production based on resales of the same item second and third hand.

6. **intermediate goods or producer goods**　中间产品

   It refers to goods used as inputs in the production of other goods, such as partly finished goods or raw materials. A firm may make then use intermediate goods, or make then sell, or buy then use them. In the production process, intermediate goods either become part of the final product, or are changed beyond recognition in the process.

   Intermediate goods are not counted in a country's GDP, as that would mean double counting, as the final product only should be counted.

7. **double counting**　重复计算

   It is an error in accounting whereby a transaction is counted more than once. In the case of a small individual business, it is unlikely that an expenditure of funds, an input or output, or an income from production will be counted twice. If it happens, that's usually just bad accounting (a math error), or else a case of fraud.

   But things are more complicated when we aggregate the accounts of many enterprises, households and government agencies ["institutional units"(机构单位) or transactors(交易者) in social accounting language]. Here, a conceptual problem arises. The basic reason is that the income of one institutional unit is the expenditure of another, and the input of one institutional unit is the output of another.

   If therefore we want to measure the total value-added(增值) by all institutional units, we need to devise a consistent system for grossing and netting the incomes and outlays of all units. Lacking such a system, we would end up double-counting incomes and expenditures of interacting units, exaggerating the quantity of value-added or investments

Exercises

I Make verb phrases by linking those in Column A and Column B.

Column A	Column B
maintain	GNP for inflation
distinguish	a base year up to date
correct	all industries in the same direction
multiply	between nominal and real GNP
affect	the prices and the quantities

II Match the following words or terms with their definitions.

double counting	final goods	intermediate goods
depreciation	GDP	GNP

1. _____ : the market value of all final goods and services produced within a country in a given period of time
2. _____ : a loss in value
3. _____ : the total market value of goods and services produced by all citizens and capital during a given period (usually 1 yr)
4. _____ : goods such as materials, parts and services used in the production of other goods
5. _____ : an error in accounting whereby a transaction is counted more than once
6. _____ : the end-products of the production process and are used by their buyers only in finished form

III Reading comprehension: decide whether the following statements are true or false according to what we have learned in the text.

1. GNP is the market value of all final goods and services produced within a country in a given period of time. (   )
2. GDP is the market value of all final goods and services produced by all nationals in a given period of time. (   )
3. Neither GDP nor GNP includes the values of intermediate goods. (   )
4. When GNP suffers a sustained decline, none of the industries in the economy can

escape a decline, whether severe or mild. (　)
5. When an economy suffers macro disturbances, many industries are more likely to make similar reaction. (　)
6. Multiply price and quantity for each good then add together these values, and you'll get the nominal GNP. (　)
7. Constantly the GNP statistics are moderately revised, including changes in the base year so as to maintain them up to date. (　)
8. Double counting must be avoided in the calculation of either nominal GNP or real GNP. (　)
9. GNP corrected for inflation refers to GNP with the effects of price changes removed by using prices held constant to those of a base year. (　)
10. A stable increase in GNP is an indicator of a healthy overall economy. (　)

Part Two　Case Study

CHINA'S "LIGHT GREEN" GDP

By **Stephen Green**[①]
From ***www.chinadialogue.net***, December 24, 2006

A RECENT "GREEN ACCOUNTING" REPORT[②] PUT A HEADLINE-GRABBING PRICE TAG ON CHINA'S GROWTH. BUT HOW FAR IS THE COUNTRY FROM CALCULATING ITS REAL "GREEN GDP"? STEPHEN GREEN REPORTS ON THE MEASURES THAT MAY HELP TO ASSESS ITS SUSTAINABILITY.

A small green bud sprouted in China's statistical forest when a report that summarized the country's first effort at "green accounting" was published in September 2006. The report was the result of two years' work by China's National Bureau of Statistics (NBS)[③] and the State Environmental Protection Administration (SEPA)[④]. It had backing from senior leaders who increasingly talk of "sustainable development[⑤]", a concept that many environmentalists understand as economic growth that does not damage the value of nature's assets.

---

① Dr. Stephen Green is a senior economist at Standard Chartered Bank in Shanghai.
② 绿色会计报表
③ 国家统计局
④ 国家环保总局
⑤ 可持续发展

There were three headline conclusions to the NBS-SEPA report. Firstly, China emitted 511.8 billion yuan (US$64 billion) worth of pollution in 2004, equivalent to 3.1% of GDP. Secondly, the estimated clean-up cost① for this pollution was calculated at 287.4 billion yuan (US$36 billion), 1.8% of GDP—around three times more than the actual money spent (100.5 billion yuan, or US$13 billion). Thirdly, if the country used current technology and today's standards to solve this pollution at the source②, it would need a one-off investment③ of 1,080 billion (US$135 billion), 6.8% of GDP. China's 11th Five Year Plan, which began this year, calls for 1.4 trillion yuan (US$175 billion) to be spent on environmental clean up — 280 billion yuan a year, a figure similar to the 2004 clean-up cost. But it still looks like NBS and SEPA are positioning this report as a call for a much larger investment.

The report was an important move, but at 10 pages — at least in the public version — it was only a start.

Economists like to measure Gross Domestic Product (GDP) — goods and services produced — since it is a straightforward concept, it is relatively easy to calculate and is comparable across time and place. But GDP does not capture the cost of using up finite resources④ and the price of environmental damage, both of which will undermine future GDP growth. Over the last 30 years, economists and environmentalists around the world have attempted to come up with alternative measures or to adjust GDP to correct for this problem. The "holy grail"⑤ has been "green GDP": a single number equal to the value of goods and services minus all the resource depletion⑥ and value of environmental damage.

It is not surprising that environmentalists and political leaders want to know their green GDP, and how fast it is growing (or declining). In theory, it allows for the sustainability of development⑦ to be easily tracked. The big attraction for China is that if local government officials were evaluated using this metric⑧, it could provide a powerful incentive⑨ for them to protect their local environments.

But the experience of places like Norway and the US is that green GDP is near impossible to calculate — and not that useful anyway. Coal is easy to price since people buy it, but how do you price clean air and how do you value a forest that is not being

---

① 治理费用
② 从源头
③ 一次性投资
④ 有限资源
⑤ 圣杯
⑥ 资源消耗
⑦ 发展的可持续性
⑧ 公共指标
⑨ 刺激,激励

cut down? How do you calculate the damage to underground water, to human health and ecological systems?① Such questions seem endless, and green GDP requires all of them to be answered consistently and accurately.

Recognizing these limitations, the surveys NBS and SEPA carried out in 2004-2005 did not attempt to assess resource depletion or any damage to China's ecological systems. On the one thing they did measure — pollution emissions② — they only tracked 10 of the more than 20 types of pollutants. In short, they only measured the tip of China's environmental iceberg.

However, not all of the issues raised by green GDP are insurmountable③. Economists recommend three ways around them, and China does appear to be adopting all of them. Firstly, China's environmental statisticians④ have begun to use "physical flow accounting"⑤: tables which allow one to track pollutants as they move around economies, even across national boundaries. These help with assessments of sustainability⑥ in various parts of the economy—and in designing policies that will lead to improvements.

Secondly, China has started to use distinct environmental measures to monitor the environment and provide incentives for local officials. Some countries go in for big measures of development, such as the "Genuine Progress Indicator": a composite index⑦ of a number of economic, social and environmental indicators. But a lot of things get mixed up in such indices, and it is ultimately more useful to break things down.

The 11th Five Year Plan has made a start at this, setting up targets in a number of different areas, such as energy efficiency⑧ (reducing energy-use per unit GDP by 20% compared to the 2005 level), and water consumption (reducing per unit industrial output by 30%). It also features targets on air pollutant emissions, water quality and protection of arable land⑨. Data for 2005 and the first half of 2006 suggest that air and water pollution indicators are going the wrong way. Energy efficiency also fell by 0.8 percentage points when it should rise four percentage points over the entire year. Local officials must be sensing that such things are beginning to make a difference to their promotion prospects.⑩

Thirdly, the NBS-SEPA team has appeared to tackle the valuation question head-on.

---

① 生态系统
② 污染排放
③ 不可逾越的，无法解决的
④ 环境统计学家
⑤ 有形污染物流动报表
⑥ 可持续性评估
⑦ 综合指数
⑧ 能源效率
⑨ 耕地
⑩ 升迁前景

For instance, they value air pollutant emissions in 2004 at 511.8 billion (US$64 billion), equivalent to 3.1% of GDP. This is a useful step — it creates press headlines① in which environmental costs come with a price tag that everyone understands, and it should also allow officials to start rationally assessing policy choices with cost-benefit analysis.

Monitoring is one thing, but enforcement② of course is another. At present, provincial, municipal and even county SEPA offices are run primarily by local governments. This is a widespread problem in China, where local directors of such bureaus owe their appointments, budgets and promotions to local leaders, and so are always under pressure to side with local interests.③ When SEPA attempt to investigate, fine or close down polluting facilities④, localities often simply ignore them. But now there is some discussion of the system being reorganized to allow SEPA to gain administrative control — with the first step being the recent establishment of five regional offices.

Sadly, however, it may require a serious crisis to trigger the kind of restructuring⑤ that would be needed. It would be regrettable, to say the least, if it took a bigger environmental disaster than the 100-tonne benzene spill⑥ into the Songhua River in Jilin Province in December 2005 to encourage this. Without better enforcement, it is difficult to be optimistic about slowing the pace of depreciation⑦ in China's natural environment — and it will be doubly painful if we can measure it.

Questions for Discussion

1. What is green accounting? What is the significance of measuring the economic growth in terms of the new metric Green GDP?

2. Is it practical to enforce green accounting in China? What obstacles and difficulties might arise? How could they be tackled?

---

① 新闻头条
② 实施,执法
③ 地方利益
④ 污染企业
⑤ 重组
⑥ 苯溢出
⑦ 贬值,降低

3. What do you think the Chinese government should and could do to enforce more rigid green policies?

___

4. Which do you think is the top priority for China, the economic growth or the environmental protection?

___

5. What's your opinion of the development-before-cleanup course, a widespread choice and popular mentality among local people, especially local governments? Can we find any alternatives? What might be better incentives to enhance the environmental awareness of officials at all levels?

___

6. What does sustainable development mean? And what are its implications to China on its way to a modern economic power?

___

7. Do you agree that environmental pollution has been so severe as to have hindered China's development? What could be done to enhance the national consciousness of environmental protection? What can each of us citizens do specifically to build an environment-friendly country?

___

 Translation

1. A small green bud sprouted in China's statistical forest when a report that summarized the country's first effort at "green accounting" was published in September 2006.

___

2. Thirdly, if the country used current technology and today's standards to solve this pollution at the source, it would need a one-off investment of 1,080 billion (US $135 billion), 6.8% of GDP.

3. But GDP does not capture the cost of using up finite resources and the price of environmental damage, both of which will undermine future GDP growth.

4. The big attraction for China is that if local government officials were evaluated using this metric, it could provide a powerful incentive for them to protect their local environments.

5. This is a useful step — it creates press headlines in which environmental costs come with a price tag that everyone understands, and it should also allow officials to start rationally assessing policy choices with cost-benefit analysis.

6. This is a widespread problem in China, where local directors of such bureaus owe their appointments, budgets and promotions to local leaders, and so are always under pressure to side with local interests.

7. Without better enforcement, it is difficult to be optimistic about slowing the pace of depreciation in China's natural environment — and it will be doubly painful if we can measure it.

Unit 9
Unemployment and Inflation

Introduction

Two closely watched indicators of economic performance are inflation and unemployment. Policymakers are eager to hear the news, economists have added together the inflation rate and the unemployment rate to produce a misery index as a measure of the health of economy. Then how are these two measures related to each other? Could government find a perfect combination of both to regulate economy as they wish?

Part One Text

The Phillips Curve

Origin of Phillips Curve

As we have learned, the long-run determinants of unemployment includes various features of the labor market, such as minimum-wage laws, the market power of unions, the role of efficiency wages, and the effectiveness of job search. By contrast, the inflation rate depends primarily on growth in the money supply, which a nation's central bank controls. In the long run, unemployment and inflation are largely unrelated but in the short run, just the opposite is true.

The short-run relationship between inflation and unemployment is often called the Phillips Curve, which was advanced by a British economist A. W. Phillips in 1958. Based on the data for the United Kingdom, Phillips showed a negative correlation between the rate of unemployment and the rate of inflation and concluded that two important macroeconomic variables — inflation and unemployment — were linked in a way that economists had not previously appreciated.

Two years later, economists Paul Samuelson and Robert Solow described a similar negative correlation between inflation and unemployment in the data for the United States. They reasoned that this correlation arose because low unemployment was associated with high aggregate demand, which in turn puts upward pressure on wages and prices throughout the economy. They believed Phillips Curve offers policymakers a menu of possible economic outcomes. By altering monetary and fiscal policy to influence aggregate demand, policymakers could choose any point on this curve. Point A offers high unemployment and low inflation. Point B offers low unemployment and high inflation. Policymakers might prefer both low inflation and low unemployment but historical data indicate such a combination is impossible. Policymakers have to face a tradeoff between inflation and unemployment and the Phillips Curve illustrates that tradeoff.

As in Figure 9 – 1, the Phillips Curve illustrates a negative association between the inflation rate and the unemployment rate. At point A, inflation rate is low and unemployment is high. At point B, inflation is high and unemployment is low.

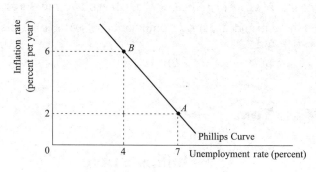

Figure 9 – 1 The Phillips Curve

Aggregate Demand, Aggregate Supply, and the Phillips Curve

The model of aggregate demand and aggregate supply provides an easy explanation for the menu of possible outcomes described by the Phillips Curve. The Phillips Curve simply shows the combinations of inflation and unemployment that arise in the short run as shifts in the aggregate-demand curve move the economy along the short-run aggregate-supply curve. An increase in the aggregate demand for goods and services leads, in the short run, to a larger output of goods and services and a higher price level. Larger output means greater employment and, thus, a lower rate of unemployment. In addition, whatever the previous year's price level happens to be, the higher the price level in the current year, the higher the rate of inflation. Thus, shifts in aggregate demand push inflation and unemployment in opposite directions in the short run — a relationship illustrated by the Phillips Curve.

Let's study Figure 9 – 2 and see how the Phillips Curve is related to Aggregate Demand and Aggregate Supply. Suppose the price level (as measured, for instance, by the consumer price index) equals 100 in the year of 2001. Figure 9 – 2 (a) shows the two outcomes using the model of aggregate demand and aggregate supply. Figure 9 – 2 (b) illustrates the same two outcomes using the Phillips curve.

In Figure 9 – 2 (a), we can see the implications for output and the price level in the year 2001. If the aggregate demand for goods and services is relatively low, the economy experiences outcome A. The economy produces output of 7,500, and the price level is 102. By contrast, if aggregate demand is relatively high, the economy experiences outcome B. Output is 8,000, and the price level is 106. Thus, higher aggregate demand moves the economy to an equilibrium with higher output and a higher price level.

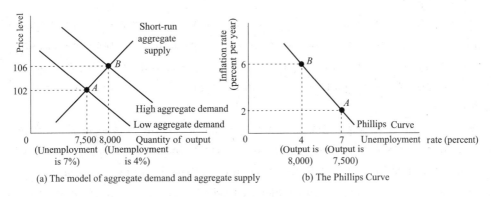

Figure 9 – 2 How the Phillips Curve is related to the model of
aggregate demand and aggregate supply

In Figure 9 – 2 (b), we can see what these two possible outcomes mean for unemployment and inflation. Because firms need more workers when they produce a greater output of goods and services, unemployment is lower in outcome B than in outcome A. In this example, when output rises from 7,500 to 8,000, unemployment falls from 7% to 4%. Moreover, because the price level is higher at outcome B than at outcome A, the inflation rate (the percentage change in the price level from the previous year) is also higher. In particular, since the price level was 100 in the year 2000, outcome A has an inflation rate of 2%, and outcome B has an inflation rate of 6%. Thus, we can compare the two possible outcomes for the economy either in terms of output and the price level (using a model of aggregate demand and aggregate supply) or in terms of unemployment and inflation (using the

Phillips Curve).

Monetary and fiscal policy can shift the aggregate-demand curve. Therefore, monetary and fiscal policy can move the economy along the Phillips Curve. Increases in the money supply, increases in government spending, or cuts in taxes expand aggregate demand and move the economy to a point on the Phillips Curve with lower unemployment and higher inflation. Decreases in the money supply, cuts in government spending or increases in taxes contract aggregate demand and move the economy to a point on the Phillips Curve with lower inflation and higher unemployment. In this sense, the Phillips Curve offers policymakers a menu of combinations of inflation and unemployment.

But does this menu remain stable over time? Is the Phillips Curve a relationship on which policymakers can rely on?

The Long-run Phillips Curve

In 1968 American economists Milton Friedman and Edmund Phelps respectively published their papers denying the existence of a long-run tradeoff between inflation and unemployment. Friedman argued that one thing monetary policy cannot do, other than for only a short time, is pick a combination of inflation and unemployment on the Phillips Curve.

Friedman and Phelps based their conclusions on classical principles of macroeconomics, which, while pointing to growth in the money supply as the primary determinant of inflation, also state that monetary growth does not have real effects — it merely alters all prices and nominal incomes proportionately. In particular, monetary growth does not influence those factors that determine the economy's unemployment rate, such as the market power of unions, the role of efficiency wages, or the process of job search. Friedman and Phelps concluded there is no reason to think the rate of inflation would, in the long run, be related to the rate of unemployment.

Here's what Friedman thought the Fed can hope to accomplish in the long run:

> The monetary authority controls nominal quantities — directly, the quantity of its own liabilities [currency plus bank reserves]. In principle, it can use this control to peg a nominal quantity — an exchange rate, the price level, the nominal level of national income, the quantity of money by one definition or another — or to peg the change in a nominal quantity — the rate of inflation or deflation, the rate of growth or decline in nominal national income, the rate of growth of the quantity of money. It can not use its control over nominal quantities to peg a real quantity — the real rate of interest, the rate of unemployment, the level of real national income or the rate of growth of the real quantity of money.

Unit 9 Unemployment and Inflation

These views have important implications for the Phillips Curve. In particular, they imply that monetary policymakers face a long run Phillips Curve that is vertical, as in Figure 9 – 3. If the Fed increases the money supply slowly, the inflation rate is low, and the economy finds itself at point A. If the Fed increases the money supply quickly, the inflation rate is high, and the economy finds itself at point B. In either case, the unemployment rate tends toward its nominal level, called the natural rate of unemployment. The vertical long-run Phillips Curve illustrates the conclusion that unemployment does not depend on money growth and inflation in the long run.

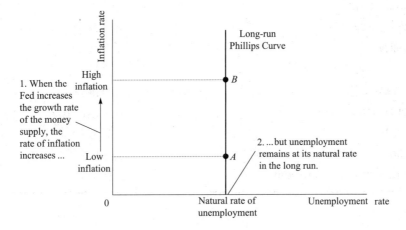

Figure 9 – 3 The long-run Phillips Curve

According to Friedman and Phelps, there is no tradeoff between inflation and unemployment in the long run. Growth in the money supply determines the inflation rate. Regardless of the inflation rate, the unemployment gravitates towards the natural rate. As a result, the long-run Phillips Curve is vertical.

Words and Expressions

variable	n.	变量
appreciate	v.	升值，理解，欣赏，评断
alter	v.	改变
contract	v.	收缩，缩小
liability	n.	债务
currency	n.	通货
peg	v.	钉住
economic performance		经济绩效

Phillips Curve	菲利普斯曲线
misery index	痛苦指数
long-run determinant	长期决定因素
minimum wage	最低工资
efficiency wage	效率工资
negative correlation	负相关
aggregate supply	总供给
aggregate demand	总需求
monetary policy	货币政策
fiscal policy	财政政策
nominal quantity	名义数量
bank reserves	银行准备金
nominal national income	名义国民收入
real quantity	实际数量
real national income	实际国民收入
natural rate of unemployment	自然失业率

Notes

1. **misery index 痛苦指数**

   The misery index was initiated by economist Arthur Okun, an adviser to President Lyndon Johnson in the 1970's. It is simply the unemployment rate added to the inflation rate. It is assumed that both a higher rate of unemployment and a worsening of inflation create economic and social costs for a country. A combination of rising inflation and more people of out of work implies a deterioration in economic performance and a rise in the misery index.

2. **minimum wage 最低工资**

   It is a minimum level of pay for the legitimate labor(合法劳工)set by the government each year based on the recommendations of relevant agencies.

3. **efficiency wage 效率工资**

   It is a higher than market-clearing wage(市场出清工资)set by employers to, for example, discourage shirking by raising the cost of being fired, encourage worker loyalty, raise group output norms, improve the applicant pool and raise morale.

4. **monetary policy 货币政策**

    It is the regulation of the money supply and interest rates by a central bank, such as the Federal Reserve Board (联邦储备委员会) in the US, in order to control inflation and stabilize currency. Monetary policy is one the two ways the government can impact the economy. By impacting the effective cost of money, the Federal Reserve can affect the amount of money that is spent by consumers and businesses.

5. **fiscal policy 财政政策**

    It's the decisions by the President and Congress, usually relating to taxation and government spending, with the goals of full employment, price stability, and economic growth. By changing tax laws, the government can effectively modify the amount of disposable income (可支配收入) available to its taxpayers. For example, if taxes were to increase, consumers would have less disposable income and in turn would have less money to spend on goods and services. This difference in disposable income would go to the government instead of going to consumers, who would pass the money onto companies. Or, the government could choose to increase government spending by directly purchasing goods and services from private companies. This would increase the flow of money through the economy and would eventually increase the disposable income available to consumers. Unfortunately, this process takes time, as the money needs to wind its way through the economy, creating a significant lag between the implementation of fiscal policy and its effect on the economy.

6. **bank reserves 银行准备金**

    It refers to the amount of money a bank sets aside, and does not lend, to meet day-to-day currency withdrawals by its customers. Since it is rare for a bank to have all its depositors withdraw all of their funds simultaneously, only a portion of total deposits is needed as reserves. The bank uses the remaining deposits to earn profit, either by issuing loans or by investing in assets such as bonds and stocks.

7. **aggregate demand 总需求**

    Aggregate demand is the demand for the gross domestic product (GDP) of a country, and is represented by this formula: aggregate demand (AD) = $C + I + G(X - M)$. In this formula, C = consumers' expenditures on goods and services; I = investment spending by companies on capital goods; G = government expenditures on publicly provided goods and services; X = exports of goods and services; M = imports of goods and services.

    It is represented by the aggregate-demand curve, which describes the relationship between price levels and the quantity of output that firms are willing to provide. Normally there is a negative relationship between aggregate demand and the price level. Also known as "total spending".

8. **aggregate supply** 总供给

   The total supply of goods and services produced within an economy at a given overall price level in a given time period. It is represented by the aggregate-supply curve, which describes the relationship between price levels and the quantity of output that firms are willing to provide. Normally, there is a positive relationship between aggregate supply and the price level. Rising prices are usually signals for businesses to expand production to meet a higher level of aggregate demand.

9. **the natural rate unemployment** 自然失业率

   It is the rate of unemployment where the labor market is in a position of equilibrium. This means that the labor supply equals to labor demand at a given real wage rate. All people willing and able to take paid employment at the going sage rate do so.

Exercises

I Make verb phrases by linking those in Column A and Column B.

Column A	Column B
describe	the economy
alter	a similar negative correlation
push upward	a nominal or real quantity
peg	a tradeoff between unemployment and inflation
face	price and nominal income proportionately

II Match the following words or terms with their definitions.

minimum wage	efficiency wage	natural rate of unemployment
misery index	monetary policy	fiscal policy
bank reserves	liabilities	currency

1. _____: a minimum level of pay set by the government each year
2. _____: financial obligations, debts, claims, or potential losses
3. _____: decisions by the President and Congress, usually relating to taxation and government spending
4. _____: any form of money that is in public circulation
5. _____: the regulation of the money supply and interest rates by a central bank

6. _____ : the amount of money a bank sets aside, and does not lend
7. _____ : the rate of unemployment where the labor supply equals labor demand at a given real wage rate
8. _____ : a higher than market-clearing wage set by employers for greater productivity
9. _____ : a combination of unemployment rate and inflation rate

III Reading comprehension: choose the best answer from the four choices.

1. Governments and economists are concerned over inflation and unemployment rates because _____.
   A. they imply a worsening economy and society on the Phillips Curve
   B. good indicators of how the economy is going on
   C. they push economy upward on the Phillips Curve
   D. they hinder the success of economic policies

2. Phillips Curve describes the short-run relationship between inflation rate and unemployment rate as _____.
   A. largely uncorrelated   B. negatively correlated
   C. interdependent   D. correlated

3. Phillips Curve describes the long-run relationship between inflation rate and unemployment rate as _____.
   A. largely uncorrelated   B. negatively correlated
   C. interdependent   D. correlated

4. The vertical long-run Phillips Curve illustrates _____.
   A. unemployment rate tends to fall with money growth and inflation
   B. unemployment rate fluctuates with inflation in the same direction proportionately
   C. unemployment rate tends to return to its natural rate in spite of inflation
   D. unemployment rate fluctuates with the nominal interest rate

5. With the Phillips Curve, policy makers and economists can expect to _____.
   A. predict the economic trends in the near future
   B. regulate and control the unemployment rate and inflation rate as they wish
   C. find a perfect combination of the unemployment rate and inflation rate
   D. none of the above

Part Two Case Study

CHINA'S LOOMING CRISIS—INFLATION RETURNS

By **Albert Keidel**
From **www.carnegieendowment.org**

ALBERT KEIDEL HAS A SEPTEMBER 2007 *POLICY BRIEF* FOR THE CARNEGIE ENDOWMENT ON THE RISKS OF INFLATION IN CHINA TITLED " CHINA'S LOOMING CRISIS — INFLATION RETURNS".

He argues that China's economy today looks much as it did before the inflationary catastrophes① of 1988 – 1989 and 1993 – 1996, and as in the past, China today faces more than inflation. If inflation gets out of control, draconian② steps to suppress it could cause hardship and social unrest.

He makes several interesting points. One point, which has not been sufficiently understood in the press or even by many research analysts, is that even though the 18% rise in food prices (which comprise one-third of the CPI basket) accounts for most of the CPI inflation, and this rise was driven largely by shortages on the supply side (especially pork), this doesn't mean inflation isn't real.

If prices for any particular good rise because of supply constraints③ the result is not inflation. As spending shifts away from other goods to take into account the higher prices of the good in short supply, the shift will cause deflation④ in those other goods, and so the net effect on inflation will be zero or very low. The rise in pork prices because of supply constraints, in other words, should be mitigated⑤ by the decline in other prices. In China that did not happen. Prices rose 6.5% in August.

This suggests that core inflation of just under 1% would have been higher if it had not been for the effect of rising food prices — without the mysterious pig disease, pork prices would have been lower but everything else would have been higher. This is not to dismiss the distinction between core (or non-cyclical) prices⑥ and prices of goods that vary greatly as supply and demand adjust. Food prices and farm production are certainly

---

① 灾难
② 严酷的
③ 供给约束，供给不足
④ 滞胀
⑤ 缓和
⑥ 核心价格，非周期性价格

cyclical, but in this case I think it may be many quarters before the cyclicality works in our favor to bring prices down. The point is to dismiss the idea that Chinese inflation was "only" food inflation, and that once food prices adjust we will be back to where we started.

A second point Keidel makes goes to the heart of an argument I have had many times. I have been often told that in China bank runs① are impossible because people have no alternative investments②, and with nowhere else to put their money, why would they ever take their money out of the banks? Aside from the fact that when you worry about the safety of your bank your first urge is to protect your liquidity③, not to find an alternative investment, there are many things you can do with money.

Value-losing deposit rates④ early in both the 1988 – 1989 and 1993 – 1996 inflation bouts⑤ sparked heavy bank withdrawals and accelerated consumer spending — pushing inflation pressures to the crisis point. <u>In 1988, as inflation rose far above deposit rates, cash rushed out of the banks and into a panic buying spree⑥ that stripped many stores bare of their goods.</u> The resulting inflation took two years to tame ... This same sequence erupted at the outset of the 1993 – 1996 inflationary period. Early, moderate inflation⑦ — again triggered by high food prices — rose far above bank deposit and lending rates. Chinese citizens quickly began withdrawing cash and spending it, and corporations pounced on bank loans that were cheaper than inflation to splurge⑧ on investment projects.

Basically Chinese savers withdrew depreciating currency⑨ from the bank and exchanged it for hard goods that retained their value⑩. I was told by a Tsinghua professor that during the last major bout of inflation it was almost impossible to buy cigarettes, whiskey, and white goods in Beijing. <u>Depositors, by the same logic, would withdraw their savings even without inflation concerns if they were ever to become nervous about the liquidity of the banks.</u>

The third interesting point is Keidel's argument that the authorities must immediately raise domestic interest rates substantially⑪ to choke off inflation. He says:

---

① 银行挤兑
② 可选投资工具
③ 流动性,变现
④ 贬值的存款利率
⑤ 阵性发作
⑥ 恐慌性抢购
⑦ 温和通胀
⑧ 挥霍
⑨ 贬值货币
⑩ 保值
⑪ 实质性地,大幅地

Some Chinese officials worry that raising domestic interest rates will attract unwanted speculative foreign capital①. This should be a secondary if not third-order concern. China's short-term capital account② is still heavily, if imperfectly, regulated. The scale of speculative inflows is manageable. The central bank has ample resources to pull foreign cash inflows out of the economy by selling either treasury bills③ or its own bonds.

Here I disagree with Keidel. As my regular blog readers know, I think the monetary expansion caused by the currency regime④ is at the heart of China's imbalances, and I do not believe any solution which does not address this problem can work. <u>Higher interest rates will drag in more speculative capital and the PBOC is unable to sterilize⑤ them in a meaningful way simply by selling bills, which are a near perfect substitute for cash</u>. The resulting monetary expansion will make inflation worse, not better.

Unfortunately the solution must involve an adjustment in the currency regime. Perhaps the RMB must appreciate⑥ at a much faster pace, as many believe, or the PBOC must engineer a one-off maxi-revaluation⑦, as I believe, but without an adjustment of the currency that reverses reserve accumulation⑧, China's monetary problems are not going to go away. Nor will inflation.

Questions for Discussion

1. Do you agree with Mr. Keidel that inflation crisis is looming in China?

2. Have you noticed similar consumption behavior among citizens as appeared in earlier inflation bouts in the 1980s and 1990s in China? What do you think is the motivation behind such behaviors?

3. Do you agree that Chinese authorities should implement a one-off maxi-revaluation as

---

① 投资性外资
② 资本账户
③ 国库券
④ 货币机制
⑤ 消毒，灭绝，制止
⑥ 升值
⑦ 一次性最大限度法定升值
⑧ 外汇储备积累

desired by American government and economists? What do you expect will happen to China's economy and society if PBoC really did so? Which do you prefer, a one-off revaluation or a progressive appreciation of RMB?

4. What's your opinion of the currency regime in China? Do you agree that China should give up its regulation of capital market?

5. Are you confident of PBoC's ability to sterilize speculative inflows of foreign capital into China and stabilize the economy? What challenges does PBOC have to face?

6. Will people stand a better chance of employment if inflation continues?

Translation

1. China's economy today looks much as it did before the inflationary catastrophes of 1988 – 1989 and 1993 – 1996, and as in the past, China today faces more than inflation.

2. As spending shifts away from other goods to take into account the higher prices of the good in short supply, the shift will cause deflation in those other goods.

3. This is not to dismiss the distinction between core (or non-cyclical) prices and prices of goods that vary greatly as supply and demand adjust.

4. In 1988, as inflation rose far above deposit rates, cash rushed out of the banks and into a panic buying spree that stripped many stores bare of their goods.

5. Depositors, by the same logic, would withdraw their savings even without inflation concerns if they were ever to become nervous about the liquidity of the banks.

6. Higher interest rates will drag in more speculative capital and the PBOC is unable to sterilize them in a meaningful way simply by selling bills, which are a near perfect substitute for cash.

Unit 10
Macro-economic Policy

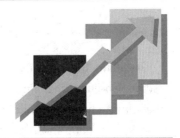

Introduction

It is not surprising that questions about these macroeconomic policies arise everyday in countries around the world. Sometimes the questions—such as the independence of the central bank, the formation of a currency bloc, or the enforcement of government budget rules—concern the fundamental design of the policy-making institutions. At other times the questions are about implementation of new monetary or fiscal policies—such as how fast to move to a non inflationary monetary policy or how soon to reach a balanced budget. Most frequently the questions concern much shorter-term operational issues, such as whether—in any given week or month—the central bank should be raising or lowering short-term interest rates.

Part One Text

Macro-economic policy refers to activities of governments that are designed to achieve full employment with price stability and equilibrium in the balance of payments. Generally, it includes (1) momentary and fiscal policies, (2) exchange-rate adjustments, (3) tariff and non-tariff trade barriers, (4) foreign-exchange controls and investments controls, and (5) export-promotion measures.

Since the 1930s, nations have actively pursued internal balance (full employment without inflation) as a primary economic objective. Nations also consider external balance (balance-of-payments equilibrium) as an economic objective. A nation realizes overall balance when it attains internal balance and external balance.

A. Policy Instrument

To attain the objectives of external balance and internal balance, policy makers enact expenditure-changing policies, expenditure-switching policies, and direct controls. Expenditure-changing policies alter the level of aggregate demand for goods and services, including those produced domestically and those imported. They include fiscal policy, which refers to changes in government spending and taxes, and monetary policy, which refers to changes in the money supply by a nation's central bank (such as the Federal Reserve). Depending on the direction of change, expenditure-changing policies are either expenditure increasing or expenditure reducing.

Expenditure-switching policies modify the direction of demand, shifting it between domestic output and imports. Under a system of fixed exchange rates, a trade-deficit nation could devalue its currency to increase the international competitiveness of its industries, thus diverting spending from foreign goods to domestic goods. To increase its competitiveness under a managed floating exchange-rate system, the nation could purchase other currencies with its currency, thereby causing the exchange value of its currency to depreciate. The success of these policies in promoting trade balance largely depends on switching demand in the proper direction and amount, as well as on the capacity of the home economy to meet the additional demand by supplying more goods.

Direct controls consist of government restrictions on the market economy, and may also be levied on capital flows so as to either restrain excessive capital outflows or stimulate capital inflows.

B. Monetary Policy and Fiscal Policy

It is known to all of us, the exchange-rate policies primarily affect the economy's external sector, while having secondary effects on its internal sector. Let's now consider monetary policy and fiscal policy as stabilization tools. These tools are generally used to stabilize the economy's internal sector, while having secondary effects on its external sector. How successful are monetary policy and fiscal policy in achieving full employment and price stability?

Let us assume that the mobility of international capital is high. This suggests that a small change in the relative interest rate across nations induces a large international flow of capital (investment funds). This assumption is consistent with capital movements among many industrial nations, such as United States and Germany, and the conclusions of many analysts that capital mobility is increasing as national financial markets have become internationalized.

Two conclusions will emerge from our discussion: (1) Under a fixed exchange-rate system, fiscal policy is successful in promoting internal balance, whereas monetary policy is unsuccessful; (2) Under a floating rate system, monetary policy is successful in promoting internal balance, whereas fiscal policy is unsuccessful.

C. Tariff and Non-tariff Trade Barriers

A tariff is a duty or fee levied on goods and service being imported into the country. These tariffs can be of two types: protective and revenue. Protective tariffs (import taxes) are designed to raise the retail price of imported products so that domestic goods will be more competitive and foreign business will be discouraged from shipping certain goods into the country. These tariffs are meant to save jobs for domestic workers and to keep industries (especially infant industries) from bankruptcy because of foreign competition. A revenue tariff is designed to raise money for the government.

Today there is still considerable debate about the degree of protectionism a government should practice. Nevertheless, almost all countries practice a policy of protective tariff and both import and export goods are subject to customs duties. Tariff (customs) duties are of three types: specific, ad valorem and compound.

Non-tariff barriers are less visible, but they are extremely effective restrictions on trade. The principal categories of NTBs are quota, license and new barriers.

D. What and How Are the Major Objectives of Macro-economic Policy?

The four major objectives are (1) full employment, (2) price stability, (3) a high, but sustainable, rate of economic growth, and (4) keeping the balance of payments in equilibrium. We will look at the way in which these objectives are measured.

The first one is full employment or low employment. Those counted must be out of work, physically able to work and looking for it, and actually claiming benefit.

Secondly, inflation is usually defined as a sustained rise in the general level of prices. Technically, it is measured as the annual rate of change of the Retail Price Index (RPI), often referred to as the headline rate of inflation. For prices to be stable, therefore, the inflation rate should be zero. Generally, governments are happy if they can keep the inflation rate down to a low percentage. This is the same as the RPI except housing costs are removed in the shape of mortgage interest payments. It makes sense for the government to use this measure because the weapon they use to control inflation, interest rates, directly affects the RPI itself.

Economic growth tends to be measured in terms of the rate of change of real GDP

(Gross Domestic Product). When the word real accompanies any statistic, it means that the effects of inflation have been removed. More on this later! GDP is a measure of the annual output (or income, or expenditure) of an economy. Much more on this later! Sometimes GNP (Gross National Product) is used, which is very similar to GDP. Growth figures are published quarterly, both in terms of the change quarter on quarter and as annual percentage changes (See Figure 10-1).

Last but not the least, keeping the balance of payments in equilibrium refers to all flows of money into, and out of a country. It is split into two: the current account and the capital and financial accounts (formerly the capital account).

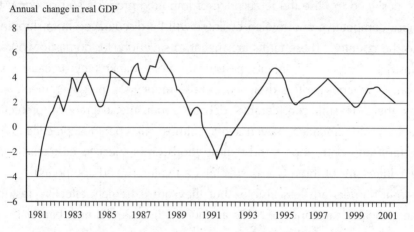

Figure 10-1 Growth of real national output

Probably the most important is the current account because this records how well the country is doing in terms of its exports of goods and services relative to its imports. If the country is to "pay its way" in the world over the long term, then it needs to keep earning enough foreign currency from its exports to pay for its imports. If this is not the case, the account will be in deficit. Japan has the largest surplus in the world. Although a surplus sounds better then a deficit, both can be bad. Japan's surplus forces other countries in the world to have deficits. In fact, while Japan's surplus is the biggest in the world, the USA's deficit is the biggest in the world. This is not a coincidence!

budget	n.	预算
	v.	做预算，编入预算
implementation	n.	执行

Unit 10 Macro-economic Policy

equilibrium	n.	平衡,平静,均衡,保持平衡的能力,沉着,安静
tariff	n.	关税,关税表,税则,(旅馆、饭店等的)价目表、价格表
	v.	课以关税
excessive	a.	过多的,过分的,额外的
mobility	n.	活动性,灵活性,迁移率,机动性
assumption	n.	假定,设想,担任,承当,假装,作态
sustainable	a.	可以忍受的,足可支撑的,养得起的
inflation	n.	胀大,夸张,通货膨胀,(物价)暴涨
annual	n.	一年生植物,年刊,年鉴
	a.	一年一次的,每年的,一年生的
mortgage	n.	抵押
	v.	抵押
surplus	n.	剩余,过剩,[会计]盈余
	a.	过剩的,剩余的
	v.	转让,卖掉
coincidence	n.	一致,相合,巧合,同时发生或同时存在(尤指偶然)的事
central bank		中央银行(指代表政府经济利益的银行,多与其他银行交易而不直接与普通人民交易)
balance of payments		贸易支付差额
trade deficit		贸易逆差
floating rate		[经]浮动汇率

1. **infant industry** 幼稚产业

   It refers to the new industries which consist of new companies in the early stages of growth.

2. **specific duties** 从量税

   Specific duties are levied at the rate of so much per unit, pound, kilo or gallon. For example, the specific duty of one product might be US$ 10 per unit, while on another it might be US$ 0.25 per pound.

3. **ad valorem duties** 从价税

   Ad valorem duties are levied on the basis of the product's value. The value of import goods usually refers to their CIF(Cost, Insurance and Freight, 包括成本、保险、运费在内的到岸价格) value, and that of export goods, their FOB (Free on Board, 船上交货) value with the export duties deducted. For example, an ad valorem duty of 7% on a particular product valued at US$100 would result in a US $7 tariff. If a firm shipped ten of these products, the tariff would be US$70.

4. **compound duties**   复合税

Compound duties are a combination of specific and ad valorem duties. For example, suits are taxed on both quantity and value, the duty on them has been, say, US$0.37 per pound and 21% ad valorem.

5. **quota**   定额,配额

A quota is a quantitative restriction, which is expressed in terms of either physical quantity or value. A quota that states that no more than 500,000 Class A deluxe limousines (豪华轿车) can be imported from Europe each year is a restriction stated in terms of physical quantity.

6. **license**   许可证制度

License is an official permission of an import that is forbidden without a license. In the importing countries, quota usually requires a licensing system and an agency to distribute the quota shares to domestic importers.

7. **new barriers**   新壁垒

There are ingenious new barriers which are constantly being developed. Some are legitimate regulatory functions, such as antipollution regulations that require automobiles to meet certain exhaust emission standards. Others may ostensibly be introduced for reasons of health, safety, or national security but are actually intended to restrict trade.

Exercises

I Make verb phrases by linking those in Column A and Column B.

Column A	Column B
promote	policies
attain	the demand
implement	export
meet	the balance
stimulate	the economy
stabilize	capital inflows

Unit 10 Macro-economic Policy

II Match the following words or terms with their definitions.

exchange rate	barriers	tariff	quota
specific duties	ad valorem duties	infant industry	
floating rate	equilibrium	surplus	

1. _____: a duty levied on goods and service being imported into the country
2. _____: a duty levied at the rate of so much per unit, pound, kilo
3. _____: a duty levied on the basis of the product's value
4. _____: a price of one currency expressed in another currency
5. _____: rate that is not stable
6. _____: the balance
7. _____: amount (of anything) in excess of requirements
8. _____: the early stages of the industrial development, especially in need of protection from predatory competition (through tariff and non-tariff barriers until it is established)
9. _____: a quantitative restriction
10. _____: the hurdles in socio-culture forces, economic and trade forces

III Reading comprehension: choose the best answer from the four choices.

1. Which of the following are not mentioned when talking about Macro-economic policy?
   A. Monetary and fiscal policies.
   B. Exchange-rate adjustments.
   C. Monetary reserves.
   D. Tariff and non-tariff trade barriers.
2. An ad valorem duty of 5% on a particular product valued at US$ 100 would result in a US$ 5 tariff. If a firm shipped 100 of these products, the tariff would be _____.
   A. US$ 5   B. US$ 5,000
   C. US$ 50   D. US$ 500
3. According to the passage, which of the following statements is not true?
   A. Since the 1930s, nations have actively pursued internal balance as a primary economic objective.
   B. Tariff duties are of three types: specific, ad valorem and quota.

C. Japan's surplus is the biggest in the world, while the USA's deficit is the biggest in the world.

D. Economic growth tends to be measured in terms of the rate of change of real GDP.

4. What is not the major objectives of macroeconomic policy?

A. Full employment.

B. A high, but sustainable, rate of economic growth.

C. Keeping the balance of payments in equilibrium.

D. Exchange rate stability.

5. Under a fixed exchange-rate system, _____ is successful in promoting internal balance.

A. fiscal policy

B. infant industry

C. monetary policy

D. trade deficit

Part Two Case Study

THE CROOKED PATH OF CAPITALISM

Capitalism has been subject to booms and busts for at least the past 300 years, notable early examples of which were the Dutch tulip mania and the British South Sea Bubble of the early 18th century. Any market system — including market socialism, if that had ever got off the ground — would probably have been subject to similar fluctuations, based as they are on human cycles of greed and fear, and alternations between unfounded optimism and unreasoning pessimism. Attempts to establish a cycle of regular duration and amplitude have failed. These fluctuations can, with a bit of luck and good policy, be tamed but not abolished.

The decade and a half of steady low inflation growth enjoyed by the UK since leaving the European exchange rate mechanism in 1992 has been quite exceptional, as have even the four years of similar behaviour enjoyed by the Group of Seven leading industrial nations as a whole. The confidence of mainstream forecasters in predicting yet another Goldilocks period for the world economy should have made one suspicious, not because of the faltering in the second quarter of this year, but because experts are never as likely to be wrong as when they speak with near unanimity.

Some economists of Austrian origin have claimed that recessions have their value in liquidating unwise investments and that attempts to keep the economy going full blast all the time only store up greater trouble for the future. It was their misfortune that their theory was promulgated during the Great Depression of the 1930s, when there really was a deficiency of purchasing power, which made them seem irrelevant. The Anglo-Austrian, Friedrich Hayek, tried to make amends by accepting the need to counter a secondary depression resulting from the multiplier effects of reduced investment spending, but he did so much too late, in the 1960s and 1970s. By then, Austrian economics had become a minority movement among US economists, who were beset by heresy hunting.

Today, the torch seems to have been taken up in Shanghai, where an economist, Andy Xie, has written that "it is time for central banks to stop bailing out markets", blaming current troubles on central banks, which after the attacks of September 11, 2001 provided the cheap credit for the leverage bubble (*Financial Times*, August 14). Some central bankers are still suffering from a guilt complex arising from the failure of the US Federal Reserve to counteract a multiple contraction at the onset of the Great Depression.

When it comes to the present turbulence, a select band of analysts is entitled to say: "We told you so." They include Paul De Grauwe, the Belgian economist; Lord Lamont, the former British chancellor; and some brave economists at the Basle-based Bank for International Settlements who have been beavering away at the need to monitor asset prices, and not just for their possible effects on consumer price inflation.

The inflationary effects of easy credit have, until now, been offset by the threat of cheap imports from the developing world. But now that China and other developing countries are themselves experiencing high and rising inflation, loose money in the west, as Mr. Xie points out, will feed straight into prices and the credibility of central banks could be fatally undermined.

The direct responsibility of central banks for controlling inflation is comparatively recent. They were traditionally bankers to the banks, in which capacity they became lenders of last resort. The art is to be ready to intervene without creating a moral hazard that unwise lenders will be painlessly rescued. The duty of such lenders was laid out in the mid-19th century by a famous early editor of The Economist, Walter Bagehot. This was not to bail out specific institutions, but to lend unlimited amounts to bona fide financial institutions at a penal rate. At first sight the European Central Bank, which has let it be known how many billions of euros it has made available, has been closely following Bagehot, but with one crucial difference. Instead of lending at a penalty rate, it has been chiefly concerned to keep the very short-term rate near the 4 per cent policy rate decided before the crisis broke.

The Bank of England was in some ways the best prepared. Under reforms introduced a year ago, 57 banks can borrow limitless cash but at a price 100 basis points above the target bank rate. But even this system will come under strain in a full-blown financial gale. There is little doubt that there would be rescues for large institutions whose failure would pose a "systemic risk", which the Barings crisis of 1890 apparently did but the one of 1995 did not. Life, as cynical Tories are fond of saying, is unfair.

Fed interventions have been more discretionary and less rule-bound. But unwise US fund managers have been berating Ben Bernanke, the US Federal Reserve chairman, for not bailing out the market. This is the voice of those who at the slightest sign of trouble call for cheap money and plenty of it. It is the mirror image of those Marxists who greet every financial shock by gloating that the long-predicted final crisis of capitalism has arrived. They deserve each other.

Questions for Discussion

1. What are the major benefits of macro-economic policy?

2. "Today, the torch seems to have been taken up in Shanghai", why did the author say so?

Translation

1. Capitalism has been subject to booms and busts for at least the past 300 years, notable early examples of which were the Dutch tulip mania and the British South Sea Bubble of the early 18th century.

2. It was their misfortune that their theory was promulgated during the Great Depression of the 1930s, when there really was a deficiency of purchasing power, which made them seem irrelevant.

3. Some central bankers are still suffering from a guilt complex arising from the failure of the US Federal Reserve to counteract a multiple contraction at the onset of the Great Depression.

4. The inflationary effects of easy credit have, until now, been offset by the threat of cheap imports from the developing world. But now that China and other developing countries are themselves experiencing high and rising inflation, loose money in the west, as Mr. Xie points out, will feed straight into prices and the credibility of central banks could be fatally undermined

Unit 11
Monetary Policy

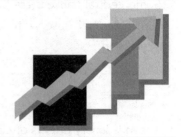

Introduction

Monetary policy is the macroeconomic policy laid down by the central bank. It involves management of money supply and interest rate and is the demand side economic policy used by the government of a country to achieve macroeconomic objectives like inflation, consumption, growth and liquidity.

Part One Text

The primary objectives of monetary policies are the management of inflation or unemployment and maintenance of currency exchange rates.

1. Inflation

Monetary policies can target inflation levels. A low level of inflation is considered to be healthy for the economy. If inflation is high, a contractionary policy can address this issue.

2. Unemployment

Monetary policies can influence the level of unemployment in the economy. For example, an expansionary monetary policy generally decreases unemployment because the higher money supply stimulates business activities that lead to the expansion of the job market.

3. Currency Exchange Rates

Using its fiscal authority, a central bank can regulate the exchange rates between domestic and foreign currencies. For example, the central bank may increase the money supply by issuing more currency. In such a case, the domestic currency becomes cheaper relative to its foreign counterparts.

The monetary policymaker, then, must balance price and output objectives. Indeed, even central banks, like the ECB, that target only inflation would generally admit that they also pay attention to stabilizing output and keeping the economy near full employment. And at the Fed, which has an explicit "dual mandate" from the US Congress, the employment goal is formally recognized and placed on an equal footing with the inflation goal.

Monetary policy is not the only tool for managing aggregate demand for goods and services. Fiscal policy—taxing and spending—is another, and governments have used it extensively during the recent global crisis. However, it typically takes time to legislate tax and spending changes, and once such changes have become law, they are politically difficult to reverse. Added to that concerns that consumers may not respond in the intended way to fiscal stimulus (for example, they may save rather than spend a tax cut), and it is easy to understand why monetary policy is generally viewed as the first line of defense in stabilizing the economy during a downturn.

Tools of Monetary Policy

Central banks use various tools to implement monetary policies. The widely utilized policy tools include:

1. Interest Rate Adjustment

A central bank can influence interest rates by changing the discount rate. The discount rate (base rate) is an interest rate charged by a central bank to banks for short-term loans. For example, if a central bank increases the discount rate, the cost of borrowing for the banks increases. Subsequently, the banks will increase the interest rate they charge their customers. Thus, the cost of borrowing in the economy will increase, and the money supply will decrease.

2. Change Reserve Requirements

Central banks usually set up the minimum amount of reserves that must be held by a commercial bank. By changing the required amount, the central bank can influence the money supply in the economy. If monetary authorities increase the required reserve amount, commercial banks find less money available to lend to their clients, and thus, money supply decreases.

Commercial banks can't use the reserves to make loans or fund investments into new businesses. Since it constitutes a lost opportunity for the commercial banks, central banks pay them interest on the reserves. The interest is known as IOR or IORR (interest on reserves or interest on required reserves).

3. Open Market Operations

The central bank can either purchase or sell securities issued by the government to affect the money supply. For example, central banks can purchase government bonds. As a result, banks will obtain more money to increase the lending and money supply in the economy.

4. Smoothing the Business Cycle

Economic growth tends to fluctuate around a long-term trend. When the economy grows too slowly because of weak demand, the Reserve Bank can loosen monetary policy, such as by lowering the cash rate to stimulate economic growth and employment. On the other hand, when the economy grows too quickly because of excessively strong demand, the Reserve Bank can tighten monetary policy, such as by raising the cash rate to dampen economic activity and contain inflation.

The Business Cycle

It is important to remember that monetary policy is a tool used to smooth fluctuations in the business cycle. While it can help support long-term economic growth by avoiding costly recessions or financial crises, it cannot create long-term economic growth by permanently stimulating demand. Any attempt to do so results in higher inflation. Long-term economic growth is ultimately determined by the availability and productivity of an economy's resources such as labour, land and capital.

Sometimes it might be difficult to achieve all three monetary policy objectives at the same time. The flexible medium-term inflation target allows the Reserve Bank to address short-run trade-offs that may occur between economic growth, employment and inflation.

For example, there could be occasions when inflation might be too high at the same time that economic growth is too low and unemployment is too high. In these cases, the Reserve Bank must carefully consider the trade-off between smoothing the business cycle (in particular economic growth and unemployment) in the short run and achieving its inflation target.

If inflation is too high, tightening monetary policy (which raises interest rates in the economy) will help to bring inflation back towards the target, but will also be likely to reduce economic growth and put upward pressure on unemployment, all else being equal. A trade-off between objectives could also occur if an easing (or tightening) of monetary policy was judged to adversely affect the Reserve Bank's broader responsibilities, such as financial stability.

Independent Policy

Although it is one of the government's most important economic tools, most economists think monetary policy is best conducted by a central bank (or some similar agency) that is independent of the elected government. This belief stems from academic research, some 30 years ago, that emphasized the problem of time inconsistency. Monetary policymakers who were less independent of the government would find it in their interest to promise low inflation to keep down inflation expectations among consumers and businesses. But later, in response to subsequent developments, they might find it hard to resist expanding the money supply, delivering an "inflation surprise." That surprise would at first boost output, by making labor relatively cheap (wages change slowly), and would also reduce the real, or inflation-adjusted, value of government debt. But people would soon recognize this "inflation bias" and ratchet up their expectations of price increases, making it difficult for policymakers ever to achieve low inflation.

To overcome the problem of time inconsistency, some economists suggested that policymakers should commit to a rule that removes full discretion in adjusting monetary policy. In practice, though, committing credibly to a (possibly complicated) rule proved difficult. An alternative solution, which would still shield the process from politics and strengthen the public's confidence in the authorities' commitment to low inflation, was to delegate monetary policy to an independent central bank that was insulated from much of the political process—as was the case already in a number of economies. The evidence suggests that central bank independence is indeed associated with lower and more stable inflation.

Words and Expressions

trade-offs	n.	平衡，协调，妥协，让步
inflation	n.	通货膨胀，通胀
liquidity	n.	资产流动性，资产变现能力；流动资产，现金

ratchet up	v.	逐步提高，逐步升高
currency exchange rates		货币汇率
dual mandate		双重任务，双重使命
interest rate adjustment		利率调整，调整利率
discount rate (base rate, interest on reserves or interest on required reserves)		贴现率（基准利率，准备金利率或法定准备金利率）

Notes

1. **monetary policy 货币政策**

   Monetary policy is a set of tools used by a nation's central bank to control the overall money supply and promote economic growth and employ strategies such as revising interest rates and changing bank reserve requirements.

   In the United States, the Federal Reserve Bank implements monetary policy through a dual mandate to achieve maximum employment while keeping inflation in check.

2. **fiscal policy 财政政策**

   Fiscal policy refers to the use of government spending and tax policies to influence economic conditions, especially macroeconomic conditions. These include aggregate demand for goods and services, employment, inflation, and economic growth.

   During a recession, the government may lower tax rates or increase spending to encourage demand and spur economic activity. Conversely, to combat inflation, it may raise rates or cut spending to cool down the economy.

   Fiscal policy is often contrasted with monetary policy, which is enacted by central bankers and not elected government officials.

3. **fiscal stimulus 财政刺激**

   An attempt to make the economy grow faster by reducing taxes.

4. **macroeconomic policy 宏观经济政策**

   Macroeconomic policy is a tool or an instrument that policymakers use to assist them in regulating an economy. It consists of two main subsets: monetary policy and fiscal policy. The functioning of the economy as a whole is what macroeconomic policy analyses and attempts to influence. Generally, the macroeconomic policy aims to create a stable economic environment that promotes robust and sustained economic growth.

5. **an expansionary monetary policy 扩张性货币政策**

   An expansionary monetary policy is a macroeconomic monetary policy that aims to increase the rate of monetary expansion to stimulate the growth of a domestic economy. It is used by a central bank to stimulate economic growth during a contractionary phase of the business cycle. The policy increases the money supply, lowers interest rates, and increases demand, which boosts economic growth. It also lowers the value of the currency, thereby decreasing the exchange rate.

6. **open market operations 公开市场操作,公开市场业务**

   Open market operation (OMO) is a term that refers to the purchase and sale of securities in the open market by the Federal Reserve (Fed). The Fed conducts open market operations to regulate the supply of money that is on reserve in US banks. The Fed purchases Treasury securities to increase the money supply and sells them to reduce it.

   By using OMOs, the Fed can adjust the federal funds rate, which in turn influences other short-term rates, long-term rates, and foreign exchange rates. This can change the amount of money and credit available in the economy and affect certain economic factors, such as unemployment, output, and the costs of goods and services.

I Make verb phrases by linking those in Column A and Column B.

Column A	Column B
stimulate	currency
decrease	fluctuations
issue	business activities
implement	unemployment
smooth	monetary policies

II Match the following words or terms with their definitions.

devalue	contractionary	alleviate	exchange rates
implement	expansionary	delegate	regulate
monetary policy	macroeconomic		

1. _____: to control or maintain the rate or speed of something so that it operates properly

2. _____ : to entrust or assign responsibility or authority to someone else
3. _____ : relating to the overall aspects and behavior of an economy, such as growth, inflation, and employment
4. _____ : the process by which a government, central bank, or monetary authority manages the supply of money and interest rates to control the economy
5. _____ : the value of one currency for the purpose of conversion into another currency
6. _____ : relating to policies or measures that aim to stimulate economic growth and increase aggregate demand
7. _____ : relating to policies or measures that aim to reduce economic growth and decrease aggregate demand
8. _____ : to make (suffering, problem, or hardship) less severe or intense
9. _____ : to put (a decision, plan, agreement, etc.) into effect
10. _____ : to reduce or underestimate the worth or importance of

III Reading comprehension: choose the best answer from the four choices.

1. What is the main objective of monetary policy?
   A. Promoting economic growth.
   B. Managing inflation levels.
   C. Controlling fiscal policy.
   D. Regulating exchange rates.
2. How does a central bank adjust interest rates to influence the economy?
   A. By changing fiscal policies.
   B. By regulating currency exchange rates.
   C. By modifying reserve requirements.
   D. By adjusting the discount rate.
3. What is the relationship between monetary policy and the business cycle?
   A. Monetary policy determines the length of the business cycle.
   B. Monetary policy influences the fluctuations in the business cycle.
   C. Monetary policy is ineffective in managing the business cycle.
   D. Monetary policy has no impact on the business cycle.
4. Why is central bank independence considered important in conducting monetary policy?
   A. It allows for political interference in monetary decisions.
   B. It ensures stability in exchange rates.
   C. It increases government control over the economy.

D. It enhances credibility and effectiveness of monetary policy.
5. What is the overall implication of the article regarding monetary policy?
   A. Monetary policy is the sole factor determining economic growth.
   B. Delegating monetary policy to an independent central bank is essential.
   C. Fiscal policy is more effective than monetary policy in stabilizing the economy.
   D. Monetary policy focuses solely on controlling inflation.

Part Two Case Study

THE GLOBAL FINANCIAL CRISIS AND THE ROLE OF MONETARY POLICY

SPEECH BY JÜRGEN STARK, MEMBER OF THE EXECUTIVE BOARD OF THE EUROPEAN CENTRAL BANK, AT THE 13TH ANNUAL EMERGING MARKETS CONFERENCE 2011, WASHINGTON, 24 SEPTEMBER, 2011.

I think it is fair to say that there was a widespread consensus over some key elements of the pre-crisis monetary policy paradigm.

In particular, against the background of the high inflation experience of the 1970s in many industrialized countries, the central bank consensus comprised three key elements:

(1) Central bank independence as a corner stone for an effective monetary policy;
(2) Price stability as the primary objective of central banks;
(3) Solidly anchored inflation expectations on the basis of transparent communication.

In addition, not least against the background of the "Great Moderation", that is, the period of low inflation and macroeconomic stability in most industrialized countries which was observed during the 20 years before the crisis, the central bank consensus also emphasized three elements, to which the ECB has never subscribed. These are:

(1) Monetary policy has a primary role in the management of aggregate demand in the short-run;
(2) Money and credit indicators can be disregarded;
(3) Monetary policy should react to asset price busts; not to asset price booms.

Let me now elaborate on the above elements and draw some conclusions.

Firstly, the crisis has, in my view, crucially underlined the importance of central bank independence as a corner stone of credible and effective monetary policy making. Of course, central bank independence is a precondition of effective monetary policy at all times. It is an important lesson which is not only evidenced by events in the history of central banking, but also by the academic literature, that any blurring of responsibilities can potentially lead to a loss of credibility for the central bank. Such a situation would ultimately undermine the effectiveness of monetary policy.

The effectiveness of monetary policy on the basis of institutional and operational independence was, however, fundamental during the crisis. During the turbulent market conditions that we experienced central banks had to implement extraordinary measures, both in terms of reducing policy rates to levels that are unprecedented, and in terms of unconventional liquidity measures. If these measures, untested as they are, are to be expected to exert any impact on economic decisions, they have to be seen by market participants as the result of an autonomous decision by the central bank. They have to be seen as consistent with its overall policy framework, rather than as the result of pressures from fiscal authorities. The reason is simple. If a central bank comes under pressure in times of crisis, and succumbs to that pressure, it is very unlikely to exit from such extraordinary measures in a timely manner. This may unanchor inflation expectations and thus undermine the effectiveness of the measures implemented during the crisis.

Secondly, regarding the objective of price stability and the anchoring of inflation expectations, the crisis taught us that well-anchored inflation expectations can act as an automatic stabilizer when uncertainty becomes destabilizing. This is always true, in good times as well. In fact, well-anchored inflation expectations in the euro area were instrumental in avoiding large interest rate hikes before the crisis, when commodity prices rose sharply. At the height of the crisis, they became a policy instrument in their own right. Thanks to well-anchored inflation expectations we could avoid deflationary spirals and real interest rates could be reduced in tandem with nominal rates. It is noteworthy that if inflation expectations are well anchored, and are not affected by transient shocks to actual inflation, there is no need to manipulate monetary policy frameworks: there is no need to increase the inflation target as a means of resisting deflationary risks in times of macroeconomic distress.

Opportunistic manipulations of the monetary policy framework of course damage the foundations on which that framework rests. So, being able to rely on the stabilizing effect of inflation expectations is clearly a preferable option.

Let me now turn to the elements of the consensus that are, from the perspective of the ECB, somewhat more controversial.

Firstly, the crisis has demonstrated that a monetary policy aimed at fine-tuning short-term objectives carries serious risks. Before the crisis, there was a widely-held conviction that monetary policy could focus more on short term demand management because inflation was firmly under control. Proponents of this view found support in the phenomenon of the "Great Moderation" observed in the twenty years before the crisis, a time of widespread macroeconomic stability and low inflation in most industrialized countries. Nonetheless, there were clear signs—and also warnings—that this short-term orientation could have negative side effects in the medium to long term.

As you know, these side effects manifested themselves in a spectacular build-up of monetary and financial imbalances. Although monetary policy frameworks oriented towards the medium term could probably not have completely prevented the current crisis, I am convinced that they would have helped to make it less disruptive.

Typically, policies of short-term demand management rely heavily on inflation forecasts and output gap measures. Experience, especially prior to the crisis, has revealed the risks of constructing policy on indicators and variables which are not sufficiently robust. Let me take the output gap as an example. As the literature has clearly shown, the empirical proxies used to capture the output gap are subject to constant revisions.

Policy-makers who base their decisions mainly on such assessments of the cyclical position can be led very much astray. For instance, The Great Inflation of the 1970s occurred, to a large extent, due to measurement errors in the real-time estimates of the output gap combined with an overreaction to output gap measures when assessing the state of the economy.

Arguably, the same can be said of the low interest rates implemented for a prolonged period in the middle of the previous decade.

Monetary policies aimed at fine-tuning short-term objectives also run a serious risk of inducing too much policy forbearance for too long. Exiting an extraordinary accommodative mode too late can sow the seeds of future imbalances. As the economy recovers from an exceptionally deep recession, real time output gap estimates and estimates of structural unemployment or the non-accelerating inflation rate of unemployment (NAIRU) are particularly uncertain. Potential output is likely to have fallen for a variety of reasons. This could be due to a mismatch between the skills of workers that lose their jobs and the skills required in new vacancies. Another phenomenon is that economic growth after a financial crisis tends to be much slower due to the debt overhang.

<u>While emphasis on measures of the output gap can give the impression that output could be increased by monetary means, it becomes an illusion if the problem is due to a mismatch of skills or a debt overhang.</u> Only structural policies can address these problems.

Secondly, with respect to the claim that money and credit do not matter for successful monetary policy making, the experiences of the past three years have proven that this conventional wisdom is simply wrong. By including an analysis of money and credit developments in their monetary policy strategy, central banks can ensure that important information stemming from money and credit, typically neglected in conventional cyclical forecasting models of the economy, is considered in the formulation of monetary policy decisions. There is compelling empirical evidence showing that, at low frequencies—that is over medium to longer-term horizons—inflation shows a robust positive association with money growth.

Monitoring credit growth can also be useful in identifying other sources of unsustainable credit developments, even if some of them cannot necessarily be eliminated by monetary policy tools, and would instead require action of a macro-prudential nature. After years of oblivion, macroeconomic theory seems to have caught up with reality and shifted its attention to credit and leverage as critical parameters that a central bank should consult regularly to measure the pulse of the economy.

The ECB had consistently used these indicators even when they were derided as relics of a defunct monetary doctrine. They proved useful. They gave information about financing conditions and the financial structure, as well as about the condition and behavior of banks, when these sources of information were critical to the assessment of the health of the transmission mechanism and, more broadly, the state of the business cycle. This dimension of monetary analysis has proven particularly valuable in shaping the ECB's response to the financial crisis. There is indeed evidence in support of the fact that, without duly taking monetary analysis into account, inflation in the euro area would have been distinctly higher at times of financial exuberance and would have fallen deep into negative territory in the wake of the financial markets' collapse, starting in the autumn of 2008. The economy as a whole would have been more volatile.

And thirdly, with regard to the pre-crisis consensus on monetary policy not to act on asset price bubbles, the crisis has vividly demonstrated that bursting asset price bubbles can be extremely costly. The public policy response to the crisis has—even when being successful in attenuating the immediate impact of a financial crisis on the real economy—carried substantial fiscal costs and has led to significant output losses. To confine ourselves to "ex-post" policies is, therefore, not enough and calls for effective "ex-ante" policies. The main policy tools in this regard are, of course, appropriate regulatory and supervisory policies. Before the crisis, these preventive tools were insufficient to deal with the building up of asset price imbalances in the pre-crisis period. Lessons have been learned, and with the re-design of the supervisory architecture in many countries around the world, and the Basel III regulatory reforms, enhanced preventive tools are underway.

But also from a monetary policy perspective, greater emphasis on "ex-ante" prevention is warranted. To the extent that financial imbalances are accompanied by excessive monetary and credit growth with possible implications for the medium term outlook on inflation, central banks do indeed have an obligation to take appropriate action. With respect to the ECB, our focus on medium term definitions of price stability, as well as the use of money and credit in our monetary pillar, already provides some 'leaning' against the build-up of asset price imbalances. Therefore, in my view, a cautious leaning against excessive money and credit growth and building up of financial imbalances as part of our general monetary policy framework cannot only contribute to financial stability, but most importantly to achieve our primary objective of maintaining price stability.

Let me now turn to the economic challenges lying ahead of us, and the role monetary policy should play in overcoming these challenges.

 ## Questions for Discussion

1. What lessons can be drawn from the crisis regarding the role of inflation expectations in maintaining macroeconomic stability? Explore the significance of well-anchored inflation expectations as automatic stabilizers and their influence on policy decisions, both in normal economic conditions and during times of uncertainty.

2. How has the global financial crisis affected the role and importance of central bank independence in monetary policy? Discuss the significance of central bank autonomy in maintaining credibility and effectiveness, particularly during times of crisis.

 ## Translation

1. It is an important lesson which is not only evidenced by events in the history of central banking, but also by the academic literature, that any blurring of responsibilities can potentially lead to a loss of credibility for the central bank.

2. While emphasis on measures of the output gap can give the impression that output could be increased by monetary means, it becomes an illusion if the problem is due to a mismatch of skills or a debt overhang.

3. The public policy response to the crisis has—even when being successful in attenuating the immediate impact of a financial crisis on the real economy—carried substantial fiscal costs and has led to significant output losses.

4. With respect to the ECB, our focus on medium term definitions of price stability, as well as the use of money and credit in our monetary pillar, already provides some "leaning" against the building up of asset price imbalances.

Unit 12

Saving, Investment and the Financial System

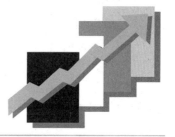

Introduction

At any time some people want to save some of their income for the future, and others want to borrow in order to finance investments in new and growing businesses. Financial system is what brings these two groups of people together.

Key issues concerning financial system are:

(1) Which are the various institutions that make up the financial system? How do they function?

(2) Which are the basic tools of finance?

(3) How interest rate balances the supply and demand for loanable funds in financial markets?

(4) How the government policies affect the interest rate and, thereby, society's allocation of scarce resources?

Part One Text

The financial system consists of the group of institutions in the economy that help to match one person's saving with another person's investment. It moves the economy's scarce resources from savers to borrowers.

Financial institutions can be grouped into two different categories: financial markets and financial intermediaries.

(1) Financial markets.
- Stock market.
- Bond market.

(2) Financial intermediaries.

- Banks.
- Mutual funds.

Financial Markets

Financial markets are the institutions through which savers can directly provide funds to borrowers.

1. The Bond Market

A bond is a certificate of indebtedness that specifies obligations of the borrower to the holder of the bond.

Characteristics of a bond are as follows:

- Term: The length of time until the bond matures.
- Credit risk: The probability that the borrower will fail to pay some of the interest or principal.

2. The Stock Market

Stock represents a claim to partial ownership in a firm and is therefore, a claim to the profits that the firm makes. The sale of stock to raise money is called equity financing. Compared to bonds, stocks offer both higher risk and potentially higher returns. Stocks are traded on exchanges such as the London Stock Exchange and the Frankfurt Stock Exchange. Most newspaper stock tables provide the following information:

- Price (of a share).
- Volume (number of shares sold).
- Dividend (profits paid to stockholders).
- Price-earnings ratio.

Financial Intermediaries

Financial intermediaries are financial institutions through which savers can indirectly provide funds to borrowers. Banks take deposits from people who want to save and use the deposits to make loans to people who want to borrow. Banks also pay depositors interest on their deposits and charge borrowers slightly higher interest on their loans. It helps create a medium of exchange by allowing people to write checks against their deposits and facilitate the purchases of goods and services. A mutual fund is an institution that sells shares to the public and uses the proceeds to buy a portfolio, of various types of stocks, bonds, or both. Mutual funds allow people with small amounts of money to easily diversify.

Other financial institutions are as follows:
- Credit unions.
- Pension funds.
- Insurance companies.
- Loan sharks.

Saving and Investment in the National Income Accounts

Recall that GDP is both total income in an economy and total expenditure on the economy's output of goods and services:

$$Y = C + I + G + NX$$

In this formula, C—consumption, I—investment, G—government spending, NX—net exports.

Assume a closed economy—one that does not engage in international trade:

$$Y = C + I + G$$

Now, subtract C and G from both sides of the equation:

$$Y - C - G = I$$

The left side of the equation is the total income in the economy after paying for consumption and government purchases and is called national saving, or just saving (S).

Substituting S for $Y - C - G$, the equation can be written as:

$$S = I$$

National saving, or saving, is equal to:
$$S = I$$
$$S = Y - C - G$$
$$S = (Y - T - C) + (T - G)$$

1. National Saving

National saving is the total income in the economy that remains after paying for consumption and government purchases.

2. Private Saving

Private saving is the amount of income that households have left after paying their taxes and paying for their consumption.

$$\text{Private Saving} = (Y - T - C)$$

3. Public Saving

Public saving is the amount of tax revenue that the government has left after paying for its spending.

$$\text{Public Saving} = (T - G)$$

4. Surplus and Deficit

If $T > G$, the government runs a budget surplus because it receives more money than it spends.

The surplus of $T - G$ represents public saving.

If $G > T$, the government runs a budget deficit because it spends more money than it receives in tax revenue.

For the economy as a whole, saving must be equal to investment.

$$S = I$$

The Market for Loanable Funds

Financial markets coordinate the economy's saving and investment in the market for loanable funds. The market for loanable funds is the market in which some people want to save supply funds and some want to borrow to invest. Loanable funds refers to all income that people have chosen to save and lend out, rather than use for their own consumption.

The supply of loanable funds comes from people who have extra income they want to save and lend out. The demand for loanable funds comes from households and firms that wish to borrow to make investments.

Interest rate:
- the price of the loan;
- the amount that borrowers pay for loans and the amount that lenders receive on their saving;

- in the market for loanable funds, the real interest rate.

Financial markets work much like other markets in the economy. The equilibrium at Point E of the supply and demand for loanable funds €1,200 determines the real rate as of 5%, as elaborated in Figure 12–1 below.

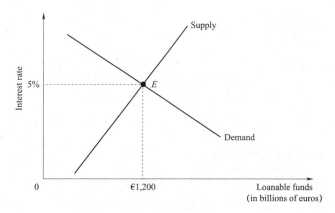

Figure 12–1 Interest rate equilibrium determined by the supply and demand

Government Policies That Affect Saving and Investment

(1) Taxes and saving.
(2) Taxes and investment.
(3) Government budget deficits and surpluses.

Policy 1: Saving Incentives

Taxes on interest income substantially reduce the future payoff from current saving and, as a result, reduce the incentive to save.

A tax decrease increases the incentive for households to save at any given interest rate.

- The supply of loanable funds curve shifts to the right.
- The equilibrium interest rate decreases from Point E_1 to Point E_2 as in Figure 12–2.
- The quantity demanded for loanable funds increases from €1,200 to €1,600 as in Figure 12–2.

If a change in tax law encourages greater saving, the result will be lower interest rates and greater investment.

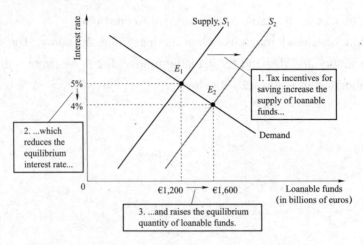

Figure 12-2 Interest rate equilibrium decreases as the supply increases

Policy 2: Investment Incentives

An investment tax credit increases the incentive to borrow.

- Increases the demand for loanable funds from €1,200 to €1,400 in Figure 12-3.
- Shifts the demand curve to the right from D_1 to D_2 as in Figure 12-3.
- Results in a higher interest rate from 5% to 6% in Figure 12-3 and a greater quantity saved.

If a change in tax laws encourages greater investment, the result will be higher interest rates and greater saving.

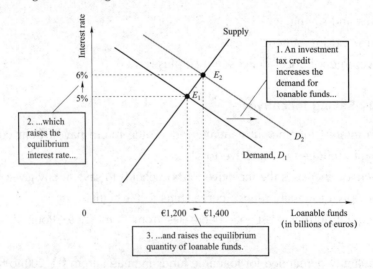

Figure 12-3 The equilibrium interest rate increases as the demand increases

Policy 3: Government Budget Deficits and Surpluses

When the government spends more than it receives in tax revenues, the short fall is

Unit 12 Saving, Investment and the Financial System

called the budget deficit. The accumulation of past budget deficits is called the government debt.

A budget deficit decreases the supply of loanable funds.

• Shifts the supply curve to the left from S_1 to S_2 as in Figure 12 – 4.
• Increases the equilibrium interest rate from Point E_1 to E_2 in Figure 12 – 4.
• Reduces the equilibrium quantity of loanable funds from € 1,200 to € 800 in Figure 12 – 4.

When government reduces national saving by running a deficit, the interest rate rises and investment falls. A budget surplus increases the supply of loanable funds, reduces the interest rate, and stimulates investment.

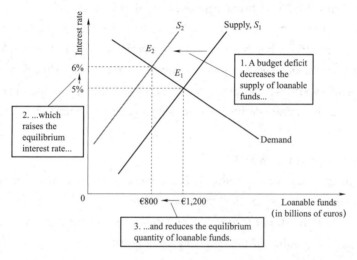

Figure 12 – 4 The equilibrium interest rate increases as the supply decreases

Words and Expressions

depositors	n.	存款人
financial intermediaries		金融中介机构，金融媒介，财务中介机构
loanable funds		可贷款资金（指金融市场上可供借贷的资金，包括储蓄、投资和信贷）
stock market		股票市场
bond market		债券市场
credit risk		信用风险（指借款人或债券发行人未能按时履行还款义务，导致投资者损失的风险）

1. **mutual funds** 共同基金(一种投资工具,由许多投资者共同出资购买股票、债券等证券的一种投资组合)

   A mutual fund is a financial vehicle that pools assets from shareholders to invest in securities like stocks, bonds, money market instruments, and other assets. Mutual funds are operated by professional money managers, who allocate the fund's assets and attempt to produce capital gains or income for the fund's investors. A mutual fund's portfolio is structured and maintained to match the investment objectives stated in its prospectus.

   Mutual funds give small or individual investors access to professionally managed portfolios of equities, bonds, and other securities. Each shareholder, therefore, participates proportionally in the gains or losses of the fund. Mutual funds invest in a vast number of securities, and performance is usually tracked as the change in the total market cap of the fund—derived by the aggregating performance of the underlying investments.

2. **price-to-earnings ratio** 市盈率

   Price-to-earnings ratio, or, P/E Ratio, is a common valuation metric used to measure a company's equity value in relation to its net earnings.

   Simply put, the P/E ratio of a company represents the amount that investors are currently willing to pay for a dollar of the company's net profit.

   $$\text{P/E ratio} = \frac{\text{market share price}}{\text{earnings per share (EPS)}}$$

   The price to earnings ratio (P/E) is one of the most widely used metrics for investors and analysts to determine stock valuation. It shows whether a company's stock price is overvalued or undervalued and can reveal how a stock's valuation compares to its industry group or a benchmark like the S&P 500 index.

   The P/E ratio helps investors determine the market value of a stock as compared to the company's earnings. It shows what the market is willing to pay for a stock based on its past or future earnings.

3. **financial portfolio** 金融投资组合

   A portfolio is a collection of financial investments like stocks, bonds, commodities, cash, and cash equivalents, including closed-end funds and exchange traded funds (ETFs). People generally believe that stocks, bonds, and cash comprise the core of a portfolio. Though this is often the case, it does not need to be the rule. A portfolio may contain a wide range of assets including real estate, art, and private investments.

   You may choose to hold and manage your portfolio yourself, or you may allow a money

Unit 12 Saving, Investment and the Financial System

manager, financial advisor, or another finance professional to manage your portfolio.

I Make verb phrases by linking those in Column A and Column B.

Column A	Column B
specify	dividends
represent	money
pay	obligations
facilitate	ownership
raise	purchases

II Match the following words or terms with their definitions.

| deflation | mitigate | extrapolate | inflation | facilitate |
| discretionary | resilient | arbitrage | volatility | unprecedented |

1. _____ : to make (an action or process) easy or easier
2. _____ : to make (something bad or unsatisfactory) less severe, serious, or painful
3. _____ : able to withstand or recover quickly from difficult conditions
4. _____ : extend the application of (a method or conclusion) to an unknown situation by assuming that existing trends will continue or similar methods will be applicable
5. _____ : the liability to change rapidly and unpredictably, especially for the worse
6. _____ : a general increase in prices and fall in the purchasing value of money
7. _____ : a reduction of the general level of prices in an economy
8. _____ : the simultaneous buying and selling of securities, currency, or commodities in different markets or in derivative forms in order to take advantage of differing prices for the same asset
9. _____ : available for use at the discretion of the user
10. _____ : never done or known before; without previous example

III Reading comprehension: choose the best answer from the four choices.

1. What is the main purpose of the financial system?
   A. To facilitate the exchange of goods and services.
   B. To connect savers and borrowers.
   C. To regulate interest rates in the market.
   D. To promote government policies on resource allocation.
2. What is the term used to describe the interest rate in the market for loanable funds?
   A. Real interest rate.   B. Stock price.
   C. Credit risk.   D. Dividend.
3. What are financial markets?
   A. Institutions that help to match savers and borrowers.
   B. Institutions that facilitate international trade.
   C. Institutions that provide tax incentives for saving.
   D. Institutions that regulate interest rates.
4. What is the relationship between national saving and investment?
   A. They are independent of each other.
   B. National saving is greater than investment.
   C. National saving is equal to investment.
   D. National saving is smaller than investment.
5. How do government budget deficits affect the market for loanable funds?
   A. They increase the supply of loanable funds.
   B. They decrease the demand for loanable funds.
   C. They decrease the supply of loanable funds.
   D. They increase the demand for loanable funds.

Part Two Case Study

GLOBAL MACRO-FINANCIAL CONDITIONS

By **Back of Canada**
From *Financial System Review*, 2022

As the global economy emerges from the COVID-19 pandemic, several factors have combined to increase volatility in financial markets and reduce investors' appetites for risky assets. Amid rising global inflationary pressures, major central banks have entered a phase of monetary policy tightening. At the same time, the Russia-Ukraine conflict has increased volatility in commodity markets and uncertainty more generally, causing significant repricing in some financial markets as investors seek safer assets. The tightening of global financial conditions could more clearly expose existing financial vulnerabilities and will test the resilience of the global financial system.

Over the past year, inflation has risen worldwide. Many economies have lifted pandemic-related restrictions, leading to robust demand, which has met with global supply constraints. In addition to causing untold human suffering, the Russia-Ukraine conflict is also adding to inflationary pressures, both by boosting commodity prices and creating additional supply chain issues.

As a result of rising inflation, investors expect major central banks to withdraw a significant amount of monetary policy stimulus. Central banks may substantially increase their policy rates and reduce their balance sheets through quantitative tightening. Expectations of both tighter monetary policy and higher inflation have led to a sharp rise in nominal sovereign bond yields around the world (see Figure 12-5). This abrupt repricing in sovereign bonds has happened alongside higher volatility in other asset classes (see Figure 12-6).

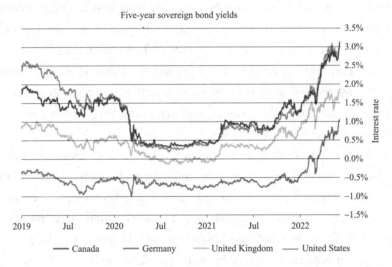

Figure 12-5 Yields on sovereign bonds have risen significantly due to expectations of tighter monetary policy

Global financial conditions are tighter than they were last year. Excluding the period of market turmoil in March and April 2020, yields on corporate bonds are at multi-year highs. Borrowing rates for households have increased substantially. Five-year fixed mortgage rates have reached levels last seen in 2010. Corporate credit spreads have widened, and most global equity indexes are down significantly in 2022. Investors' appetites for risky assets have weakened, particularly for technology stocks and cryptoassets, leading to sharp declines in prices and valuations.

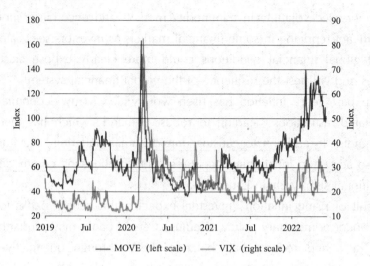

Figure 12-6　Volatility has increased in many asset classes

　　The tightening of global financial conditions could expose existing financial vulnerabilities. It could reignite concerns about market liquidity in the event of an episode of severe financial stress. Tightening could also interact with vulnerabilities in emerging-market economies (EMEs)—such as high public and private debt, foreign exchange exposures and large current account deficits—and trigger capital outflows. Concerns about corporate leverage in the property sector in China could intensify further. Finally, tighter financial conditions will put pressure on government finances given higher levels of debt taken on during the pandemic. Fiscal sustainability is a particularly acute concern for some EMEs.

　　The Russia-Ukraine conflict is compounding the risks to global financial stability. The war is affecting the global economy through many channels. It has increased global uncertainty. As mentioned, the sharp rise in commodity prices and the additional disruptions to supply are adding to already elevated inflationary pressures. In this context, central banks face a delicate balancing act. They must reduce inflation while seeking to safeguard both the recovery from the pandemic and overall financial stability. <u>Failure to balance these competing objectives could lead to a further global repricing of risk and a sharp tightening of global financial conditions, potentially triggering risks associated with high leverage.</u> The conflict in Europe has also introduced a short-term trade-off between energy security and transition plans in response to climate-related risks and has increased cyber risks.

　　The financial health of households has generally improved since the start of the pandemic, particularly over 2021. Net worth increased on average by \$230,000 per household between the fourth quarter of 2019 and the fourth quarter of 2021, reflecting three key factors:

(1) Increased residential assets (Figure 12-7, blue bars)—House prices rose strongly across the country (Vulnerability 2), boosting homeowners' wealth. Real estate assets account for two-thirds of the growth in net worth since the fourth quarter of 2019.

(2) Increased financial assets (Figure 12-7, green bars)—With stock markets reaching new highs during the pandemic, households that have financial assets tied to the stock market (either directly or through mutual or pension funds) generally saw the value of their equity portfolios grow. The recent decline in stock markets still leaves equity valuations about 15% higher than their pre-pandemic levels.

(3) Higher bank deposits (Figure 12-7, yellow bars)—In addition to paying down debt and increasing investments in residential and financial assets, households have expanded their holdings of liquid assets.

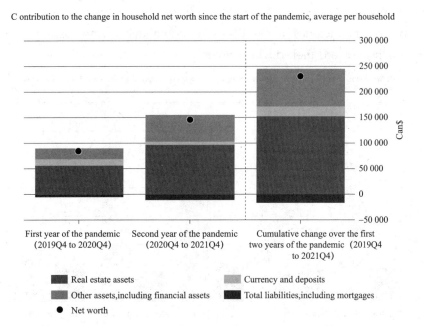

Figure 12-7 Household net worth has increased by about $230,000 on average since the pandemic began, largely reflecting higher house prices

Overall, households have also increased their liabilities (Figure 12-7, red bars), with higher mortgage debt more than offsetting lower consumer debt. Many households have taken on large mortgages relative to their income in the context of elevated house prices. At the same time, households have reduced their use of other forms of credit. For instance, in March 2022, total outstanding balances on credit cards were 9% lower than they were in February 2020. Balances on home equity lines of credit were 6% lower. The share of Canadians falling behind on consumer debt payments, at about 2%, remains close to its historical low.

Looking beyond average balance sheet statistics to evaluate household vulnerabilities is important. The increase in overall net worth seen in 2020 and 2021 hides important changes to its distribution and composition across households. Also unclear is the capacity for some households to service their debt in the event of a loss in income. Typically, when households allocate a larger share of their income to debt payments and have fewer liquid assets or limited access to credit, they must cut back on consumption by more if their disposable income declines.

Many aspects of the ongoing vulnerability related to elevated household indebtedness have evolved in opposing directions since the start of the pandemic.

The Bank's analysis suggests that households across different levels of indebtedness have generally increased their holdings of liquid assets relative to 2019, adding to their financial resilience. However, the Bank estimates that the increase in liquidity buffers during the pandemic is smallest for highly indebted households (Figure 12 – 8). This group of borrowers includes many first-time homebuyers who have put their extra pandemic savings toward their down payment.

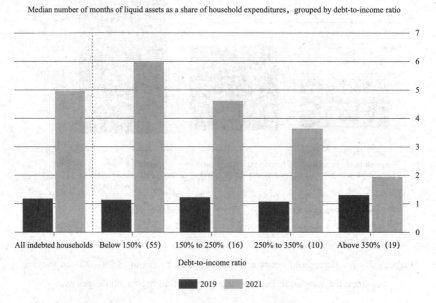

Figure 12 – 8 Simulations suggest that households of all levels of indebtedness have increased their liquidity buffers, but highly indebted households have done so the least

Most homeowners have more home equity to borrow against if they experience an income shock, but the gains are lowest for those who purchased a house most recently. Households that have enough equity in their house can use home equity lines of credit or mortgage refinancing to access some of this capital in times of financial stress. Given the large increase in house prices since 2020, most highly indebted households have improved their equity positions. However, households that bought a property in recent quarters have generally seen the smallest gains and have increasingly made small down payments relative to the purchase price. The number of new mortgages with a loan-to-value ratio of 75% or more increased 40% over this period. Combined, these developments suggest that many recent homebuyers would have limited access to secured forms of credit in the event of a decline in income.

A rising number of households have financially stretched to purchase a house amid elevated house prices. Increasingly over the past year, households have taken on mortgages that are large relative to their income and have opted for variable mortgage rates and longer amortization periods (Figure 12 – 9). The growing share of new mortgages taken out by borrowers with elevated loan-to-income ratios implies that the overall proportion of highly indebted households likely surpassed its pre-pandemic peak in 2021 (Figure 12 – 10), increasing the risk to macro-financial stability.

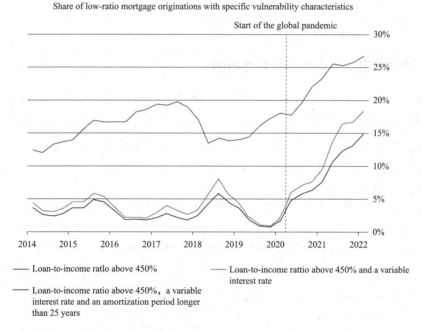

Figure 12 – 9 An increasing share of households are stretching financially to purchase a house

Higher interest rates will increase the vulnerability of highly indebted households. Even with a high debt load, households have generally been able to manage their debt servicing costs due to low interest rates since the start of the pandemic. But as mortgages are renewed at higher rates, some households—particularly those that took on a sizable mortgage since the start of the pandemic—will face significantly larger mortgage payments (Box 1). All else being equal, higher interest costs would greatly reduce their financial flexibility in the event of an income shock.

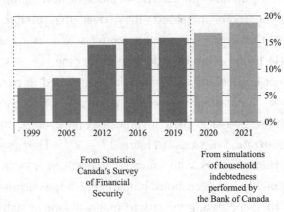

Figure 12-10 The share of highly indebted households in 2021 will likely surpass pre-pandemic highs

Questions for Discussion

1. In what ways do you think the COVID-19 pandemic has influenced people's attitudes towards financial stability and their approach to managing personal finances?

2. Reflect on the role of government policies in addressing the challenges posed by global financial conditions. What measures can governments take to promote financial stability and protect individuals and households from economic shocks?

Translation

1. As the global economy emerges from the COVID-19 pandemic, several factors have combined to increase volatility in financial markets and reduce investors' appetites for risky assets.

Unit 12 Saving, Investment and the Financial System

2. In addition to causing untold human suffering, the Russia-Ukraine conflict is also adding to inflationary pressures, both by boosting commodity prices and creating additional supply chain issues.

   _____
   _____
   _____

3. Failure to balance these competing objectives could lead to a further global repricing of risk and a sharp tightening of global financial conditions, potentially triggering risks associated with high leverage.

   _____
   _____
   _____

4. Typically, when households allocate a larger share of their income to debt payments and have fewer liquid assets or limited access to credit, they must cut back on consumption by more if their disposable income declines.

   _____
   _____
   _____

Unit 13
Economic Growth

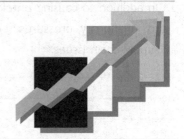

Introduction

Economic growth is the increase in value of the goods and services produced by an economy. It is conventionally measured as the percent rate of increase in real Gross Domestic Product, or GDP. Growth is usually calculated in real terms in order to net out the effect of inflation on the price of the goods and services produced. In economics, "economic growth" or "economic growth theory" typically refers to growth of potential output, which is caused by growth in aggregate demand or observed output. As economic growth is measured as the annual percent change of Gross Domestic Product, it has all the advantages and drawbacks of that measure.

Part One Text

A. Origins of the Concept and Theories of Economic Growth

In the early modern period, some people in Western European nations began conceiving of the idea that economies could "grow", that is, produce a greater economic surplus which could be expended on something other than mere subsistence. This surplus could then be used for consumption, warfare, or civic and religious projects. The previous view was that only increasing either population or tax rates could generate more surplus money for the Crown or country.

Now it is generally recognized that economic growth also corresponds to a process of continual rapid replacement and reorganization of human activities facilitated by investment motivated to maximize returns. This exponential evolution of our self-organized life-support and cultural systems is remarkably creative and flexible, but highly unpredictable in many ways. Since science still has no good way of modeling complex self-organizing systems, various efforts to model the long term evolution of economies have produced few useful results.

During much of the "Mercantilist" period, growth was seen as involving an increase in the total amount of specie, that is circulating medium such as silver and gold, under the control of the state. This "Bullionist" theory led to policies to force trade through a particular state, the acquisition of colonies to supply cheaper raw materials which could then be manufactured and sold.

Later, such trade policies were justified instead simply in terms of promoting domestic trade and industry. Under this system high tariffs were erected to allow manufacturers to establish "factories". (The word comes from "factor", the term for someone who carried goods from one stage of production to the next.) Local markets would then pay the fixed costs of capital growth, and then allow them to export abroad, undercutting the prices of manufactured goods elsewhere. Once competition from abroad was removed, prices could then be increased to recoup the costs of establishing the business.

Under this theory of growth, the road to increased national wealth was to grant monopolies, which would give an incentive for an individual to exploit a market or resource, confident that he would make all of the profits when all other extra-national competitors were driven out of business. The "Dutch East India Company" and the "British East India Company" were examples of such state-granted trade monopolies.

In this period the view was that growth was gained through "advantageous" trade in which specie would flow in to the country, but to trade with other nations on equal terms was disadvantageous. It should be stressed that Mercantilism was not simply a matter of restricting trade. Within a country, it often meant breaking down trade barriers, building new roads, and abolishing local toll booths, all of which expanded markets. This corresponded to the centralization of power in the hands of the Crown (or "Absolutism"). This process helped produce the modern nation-state in Western Europe.

Internationally, Mercantilism led to a contradiction: growth was gained through trade, but to trade with other nations on equal terms was disadvantageous. This — along with the rise of nation-states — encouraged several major wars.

B. Solow-Swan Growth Model

Economic growth occurs whenever people take resources and rearrange them in ways that are more valuable. This notion of growth as increased stocks of capital goods (means of production) was codified as the Solow-Swan Growth Model, which involved a series of equations which showed the relationship between labor-time, capital goods, output, and investment. In this modern view, the role of technological change became crucial, even more important than the accumulation of capital. This model, developed by Robert Solow and Paul Samuelson in the 1950s, was the first attempt to model long-run growth analytically. This model assumes that countries use their resources efficiently and that there are diminishing returns to capital and labor increases. From these two premises, the neo-classical model makes three important predictions. First, increasing capital relative to labor creates economic growth, since people can be more productive given more capital. Second, poor countries with less capital per person will grow faster because each investment in capital will produce a higher return than rich countries with ample capital. Third, because of diminishing returns to capital, economies will eventually reach a point at which no new increase in capital will create economic growth. This point is called a "steady state".

The model also notes that countries can overcome this steady state and continue growing by inventing new technology. In the long run output per capita depends on the rate of saving but the rate of growth of output should be equal for any saving rate! In this model the process by which countries continue growing despite the diminishing returns is "exogenous" and represents the creation of new technology that allows production with fewer resources. Technology improves, the steady state level of capital increases and the country invests and grows. The data does not support some of this model's predictions, in particular, that all countries grow at the same rate in the long run, or that poorer countries should grow faster until they reach their steady state. Also, the data suggests the world has slowly increased its rate of growth.

In the early 20th century, it became the policy of most nations to encourage growth of this kind. To do this required enacting policies, and being able to measure the results of those policies. This gave rise to the importance of econometrics, or the field of creating measurements for underlying conditions. Terms such as "unemployment rate", "Gross Domestic Product" and "rate of inflation" are part of the measuring of the changes in an economy.

In mainstream economics, the purpose of government policy is to encourage economic activity without encouraging the rise in the general level of prices (in other words, increase GDP without creating inflation). This combination is seen as, at the macro-scale (see macroeconomics) to be indicative of an increasing stock of capital. The argument runs that if more money is changing hands, but the prices of individual goods are relatively stable, then it is proof that there is more productive capacity, and therefore more capital, because it is capital that is allowing more to be made at a lower cost per unit.

The late 20th century, with its global economy of a few very wealthy nations, and many very poor nations, led to the study of how the transition from subsistence and resource-based economies, to production and consumption based-economies occurred, leading to the field of Development economics, including the work of Amartya Sen and Joseph Stiglitz.

The short-run variation of economic growth is termed the business cycle, and almost all economies experience periodical recessions. The cycle can be a misnomer as the fluctuations are not always regular. Explaining these fluctuations is one of the main focuses of macroeconomics. There are different schools of thought as to the causes of recessions but some consensus — see Keynesianism, Monetarism, New Classical Economics and New Keynesian Economics. Oil shocks, war and harvest failure are obvious causes of recession. Short-run variation in growth has generally dampened in higher income countries since the early 90s and this has been attributed, in part, to better macroeconomic management.

C. Measuring Growth

The real GDP per capita of an economy is often used as an indicator of the average standard of living of individuals in that country, and economic growth is therefore often seen as indicating an increase in the average standard of living. However, there are some problems in using growth in GDP per capita to measure general well-being. Economists are well aware of these deficiencies in GDP, thus, it should always be viewed merely as an indicator and not an absolute scale. Economists have developed mathematical tools to measure inequality, such as the Gini Coefficient. There are also alternate ways of measurement that consider the negative externalities that may result from pollution and resource depletion.

The flaws of GDP may be important when studying public policy, however, for the purposes of economic growth in the long run it tends to be a very good indicator. There is no other indicator in economics which is as universal or as widely accepted as the GDP.

Other measures of national income, such as the Index of Sustainable Economic Welfare or the Genuine Progress Indicator, have been developed in an attempt to give a more complete picture of the level of well-being, but there is no consensus as to which, if any, is a better measure than GDP. GDP still remains by far the most often-used measure, especially since, all else equal, a rise in real GDP is correlated with an increase in the availability of jobs, which are necessary to most individuals' survival.

D. Criticism

Four major critical arguments are generally raised against economic growth.

(1) Growth has negative effects on the quality of life: many things that affect the quality of life are not traded in the market and measured in the market, and they generally lose value when growth occurs, such as the environment.

(2) Growth encourages the creation of artificial needs: industry causes consumers to develop new tastes, and preferences for growth to occur. Consequently, "wants are created, and consumers have become the servants, instead of the masters, of the economy."

(3) Resources: similar to the arguments made by Thomas Malthus, economic growth depletes non-renewable resources rapidly.

(4) Distribution of income: growth may reinforce and propagate unequal distribution of income.

The concept of economic growth is also refuted by adherents to the school of economics. According to the economists, the concept of "growth" or the creation and acquisition of more goods and services is dependent upon the relative desires of the individual. Someone may favour spending more leisure time preferable over acquiring more goods and services. Also, they claim that the notion of growth implies the need for a "central planner" within an economy.

E. Growth and Recipes

A useful metaphor for production in an economy comes from the kitchen. To create valuable final products, we mix inexpensive ingredients together according to a recipe. The cooking one can do is limited by the supply of ingredients, and most cooking in the economy produces undesirable side effects. If economic growth could be achieved only by doing more and more of the same kind of cooking, we would eventually run out of raw materials and suffer from unacceptable levels of pollution nuisance. Human history teaches us, however, that economic growth springs from better recipes, not just from more cooking. New recipes generally produce fewer unpleasant side effects and generate more economic value per unit of raw material.

Unit 13　Economic Growth

Words and Expressions

conceive	v.	构思，以为，持有
	v.	怀孕，考虑，设想
exponential	n.	［数］指数，倡导者，演奏者，例子
	a.	指数的，幂数的
specie	n.	硬币
recoup	v.	赔偿，补偿，扣除
	v.	补偿损失
incentive	n.	动机
	a.	激励的
codify	v.	编成法典，使法律成文化
exogenous	a.	［生］外生的，［地］外成的，［医］外因的
misnomer	n.	用词不当，［律］（在诉讼等中）写错姓名（或地名）
consensus	n.	一致同意，多数人的意见，舆论
refute	v.	驳倒，反驳
preferable	a.	更可取的，更好的，更优越的

Notes

1. **Mercantilism**　重商主义（一般是指17—18世纪的经济政策体系和经济学说①）

   Mercantilism is a doctrine asserting that power and wealth are closely interrelated and are legitimate goals of national policy. Wealth is necessary for power, and power can be used to obtain wealth. Power is a relative concept because one country can gain it only at the expense of another like a zero-sum game. States thus are locked in conflict in the international political economy. Mercantilist trade restrictions were under widespread attack (by Adam Smith, David Ricardo（大卫·李嘉图）, Richard Cobden（理查德·柯布登）and other Manchester Industrialists).

---

① 关于对重商主义这个名词的确切定义一直是有争论的问题，不同观点的争论，参见罗尔的《经济思想史》，1973。

2. **Bullionism** 重金主义，金银通货主义①

   Bullionism is an advocate for a metallic currency, or a paper currency always convertible into gold.

3. **Keynesianism** 凯恩斯理论(学说)

   It is named for economist John Maynard Keynes（约翰·梅纳德·凯恩斯，1883—1946）. It is an economic theory which advocates government intervention, or demand-side management of the economy, to achieve full employment and stable prices.

4. **Monetarism** 货币主义②

   It is a theory holding that economic variations within a given system, such as changing rates of inflation, are most often caused by increases or decreases in the money supply. It also refers to a policy that seeks to regulate an economy by altering the domestic money supply, especially by increasing it in a moderate but steady manner.

5. **New Keynesian Economics** 新凯恩斯主义经济学

   New Keynesian Economics is a school of contemporary macroeconomics that strives to provide microeconomic foundations for Keynesian Economics. It developed partly in response to the New Classical School's（新古典学派）criticisms of earlier versions.

I Make verb phrases by linking those in Column A and Column B.

Column A	Column B
generate	returns
maximize	the costs
erect	technology
recoup	a surplus
improve	the steady state
overcome	high tariffs

---

① 早期重商主义的货币学说，即所谓的重金主义（又译作硬币主义），起源于中世纪后期的大部分时期里流行的"重金主义"思想（形成于14世纪末和15世纪初）。但是后者与前者的联系，只是在重视"金银"这一点上才是正确的。

② 货币主义是1960年代形成的一个经济学流派，以挑战凯恩斯主义的面貌出现，其领袖人物为米尔顿·弗里德曼。货币主义的核心命题是货币在经济活动中最重要。其政策主张是货币发行增长率要保持一个不变的速度，让经济中的个体对通货膨胀有完全的预期。

Unit 13 Economic Growth

II Match the following words or terms with their definitions.

Mercantilism	economic growth	Gross Domestic Product
surplus	Keynesianism	Monetarism
rate of inflation	national income	a steady state
Bullionism		

1. _____ : the increase in value of the goods and services produced by an economy
2. _____ : the amount that remains when use and need are satisfied
3. _____ : a doctrine asserting that power and wealth are closely interrelated and are legitimate goals of national policy
4. _____ : an advocate for a metallic currency, or a paper currency always convertible into gold
5. _____ : an economic theory which advocates government intervention, or demand-side management of the economy, to achieve full employment and stable prices
6. _____ : a theory holding that economic variations within a given system, such as changing rates of inflation, are most often caused by increases or decreases in the money supply. It also refers to a policy that seeks to regulate an economy by altering the domestic money supply, especially by increasing it in a moderate but steady manner.
7. _____ : the total net value of all income earned within a country by its people during a given period (typically 1 year), representing the sum of all wages, profits, interest, rent income, and pension payments earned by the residents of the country
8. _____ : the total market value of all final goods and services produced in a country in a given year, equal to total consumer, investment and government spending, plus the value of exports, minus the value of imports
9. _____ : the percentage increase in the price of goods and services, usually annually
10. _____ : a point because of diminishing returns to capital, economies will eventually reach a point at which no new increase in capital will create economic growth

III Reading comprehension: choose the best answer from the four choices.

1. According to your understanding, which factor could not generate more surplus money?
    A. Increasing population.
    B. Increasing tax rates.
    C. A process of continual rapid replacement and reorganization of human activities facilitated by investment motivated to maximize returns.
    D. Consumption, warfare, or civic and religious projects produce a greater economic surplus which could be expended on something other than mere subsistence.

2. In the following statements, which is the post-Bullionist's point of view?
    A. Growth was seen as involving an increase in the total amount of specie, which is circulating medium such as silver and gold, under the control of the state.
    B. The increasing capability of manufacturing encouraged manufacturing in itself, and the formula of importing raw materials and exporting finished goods.
    C. Power can be used to obtain wealth.
    D. Expanding exports and imports encouraged several major wars.

3. "Once competition from abroad was removed, prices could then be increased to recoup the costs of establishing the business." Which of the following strategies can be explained by the statement?
    A. Establish factories.
    B. Grant monopolies.
    C. High tariffs.
    D. Expand markets.

4. According to the passage, which of the following statements is not true?
    A. Many things that affect the quality of life are not traded in the market and measured in the market, and they generally lose value when growth occurs, such as the environment.
    B. This combination is seen as, at the micro-scale, to be indicative of an increasing stock of capital. The argument runs that if more money is changing hands, but the prices of individual goods are relatively stable, then it is proof that there is more productive capacity, and therefore more capital, because it is capital that is allowing more to be made at a lower cost per unit.
    C. The real GDP per capita of an economy is often used as an indicator of the average standard of living of individuals in that country, and economic growth is therefore often seen as indicating an increase in the average standard of living.
    D. The "Dutch East India Company" and the "British East India Company" were

examples of such state-granted trade monopolies.
5. There are different schools of thought as to the causes of recessions but some consensus. Which of the following is not the cause of recession?
   A. Inflation.   B. Oil shocks.   C. War.   D. Harvest failure.

Part Two Case Study

AVOIDING THE CRUSH

Being a developing country used to be easy. You followed leaders — Japan, Singapore, South Korea — up a well-trodden ladder from agriculture through manufacturing to services. Starting with tilling the soil, you moved on to turning out T-shirts, then toys, then tractors, then television sets, and ended up trading Treasuries.

The rise of China has made that less straightforward. Not only is the first rung harder to reach, thanks to the hundreds of millions of rural migrants to Chinese cities still willing to work for low wages stitching garments, but also exports of goods from China's coastal industrial fringe are rapidly becoming more sophisticated, threatening those halfway or more up the ladder. While the shoemakers of Italy and the steelmakers of Pennsylvania may complain loudly about Chinese competition, those with more to worry about are middle-income Asian countries geographically and economically close to the Middle Kingdom.

As Frederick Burke, a lawyer in Ho Chi Minh City, says of south-east Asia: "Looking around the region, you can see a lot of countries with a bright future behind them." Economies such as Indonesia and the Philippines — and, further afield, Brazil and Egypt — risk being stuck in what the World Bank has called a "middle-income trap", having achieved basic industrialisation but struggling to find new areas of high growth where they can compete with the Chinese.

The Philippines is a good example. Having slipped from one of the richest countries in Asia 50 years ago to one of the poorer ones at the beginning of the 1990s, the country's trend economic growth, unusually in the region, has increased following the 1997 – 1998 Asian financial crisis. But it is a long way from catching up with Malaysia and Thailand, let alone with Taiwan or Singapore.

Economic growth has recently averaged about 4 – 5 per cent, respectable but not dramatic for a country with nearly 2 per cent population growth a year. The economy remains well short of the 7 – 8 per cent growth that would give the Philippines the roar of an Asian tiger.

Business people and politicians in the Philippines are acutely aware of the need to find niches in the global economy. They closely scan the various competitiveness indices published by the World Economic Forum and others that give international benchmarks for costs and productivity.

While economists spend a great deal of time trying to correct the misapprehension that countries compete with each other in the same way that companies do, Philippine businesses still have to spend much time searching for somewhere they have a relative advantage. World Bank research confirms anecdote: other east Asians do least well when they compete head-to-head against Chinese exporters in European or American markets. They do better by complementing them, going up the value chain in existing industries and creating high-value sectors in which China is relatively weak. The Philippines has found some such activities, but so far not enough of them.

Sanjiv Mehta, head of Unilever in the Philippines, says the quality of the workforce has kept much manufacturing in the country despite the rise of China, although power is among the priciest in Asia and minimum wage rates are high. Unilever has closed its manufacturing operations in Malaysia, a richer country with higher labour costs and a relatively small market, but retained about 80 per cent of its historical production in the Philippines.

Thanks to cheaper transport and lower trade barriers, it is now easier to supply an entire region from a single manufacturing base. But Mr. Mehta warns against trying to do everything from one place: "It used to be said that Unilever was hopelessly local, but we don't want to go mindlessly global."

Unilever has established an international supply centre in the Philippines for deodorant sticks, whose manufacture requires little power but good quality management. "It helps that the Philippines is the texting capital of the world[①]," Mr. Mehta says — Filipinos' obsessive need to stay in mobile phone contact with each other means ideas to boost productivity and feedback on hitches flit quickly around the shop floors.

The Philippines has exploited its relatively good education system and high standards of English, a legacy of American occupation, to develop service industries at which China is poor. It is a growing centre for outsourced business processing, writing and editing websites for foreign companies and teaching English as a foreign language. As well as language skills, the Philippines' press freedom and democracy give it an edge over China, where internet sites are heavily monitored and censored.

But by no means have these bits and pieces added up to the kind of mass-employment, high-growth engine that a country of 90m people needs — and the threat

---

① According to Anthony Ian Cruz, a spokesman for TXTPower (a consumer advocacy group), the Philippines, which has a population of almost 80 million, has 14 million to 16 million mobile phone users generating 150 million to 200 million text messages a day-one of the largest volumes in the world.

of Chinese competition remains potent. Manila has long regarded itself as a hub for transport and communications, but FedEx of the US is moving its regional distribution centre from the Philippines to Guangzhou in China, citing trends in manufacturing and trading. The country attracts little foreign direct investment and Filipinos still go in their millions to work abroad. Remittances form more than 10 per cent of gross domestic product, the highest ratio in the world.

Business people say high telecommunications and transport costs and the persistence of government-sanctioned cartels and regulation prevent the economy adapting. "The electronics industry we have remains competitive despite everything, even against China," says Donald Dee, chairman of the national chamber of commerce in Manila. But it does not create as much value as it could. "Our strongest asset, our labour, still goes abroad, and when they come back they say: nothing works properly in the Philippines."

Yet the limits to the remedies prescribed by Manila's business community are telling. With the exception of farmers undercut by Chinese imports, few think trade protection or outright subsidies are the answer.

Questions for Discussion

1. Being a developing country used to be easy. Compared with the past, what is the difference? Why now is it not easy to be a developing country?

___

___

2. What kind of industry do we Chinese remain competitive despite everything? According to your understanding, what are advantageous trade in China and in the Philippines?

___

___

___

Translation

1. Not only is the first rung harder to reach, thanks to the hundreds of millions of rural migrants to Chinese cities still willing to work for low wages stitching garments, but also exports of goods from China's coastal industrial fringe are rapidly becoming more sophisticated, threatening those halfway or more up the ladder.

2. Economies such as Indonesia and the Philippines — and, further afield, Brazil and Egypt — risk being stuck in what the World Bank has called a "middle-income trap", having achieved basic industrialisation but struggling to find new areas of high growth where they can compete with the Chinese.

3. Having slipped from one of the richest countries in Asia 50 years ago to one of the poorer ones at the beginning of the 1990s, the country's trend economic growth, unusually in the region, has increased following the 1997–1998 Asian financial crisis. But it is a long way from catching up with Malaysia and Thailand, let alone with Taiwan or Singapore.

4. With the exception of farmers undercut by Chinese imports, few think trade protection or outright subsidies are the answer.

Unit 14
An Overview of International Economics

Introduction

International economics deals with flows across national boundaries of goods, services, capital, and labor. It is the conduct of trade, rather than in benefits that flow from it, which distinguishes international from domestic transactions. The field of international economics has been in a creative ferment in recent years, with new views emerging on such issues as the political economy of trade policy, strategic trade policy, exchange rate determination, and the international coordination of macro-economic policies.

Part One Text

The peoples of the nations of the world continually seek to maximize their welfare by a wide variety of interactions and exchanges across boundaries. Differences in aspirations; human, natural, and capital resources; technology; culture; social and political systems; and other factors are always apparent and lay the foundation for mutually advantageous economic relationships.

How Nations Are Classified

Nations are commonly classified into groups that indicate their economic strengths and weaknesses as well as their stage of development.

Industrial or developed nations are those which have achieved substantial manufacturing and service capability in addition to advanced techniques in agriculture and raw material extraction.

Developing nation are usually those whose production sector is dominated by agriculture and mineral resources and are in the process of building up industrial capacity.

Much attention in international economic and political affairs understandably focuses on the welfare gap between the developed and developing nations. Comparisons are frequently made among countries concerning such measures of economic progress and competitive strength as cultivated land area, population, per capita income and wealth, unit labor costs, prices, external debt, and monetary reserves.

Most of the trade of the world occurs between the industrialized countries. The remaining nations strive to strengthen their economies by trade, barter and aid from the major developed nations.

The generalization is often made that most of the richer nations are located in the Northern Hemisphere and the poorer nations in the Southern Hemisphere. This gives rise to the expression "North/South" in reference to many international problems, confrontations, and dialogues.

Official International Organizations

Many official international bodies have been formed through the years to facilitate trade and to solve pressing problems, for example: (1) to provide a means for discussing and addressing grievances among nation, e. g., United Nations; (2) to formulate rules and procedures for commercial and other interactions between countries, e. g., Organization for Economic Cooperation and Development (OECD), United Nations Conference for Trade and Development (UNCTAD), European Economic Community (EEC); (3) to supervise and monitor global monetary and related affairs, e. g., International Monetary Fund (IMF); (4) to assist in planning and financing development projects, e. g., International Bank for Reconstruction and Development (World Bank); and (5) to offer direct aid, e. g., as offered by various regional development banks around the world.

Few nations are willing to give up much of their sovereignty and accede to direction in their economic affairs from the outside unless they see offsetting gains or they have no other choice.

Developing nations with natural resources or commodities to sell usually strive for international agreements — sometimes in the form of cartels such as OPEC — which will reduce price fluctuations (mainly on the down side) and ensure steadily increasing demand and revenues for their goods.

Population in many respects determines and foreshadows the world's and each nation's needs and demands for goods, services, and jobs. The more than 4 billion people already living in the earth and the prevailing excess rate of births over deaths indicate that international economic and related questions merit high priority attention throughout the world if future tensions and conflicts are to be minimized. For developing nations — in particular, for those with large and growing populations — the problem of unemployment poses a constant threat to social and political stability.

Protectionism and Free Trade

Protectionism takes many forms. Tariff and non-tariff barriers are the subject of continuing global debate and confrontation. Periodically, the principal nations join the detailed and lengthy negotiations to reduce trade barriers. These are mainly under the aegis of the General Agreement on Tariffs and Trade (GATT). The overriding objectives is to try to keep trade as free and open as possible so as to encourage greater world growth, employment, income, and investment. History records many instances where growing protectionism has led to international trade wars and eventually has caused wars among belligerents.

Few nations can survive for long in economic isolation from the rest of the world simply because political geographical boundaries do not coincide with the natural resources, skills, and other essentials for the betterment of human welfare.

Foreign Investment and Transnational Corporations

Investment in one country by individuals and organizations from another is an important aspect of international economics. Investment may be for portfolio, (i.e., in the form of securities) or direct capital (i.e., productive facilities).

Developing nations in particular face some dilemma in formulating policies covering investments by foreigners. They usually have an urgent need for foreign investment assistance, but domestic political considerations often dictate severe tax and other laws, including nationalization laws, which discourage new foreign investment. Many developing nations have been successful, however, in providing attractive tax and other incentives to foreign investors for sufficient time periods to ensure a satisfactory return on the original investment.

Words and Expressions

interaction	n.	合作，配合
aspiration	n.	渴望，志气，抱负
extraction	n.	抽出，取出，[化] 提取（法），萃取法
grievance	n.	委屈，牢骚，抱怨（against）
accede	v.	（与 to 连用）同意，答应，批准
offsetting	n.	补偿，抵消
foreshadow	v.	预示
prevailing	a.	占优势的，主要的，流行的
overriding	a.	最重要的，高于一切的
belligerent	n.	交战国，交战者
dilemma	n.	进退两难的局面，困难的选择
dictate	v.	指示，命令，规定
welfare gap		福利差距
Northern Hemisphere		北半球
Southern Hemisphere		南半球
under the aegis of		在……的保护下，支持下
coincide with		与……相符

Notes

1. **welfare** 福利

    It refers to well-being, quality of life, financial assistance paid by taxpayers to people who are unable to support themselves.

2. **Organization for Economic Cooperation and Development (OECD)**
    经济合作发展组织

    Organization for Economic Cooperation and Development is an organization that acts as a meeting ground for 30 countries which believe strongly in the free market system. The OECD provides a forum for discussing issues and reaching agreements, some of which are legally binding.

3. **United Nations Conference for Trade and Development (UNCTAD)**
    联合国贸易和发展会议

    It is a part of the UN General Assembly(联合国大会) which promotes international trade and seeks to increase trade between developing countries and countries with different social and economic systems.

4. **European Economic Community (EEC)** 欧洲经济共同体

   It is an economic organization established in 1958 to reduce tariff barriers and promote trade among the countries of Belgium, Luxembourg, the Netherlands, France, Italy, and West Germany. These countries became the original members of the European Community in 1965.

5. **International Monetary Fund (IMF)** 国际货币基金组织

   It is an organization set up in 1944 to lower trade barriers between countries and to stabilize currencies by monitoring the foreign exchange systems of member countries, and lending money to developing nations.

6. **International Bank for Reconstruction and Development (World Bank)** 国际复兴开发银行(世界银行)

   It is an international financial institution that offers loans for development to middle-income and creditworthy poorer countries. Most of its funds come from sales of bonds in international capital markets. More than 180 countries are members of the IBRD. Each member's voting power is linked to its capital subscription; the US, with some one-sixth of the shares in the IBRD, has veto power over any proposed changes to the bank.

7. **OPEC** 石油输出国组织(或称"欧佩克")

   Organization of Petroleum Exporting Countries (OPEC) is a collective of countries founded in 1960 that choose to collaborate in order to manage the exportation of their crude oil to the rest of the world. Because of their ability to adjust production levels, they possess a great deal of influence on the price or oil.

8. **cartel** 卡特尔

   It refers to a group of companies or countries which collectively attempt to affect market prices by controlling production and marketing. It is illegal in the US, and also called **trust**(托拉斯).

9. **protectionism** 贸易保护主义

   It refers to the advocacy, system, or theory of protecting domestic producers by impeding or limiting, as by tariffs or quotas, the importation of foreign goods and services. It is the opposite to Free Trade(自由贸易), which means the free flow of goods and/or services across the national boundaries without any artificial barriers from governments or any economic organizations.

10. **tariff barrier** 关税壁垒

    A tariff is a duty or fee levied on goods being imported into the country. These tariffs can be of two types: protective and revenue. Protective tariffs (保护性关税) are designed to raise the retail price of imported products so that domestic goods will be more competitive and foreign business will be discouraged from shipping certain goods into the country. These tariffs are meant to save jobs for domestic workers and to keep industries (especially infant industries) from bankruptcy because of foreign competition. A revenue tariff (财政关税) is designed to raise money from imports for the government. Revenue tariffs are also commonly used by developing countries to help infant industries compete in global markets.

11. **non-tariff barrier 非关税壁垒**

    It refers to any number of import quotas (进口配额) or other quantitative restrictions (数量限制), non-automatic import licensing (非自动进口许可), customs surcharges (海关附加税) or other fees and charges, customs procedures (海关手续), export subsidies (出口补贴), unreasonable standards or standards-setting procedures, government procurement restrictions (政府采购限制), inadequate intellectual property protection and investment restrictions which deny or make market access excessively difficult for goods or services of foreign origin.

12. **General Agreement on Tariffs and Trade (GATT) 关税与贸易总协定**

    It was originally created by the Bretton Woods Conference as part of a larger plan for economic recovery after World War II. The GATT's main objective was the reduction of barriers to international trade. This was achieved through the reduction of tariff barriers, quantitative restrictions and subsidies on trade through a series of agreements. The GATT was an agreement, not an organization. The functions of the GATT were taken over by the World Trade Organization which was established during the final round of negotiations in the early 1990s.

13. **investment 投资**

    In general terms, investment means the use of money in the hope of making more money. In business, the purchase by a producer of a physical good, such as durable equipment or inventory, in the hope of improving future business. In finance, the purchase of a financial product or other item of value with an expectation of favorable future returns.

14. **portfolio 投资组合**

    It refers to a collection of investments all owned by the same individual or organization. These investments often include stocks, which are investments in individual businesses; bonds, which are investments in debt that are designed to earn interest; and mutual funds, which are essentially pools of money from many investors that are invested by professionals or according to indices.

Unit 14 An Overview of International Economics

I Make verb phrases by linking those in Column A and Column B.

Column A	Column B
formulate	profits
maximize	rules and regulations
supervise	economic growths
strengthen	global monetary affairs
reduce	tariff barriers

II Match the following words or terms with their definitions.

welfare	investment	capital	income	trade
cost	barter	revenue	tax	Protectionism

1. _____ : money gained from business
2. _____ : trade without money
3. _____ : something that aids or promotes well-being
4. _____ : money, property, or stock employed in trade, manufactures
5. _____ : the purchase of property with the expectation that its value will increase
6. _____ : trade hurdle, import barrier, or system, and theory of protecting domestic products by impending of limiting the flow of goods and/or services between nations
7. _____ : something expended to obtain a benefit or desired result
8. _____ : a charge levied upon persons or things by a government
9. _____ : the buying and selling of goods and services
10. _____ : the entire amount of income before any deductions are made

III Reading comprehension: choose the best answer from the four choices.

1. Which of the following is not mentioned when comparing economic progress and competitive strength of different countries?
    A. Population.
    B. Monetary reserves.
    C. Cultivated land area.
    D. Mineral resources.

2. How does the expression "North/South" come into being?
   A. Because most of the richer nations are located in the Northern Hemisphere and the poorer Southern Hemisphere.
   B. Because nations in the Northern Hemisphere are mainly capitalist and nations in the Southern Hemisphere are socialist.
   C. Because most people in the Northern Hemisphere are white people and people the Southern Hemisphere are colored people.
   D. It is not mentioned in the passage.
3. How many international organizations are mentioned in the first paragraph of the section "Official International Organizations"?
   A. 4.　　　　B. 5.　　　　C. 6.　　　　D. 7.
4. According to the passage, which of the following statements is not true?
   A. Principal nations join negotiations periodically to try to reduce trade barriers.
   B. The negotiations concerning protectionism and free trade are mainly guided by GATT.
   C. The objectives of the negotiations are to try to keep trade as free and open as possible.
   D. Only nations whose natural resources, skills and other essentials are remarkably self-sufficient don't have to get involved into the world trade.
5. Why developing nations in particular face dilemma in formulating policies covering foreign investments?
   A. They don't know the precise amount of foreign investments they need for their economic growth.
   B. They have to balance domestic political considerations and foreign investment assistance.
   C. Different ideologies have hindered them in their efforts to attract foreign investment.
   D. Not mentioned.

Part Two　Case Study

KEYNES VERSUS FRIEDMAN: BOTH MEN CAN CLAIM VISTORY

By **Martin Wolf**
From *Financial Times*, Thursday, November 23, 2006

John Maynard Keynes, who died in 1946, and Milton Friedman, who died last week, were the most influential economists of the 20th century. Since Friedman spent much of his intellectual energy attacking the legacy of Keynes, it is natural to consider them opposites. Their differences were, indeed, profound. But so was what they shared. More interesting, neither won and neither lost: today's policy orthodoxies are a synthesis of their two approaches.

<u>Keynes concluded from the great depression that the free market had failed; Friedman decided, instead, that the Federal Reserve had failed.</u> Keynes trusted in discretion for sophisticated mandarins like himself; Friedman believed the only safe government was one bound by tight rules. Keynes thought that capitalism needed to be in fetters; Friedman thought it would behave if left alone.

These differences are self-evident. Yet no less so are the similarities. Both were brilliant journalists, debaters and promoters of their own ideas; both saw the great depression as, at bottom, a crisis of inadequate aggregate demand; both wrote in favour of floating exchange rates and so of fiat (or government-made) money; and both were on the side of freedom in the great ideological struggle of the 20th century.

If it were not for the fact that the UK and US are two nations divided by a common language, one might even call both "liberals" in the 18th and 19th century English sense of that word. But Keynes, though temperamentally a liberal, was also a pessimistic member of the upper middle classes of a declining country: he thought the survival of a measure of freedom required jettisoning large elements of 19th century orthodoxy. Friedman, a child of poor Jewish immigrants and thoroughly American, was optimistic: he hoped to restore free markets and limited government.

<u>To achieve this end, Friedman sought to demolish what he saw as the mistakes made by Keynes and his successors: the assumption that a fixed propensity to consume out of current income drove aggregate demand; the trust in fiscal policy as the most potent instrument in the policy armoury; the belief that changes in nominal demand would secure durable changes in real output; and confidence in the exercise of discretion by governments.</u>

In his work of the 1950s and 1960s, Friedman took on all these propositions in turn. In a celebrated paper published in 1957 he argued that consumption depended not on current, but on permanent or long-term, income; in A Monetary History of the United States (1963), co-authored with Anna Schwartz, and a number of empirical studies co-authored with David Meiselman, he sought to reinstate the quantity theory of money, the view that a stable relationship exists between the money supply and nominal demand; and in his famous presidential address to the American Economic Association in 1968 he advanced the "natural rate of unemployment", also known as the "non-accelerating inflation rate of unemployment" (NAIRU), in place of the trade off between inflation and output implied by the then-fashionable "Phillips Curve".

In the 1960s, most economists regarded Friedman's belief in the free market and rejection of Keynesian ideas as evil, misguided or, more often, both. I remember the shock when, at Oxford, I read his arguments supporting the idea of a natural rate of unemployment just after its appearance. The great inflation of the 1970s — unprecedented in peacetime — transformed the climate of opinion (see chart). So, too, did the collapse of the fixed exchange rate regime in 1971 and move to free floating, which preceded the price surge.

A new theory was required to guide this world of more or less freely floating exchange rates and soaring inflation. The answer, it was hoped, was Friedman's monetarism — the targeting of some measure of the money supply. As chairman of the Federal Reserve, Paul Volcker tried that experiment in the US between 1979 and 1982. Margaret Thatcher's government tried it in the UK between 1979 and the mid-1980s. In both cases inflation was crushed. But the relationship between money and nominal demand also crumbled. Keynesianism had, indeed, died. But so, too, did Friedman's monetary rule.

From the ashes, a new orthodoxy has emerged: policy should, as Friedman argued, target a nominal variable, not a real one; that target should be the goal, inflation, not the instrument, money; central banks should be free to move the interest rate as needed to hit their target. This, then, is a regime of rules-bound discretion. Friedman would approve of the rules; Keynes would approve of the discretion. Friedman has won on the primacy of monetary policy; but Keynes has won on the rejection of the quantity theory.

Yet both have won in the most important sense. Over the past two decades, a world of fiat money has supplied modest inflation and supported stable growth. This is unprecedented. Friedman himself stated early this year that "Alan Greenspan's great achievement is to have demonstrated that it is possible to maintain stable prices". Thus did the great proponent of rules commend the great employer of discretion.

Are the inflation-targeting independent central bank and floating currencies "the end of history" in macroeconomic policy? I suspect not. The vagaries of floating exchange rates seem to cry out for yet another experiment in monetary integration, perhaps even a stab at a world currency.

The march of technology may even make money redundant as anything more than a unit of account.

Policy debate, too, continues. The European Central Bank may yet persuade its peers that the monetary data tell one something useful. Central banks may learn, as well, that they ignore asset prices at their peril. Even expansionary fiscal policy may again be needed, as proved the case in Japan during the deflationary 1990s.

Also uncertain is the future of the market economy. Here, too, the present position is a draw. Keynes would have worried about the destabilising consequences of the freeing of capital flows. But Friedman had to recognise that a comprehensive rolling back of the state was not on the agenda. The market has indeed been freed from many of its mid-20th century shackles. But the state commands resources and regulates economies on a scale unimaginable a century ago. Globalization itself may yet founder.

Keynes and Friedman were the protagonists of the policy debate of the last century. But today, we can see that neither won and neither lost.

Questions for Discussion

1. In order to achieve the purpose of restoring free markets and limited government, what effort did Friedman make?

2. Friedman's monetarism was adopted by the US government between 1979 and 1982 and the UK government between 1979 and the mid-1980s. What did the two experiments prove?

3. In the author's opinion, are the inflation-targeting independent central bank and floating currencies "the end of history" in macroeconomic policy? Why?

4. What are the differences between Keynes' and Friedman' theory? And what are the similarities?

Translation

1. Keynes concluded from the great depression that the free market had failed; Friedman decided, instead, that the Federal Reserve had failed.

2. To achieve this end, Friedman sought to demolish what he saw as the mistakes made by Keynes and his successors: the assumption that a fixed propensity to consume out of current income drove aggregate demand; the trust in fiscal policy as the most potent instrument in the policy armoury; the belief that changes in nominal demand would secure durable changes in real output; and confidence in the exercise of discretion by governments.

3. From the ashes, a new orthodoxy has emerged: policy should, as Friedman argued, target a nominal variable, not a real one; that target should be the goal, inflation, not the instrument, money; central banks should be free to move the interest rate as needed to hit their target.

4. The vagaries of floating exchange rates seem to cry out for yet another experiment in monetary integration, perhaps even a stab at a world currency.

Unit 15
World Trade and National Economy

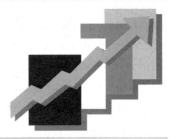

Introduction

World trade, also international trade, concerns the flow of commodities, services, and productive factors (capital and labor) across national boundaries. Trade in commodities refers to imports and exports of merchandise. Service transactions involve such activities as shipping, travel, insurance, or tourist services performed by companies of one country for the residents of another. Capital flows represent the establishment of manufacturing plants in foreign countries, or the acquisition of foreign bond, stocks, and band accounts. Labor flows describe the international migration of workers. World trade contributes a lot to the development of the global and the national economy.

Part One Text

World trade constitutes an extension of the domestic trade of one nation. In both cases, trade offers the benefits of specialization. Exchanges of goods and services among individuals enable them to specialize in what they do best. Likewise, domestic exchange enables regions of the county to specialize in the same manner. Thus, the exchange of Florida oranges, Washington-produced aircraft, and Michigan-made cars enhances efficiency of production and improves living standards for each of these states. Internationally, US import of German cameras, Japanese cars, and Brazilian coffee, and US export of grains, jet aircraft, and sophisticated computers fosters specialization of the participating countries, thereby producing more than they could without trade and increasing the living standards of all.

The reason for and the benefits from international transactions are no different from the reasons for and the benefits from domestic transactions: to reap the fruits of increased output from a given amount of resources attendant upon greater specialization.

Why then is it necessary to distinguish between domestic and international economic relations? Why study international economics as a separate field? Because the existence of national boundaries has profound implications for the conduct of trade. The following are a few of the differences between domestic and foreign trade that emanate from this fact.

Exchange Rates

Transactions within a country are financed by that country's own currency, usually through the writing of checks. But a universal currency does not exist. Instead, each country issues its own currency. An exchange rate — the price of one currency in terms of another — is used to translate values from one currency to another. For example, if the dollar is worth 100 Japanese yen ($1 = ¥100) then a ¥10,000 Japanese camera would cost $100 in the United States, and a $10 million American jet aircraft would be valued at 1 billion yen in Japan. Many exchange rates vary from day to day in response to changes in supply and demand conditions in the foreign exchange markets. International transactions require payments or receipts in foreign currencies, and these must be converted to the domestic currency through the exchange rates, which themselves are subject to change. This process introduces risks and complications that are unknown in domestic trade.

Commercial Policies

A national government can introduce a variety of restrictions upon international transactions that cannot be imposed on domestic transactions. These could include the following.

(1) A tariff, which is a tax on an imported commodity.

(2) An import quota, which places a maximum limitation on the amount of the commodity that may enter the country.

(3) A voluntary export restraint (VER), where the governments of an importing country and an exporting country (say, the United States and Japan) negotiate a quantitative limitation on the export of a certain commodity. The Japanese government limited automobile shipments to the United States during the years 1981-1986 under such an agreement.

(4) An export subsidy, where a government pays exporters a sum of money for each unit of the product they export in order to make them more competitive

abroad.

(5) Exchange control, where a country, such as India, restricts the ability of its citizens to convert their money (rupees) to foreign currencies, such as US dollar.

Such measures may have profound effects on the economy. Yet they only concern international, not domestic, transactions.

Different Domestic Policies

Each country has its own central bank and finance ministry, and hence its own monetary and fiscal policies. These in turn determine its rates of inflation, economic growth, and unemployment. While these policies apply to all regions or states within a country, they vary from one country to another. Consequently while the rate of inflation is the same throughout the regions of the United Kingdom it offers between the United Kingdom and Germany. This differential rate not only affects the competitive position between the two countries, but their competition with third countries as well.

Statistical Data

We know more about the composition, size, and direction of international trade than we do about the same features of domestic transactions. Since there are no "border checkpoints" along state lines to compile such information, it is uncertain what particular commodities and their quantities are being traded between New York and California. But when a shipment of merchandise leaves or enters the country, the exporter or importer must fill out an export or import declaration describing the shipment in terms of its weight, value, destination or source, and other characteristics. From these trade declarations, which are required by all countries, detailed statistics can be compiled on international trade that are not available for domestic trade.

Relative Immobility of Productive Factors

Factors of productions are much more mobile domestically than they are internationally. No one can prevent workers from moving between Virginia and Texas. But immigration restrictions, language barriers, and different social customs constitute formidable barrier to people's mobility between countries. While capital can move between countries much more easily than labor, it is also more domestically than internationally.

Marketing Considerations

Differences in demand patterns, sales techniques, market requirements, and the like make international transactions more difficult than domestic ones. Many Japanese sleep in futon beds and have little use for American sheets and pillowcases. American exports of electrical appliances to Europe must be adjusted for the different electric current. And automobiles exported to the United Kingdom or Japan require steering wheels on the right side of the vehicle, as the British and Japanese drive on the left side of the road. In sum, exporters often need to make special adjustments in their product design in order to penetrate a foreign market.

The preceding six areas of significant difference between domestic and foreign transaction refer to the conduct of trade, rather than its rationale and benefits. They highlight important and unique features that require their own special field of international economics.

However, commodity trade is not the only component of international transactions that has expanded rapidly. As the share of services in Gross Domestic Product (GDP) (services make up two thirds of GDP, in the industrial countries) rises, so do international service transactions. Global trade in these services was 1.76 trillion in 2003. Finally, there has been a massive increase in private capital flows, with transfers of capital between countries amounting to many trillions of dollars each year. Direct foreign investment, involving the establishment of manufacturing plants in foreign countries, is also growing rapidly. The global "stock" of direct foreign investment has been estimated at about $408 trillion, with the United States being the leading "host" country, followed by the United Kingdom and China. A global marketplace is emerging for the production and distribution of most goods and services, a process often referred to as globalization.

These trading relationships are experiencing profound changes with the transformation of the global economy. As Eastern Europe becomes integrated into the world trading and financial system, its share in world trade is likely to rise. Far outstripping the growth rate of the industrial countries, the Asian Pacific Rim countries are developing rapidly with annual GDP growth of 6 to 10 percent up to 2007. They include China (particularly its coastal regions) where the government of the population numbering 1.2 billion has adopted a market economic system along with political dictatorship, and the Newly Industrial Economies (NIEs) of South Korea, Taiwan, Hong Kong, and Singapore, which are on the threshold of a fully developed status. Even the Indian economy is beginning to stir, with its relaxation of government controls.

Last but not the least, many Latin American countries have adopted democratic

Unit 15 World Trade and National Economy

governments, and are pursuing sensible macroeconomic policies while allowing market forces to replace government regulations — thus accelerating their growth rates. It is quite likely that in the next century the distinction between developed and underdeveloped countries will become blurred — significantly affecting global trade and investment flow.

Words and Expressions

sophisticated	a.	老练的，复杂的，精密的
implication	n.	牵连，暗示
emanate	v.	发出，发散，流出
receipt	n.	收据，收条
convert	v.	兑换，换算
compile	v.	编纂，编辑，收集
globalization	n.	全球化
outstrip	v.	越过，胜过
exchange control		外汇管制，汇兑管理
border checkpoint		边卡
Newly Industrial Economies (NIEs)		新兴工业化经济
macroeconomic policy		宏观经济政策

Notes

1. **specialization** 专业化分工

   In the economic sense, the social phenomenon of individual human beings or organizations each concentrates their productive efforts on a rather limited range of tasks.

2. **exchange rate** 汇率，兑换率

   In finance, the exchange rate (also known as the foreign-exchange rate) between two currencies specifies how much one currency is worth in terms of the other.

3. **currency** 通货，货币

   A currency is a unit of exchange, facilitating the transfer of goods and services. It is one form of money, where money is anything that serves as a medium of exchange, a store of value, and a standard of value.

4. payment 支付，支付款额

The partial or complete discharge of an obligation by its settlement in the form of the transfer of funds, assets, or services equal to the monetary value of part or all of the debtor's obligation.

5. import quota 进口配额

An import quota is a type of protectionist trade restriction that sets a physical limit on the quantity of a good that can be imported into a country in a given period of time. For example, a country might limit sugar imports to 50 tons per year.

6. voluntary export restraint (VER) 自愿出口限制

A voluntary export restraint is a restriction set by a government on the quantity of goods that can be exported out of a country during a specified period of time. Often the word voluntary is placed in quotes because these restraints are typically implemented upon the insistence of the importing nations.

7. export subsidy 出口补贴

Export subsidy is a government policy to encourage export of goods and discourage sale of goods on the domestic market through low-cost loans or tax relief for exporters, or government financed international advertising or R&D. An export subsidy reduces the price paid by foreign importers, which means domestic consumers pay more than foreign consumers. The WTO prohibits most subsidies directly linked to the volume of exports.

8. inflation 通货膨胀

Inflation is the overall general upward price movement of goods and services in an economy, usually as measured by the consumer price index and the producer price index.

9. Pacific Rim 太平洋地区

The Pacific Rim refers to the countries and cities located around the edge of the Pacific Ocean. There are many economic centers around the Pacific Rim, such as Shanghai, Hong Kong, Singapore, Seoul, Tokyo, Manila, Los Angeles, Taipei, Sydney, Melbourne, Brisbane, Auckland, Santiago, San Francisco, Seattle, San Diego, Portland, and Vancouver.

Unit 15 World Trade and National Economy

I Make verb phrases by linking those in Column A and Column B.

Column A	Column B
compile	high taxes
impose	dollar to yen
specialize	in Italian food
conduct	information
convert	a trade

II Match the following words or terms with their definitions.

investment	export subsidy	capital	transaction	check
globalization	domestic	quota	payment	receipt

1. _____ : a government policy to encourage export of goods and discourage sale of goods on the domestic market
2. _____ : the transfer of wealth from one party to another
3. _____ : an allotment or limited amount
4. _____ : the process of increasing the connectivity and interdependence of the world's markets and businesses
5. _____ : cash or goods used to generate income
6. _____ : a negotiable instrument drawn against deposited funds, to pay a specified amount of money
7. _____ : within the given country
8. _____ : the purchase by a producer of a physical good in the hope of improving future business
9. _____ : a written acknowledgement which grants legal validation to a repayment of all or part of a debt
10. _____ : an agreement between a buyer and a seller to exchange an asset for payment

III Reading comprehension: choose the best answer from the four choices.

1. How many Newly Industrial Economies are mentioned?

A. 3   B. 4   C. 5   D. 6

2. A national government introduces a variety of restrictions upon international transactions which do not include _____.

   A. a tariff   B. an export quota
   C. an export subsidy   D. exchange control

3. A country's monetary and fiscal policies do not determine its _____.

   A. rates of inflation   B. economic growth
   C. unemployment   D. import quota

4. Which of the following is not a fiscal policy?

   A. Increasing the total money supply.
   B. Lowering interest rates.
   C. Raising taxes.
   D. Decreasing the total money supply.

5. Which of the following descriptions about the differences between domestic and foreign trade is not true?

   A. Detailed statistics from trade declarations which are not available for domestic trade can be compiled on international trade.
   B. Factors of productions are much more mobile internationally than they are domestically.
   C. A national government can introduce a variety of restrictions upon international transactions that cannot be imposed on domestic transactions.
   D. Differences in demand patterns, sales techniques, market require-ments, and the like make international transactions more difficult than domestic ones.

Part Two Case Study

WHY CHINA MUST TURN AWAY FROM ECONOMIC NATIONALISM

From *Wallstreet*, November 23, 2006

After opening up its economy to the outside world and seeing decades of growth, is China turning its back on foreign investment? Is a populist response to public resentment heralding① a new era of economic nationalism②?

---

① 预示
② 经济民族主义

Unit 15 World Trade and National Economy

The international business community is worried. Several high-profile foreign takeovers① of Chinese companies have recently ground to a halt. Carlyle, the US private equity group, said last October that it had agreed to pay $375m for 85 per cent of Xugong, a state-owned machinery company. After facing resistance from authorities the deal was watered down② to a 50 per cent joint venture. A fund led by Goldman Sachs has been waiting since May for approval to buy Shineway, China's largest meat-processor. Schaeffler, the German company, also hit snags③ at the approval stage of its acquisition of Luoyang, a state-owned machinery maker. The list goes on.

A raft of new legislation primarily aimed at foreign investors is adding to concerns. Wu Yi, a Chinese vice premier, sought to reassure senior executives from multinationals last month that China "welcomes foreign investment in all forms". However, other officials have expressed divergent views. There are clear signs that a big rethink is under way. Li Deshui, former head of the National Bureau of Statistics, told an audience including Wen Jiabao, China's premier, that it was dangerous to allow "malicious takeovers"④ of Chinese enterprises go on.

Those businesses feeling threatened have been even more outspoken. Xiang Wenbo, chief executive of Sany, the Carlyle Group's main rival in the contest for Xugong, launched what has been called an internet "war" to incite nationalistic objections to the deal.

His blog is peppered with comments such as "selling anything is fine but selling out the country is wrong!"

His views have received widespread popular support.

Economic nationalism is also a reaction to US protectionism. Chinese companies have recently been involved in two large takeover attempts of American companies which have foundered, partly for political reasons. The China National Offshore Oil Corporation's $18.5 bn bid for Unocal, a US oil company with considerable interests in Asia, was considered by conservatives as impinging on energy security. Haier's proposed acquisition of Maytag, a venerable US white-goods brand, aroused similar patriotic sentiment.

Domestic issues also are driving this trend. High-profile takeovers are new to China. <u>There is widespread concern, verging on paranoia, that the privatization of state-owned companies is being used by corrupt officials as an opportunity to drain the country's coffers⑤.</u> Stricter control is seen as necessary.

At the same time, Chinese confidence on the world stage is growing. Young people

---

① 备受关注的外资收购
② 加水冲淡,此处译为"改为,组建成……"。
③ 遭遇阻滞
④ 恶意并购
⑤ 盗空国家资产

no longer see China as a developing country but as an emerging world power. China might have once been desperate for foreign capital but this is no longer the case. Foreign investment should now be on China's own terms①.

Digging deeper into Ms Wu's remarks last month, it appears the free-for-all② is over. While foreign investment might still be welcome in principle, China wants to make sure it gets some bang for its buck. Multinationals have hit an investment ceiling. But it is too early to tell whether this bout of economic nationalism will last. We do not know whether this is part of an explicit government policy or merely a fad.

This indicates China is at a turning point. Investors must continue lobbying③ the Chinese government to resist the temptation of economic nationalism. As well as stating the case for individual transactions, foreign investors need to also demonstrate the benefits of investment both for the sector concerned and the broader economy. If a potential transaction risks provoking "nationalistic" objections, investors will need to couch the deal in the language of mutual benefit.

The concern is that the current climate is indicative of a deeper policy shift — but it is not too late. Any further move towards economic nationalism will ultimately harm China. Some Chinese commentators argue opposition to foreign investment is a sign of economic maturity but this is short sighted. They ignore the harsh realities of competition in an international economy that rewards nations and businesses able to allocate capital and resources efficiently — that is, by letting the market decide. China's open-door policy has brought tremendous results over the past 30 years. Beijing needs to resist the urge to turn away from further liberalization.

Questions for Discussion

1. After reading the article, try to give a definition to economic nationalism.

2. Why did Xiang Wenbo's comments in his blog that "selling anything is fine but selling out the country is wrong" receive popular support?

---

① 遵从中国的条件
② 自由参与
③ 劝说

Unit 15 World Trade and National Economy

3. What should foreign investors do to respond to the trend of economic nationalism in China?

4. What position does the Chinese government take on foreign investment? What's your attitude?

Translation

1. There is widespread concern, verging on paranoia, that the privatization of state-owned companies is being used by corrupt officials as an opportunity to drain the country's coffers.

2. While foreign investment might still be welcome in principle, China wants to make sure it gets some bang for its buck.

3. If a potential transaction risks provoking "nationalistic" objections, investors will need to couch the deal in the language of mutual benefit.

4. The concern is that the current climate is indicative of a deeper policy shift — but it is not too late.

Unit 16
Import and Export Practices

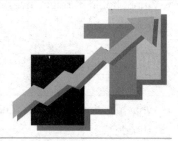

Introduction

Exporting is selling products to another country. Importing is buying products from another country. International trade, economic transactions that are made between countries. Among the items commonly traded are consumer goods, such as television sets and clothing; capital goods, such as machinery; and raw materials and food. Other transactions involve services, such as travel services and payments for foreign patents. International trade transactions are facilitated by international financial payments, in which the private banking system and the central banks of the trading nations play important roles.

Part One Text

Role of Trade Terms

In international trade, trade terms are an important components of a unit price of the traded goods. Trade terms define the obligations, risks, and costs of the buyer and seller involving the delivery of goods that comprise the export transaction. These terms are commonly known as Incoterms.

Incoterms are a set of rules which define the responsibilities of sellers and buyers for the delivery of goods under sales contracts. They are published by the International Chamber of Commerce (ICC) and are widely used in commercial transactions. A freight forwarder can also advise you on selecting the most appropriate Incoterms for your business, defining delivery responsibilities for you and your overseas buyer. You may decide on a company policy of the Incoterm you will use in all but exceptional circumstances. This makes your pricing and sales terms clear. However, an overseas buyer may insist on which of you organizes the freight and that will determine the Incoterm you eventually use.

Since its founding in 1919, ICC has been committed to the facilitation of international trade. Different practices and legal interpretations between traders around the world necessitated a common set of rules and guidelines. As a response, ICC published the first Incoterms rules in 1936. Since its first version, Incoterms were revised by ICC in 1953, 1982, 1990, 2000, 2010 and again in 2020 in order to bring the rules in line with current international trade practices. Incoterms 2020 came into effect on Jan. 1, 2020. Please note that all contracts made under Incoterms 2020 or even any earlier version remain valid even after 2020. Contracts are interpreted by the version of Incoterms referred to in the contract. Therefore, only a contract that refers to Incoterms 2020 will be governed by rules from that version. "Incoterms" is a registered trademark of the ICC.

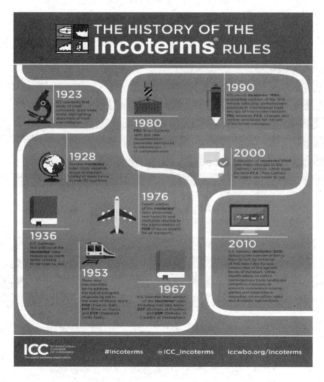

Figure 16-1　The history of the Incoterms rules

Incoterms are not laws enacted by governments. Rather, they are rules agreed to by parties to a contract. Also, Incoterms are not implied into contracts for the sale of goods. If you desire to use Incoterms, you must clearly specify the chosen version INCOTERMS 2020, INCOTERMS 2010 or any earlier version in your contract. For example: CIF Oakland, California, USA, Incoterms 2020.

The current prevailing INCOTERMS is Incoterm 2020, which is listed by four categories as elaborated in Figure 16 – 2: namely starting with the term whereby the seller only makes the goods available to the buyer at the seller's own premises (the "E"-term, Ex Works); followed by the "F"-terms whereby the seller is called upon the deliver the goods to a carrier appointed by the buyer (FCA, FAS and FOB); continuing with the "C"-terms where the seller is responsible for delivering the goods on board the ship at the port of shipment, contracting and paying for carriage to the "named port of destination. "C" terms evidence "shipment" (as opposed to "arrival") contracts without assuming the risk of loss of or damage to goods or additional costs due to events occurring after shipment and dispatch (CFR, CIF, CPT and CIP); and finally, the "D"-terms whereby the seller has to bear all costs and risks needed to bring the goods to the place of destination (DAP, DPU and DDP).

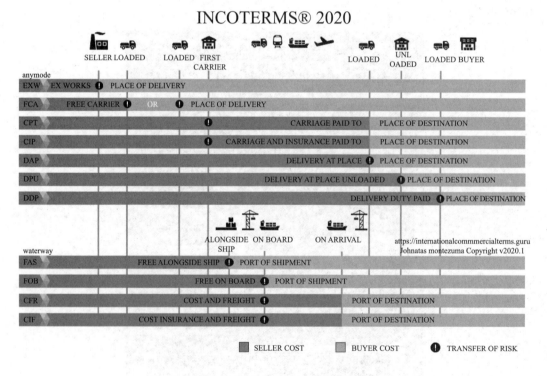

Figure 16 – 2 Incoterms 2020, four categories

Export and Import Documents

International trade involves complex flows of goods and services between many countries. Therefore, a set of documents are used by countries to monitor and control these flows. These usually include:

1. Air Waybill

An air waybill is a receipt issued by an international airline for goods, and evidence of the contract of carriage. It obliges the carrier to carry the goods to the airport of destination, according to specified conditions. It is a document of title, which proves ownership, and is non-negotiable.

2. Bill of Lading

A bill of lading is a contract between the owner of the goods and the carrier. It is a receipt, contains the terms of the carriage contract, and importantly, is a document of title, which proves ownership of the goods. For ships, there are two types:

(1) A straight bill of lading. This is not negotiable. It indicates that the carrier has accepted the goods listed, and obliges the carrier to carry the goods to the port of destination, according to specific conditions.

(2) A shipper's orders bill of lading. This is negotiable. It can be bought, sold or traded whilst the goods are in transit.

3. Certificate of Conformity

A certificate of conformity is a signed statement from a manufacturer guaranteeing that a product meets certain technical standards.

4. Certificate of Origin (COO)

A certificate of origin is a signed statement guaranteeing the origin of the export item. Certificates of origin are usually validated by a chamber of commerce in the UK.

5. Commercial Invoice

A commercial invoice provides the information needed to clear your goods through customs in the destination country. It is prepared by the exporter or freight forwarder, and required by the buyer to arrange for payment to the exporter. It should provide a description of goods, the address of the shipper and seller, and the delivery and payment terms. In most cases, the commercial invoice is used to assess customs duties and taxes.

6. Consignment

A consignment is an arrangement where an exporter delivers goods to a distributor, who agrees to only pay the exporter once they have sold it. The exporter retains ownership of the goods until they are sold, but also carries all of the financial burden and risk.

7. Consular Invoice

An invoice covering a shipment of goods certified by the embassy or consulate of the country for which the merchandise is destined. A consular invoice describes the shipment of goods and shows information such as the consignor, consignee, and value of the shipment. It is used by the country's customs officials to verify the value, quantity, and nature of the shipment.

8. Customs Declaration

A customs declaration needs to be made in the UK for any goods that are being exported out of the country. HMRC is replacing the Customs Handling of Import and Export Freight (CHIEF) system, with the Customs Declaration Service (CDS). A freight forwarder can make a customs declaration for you.

9. Customs Invoice

A customs invoice is a document used to clear goods through customs in the country you are exporting to. It provides evidence for the value of the goods. In some countries, it might be sufficient to use the commercial invoice for this.

10. Export License

An export license is a government document that authorizes the export of restricted goods. Learn about the type of goods which may require a license for export from the UK.

11. Export Packing List

An export packing list is a document that indicates the type of package being used to transport goods for export, such as a box, crate, drum or carton. It also itemizes the goods for export in each package. An export packing list is considerably more detailed than a standard domestic packing list. For example, it shows individual weights and measurement for each package.

12. Freight Forwarder

A freight forwarder is a third party agent that you can hire to move your goods from the UK to the country you are exporting to. Most UK companies choose to use a freight forwarder to move their goods. A freight forwarder can take on full responsibility for the documentation required to clear UK and foreign customs, and the movement of goods between these points. The split of responsibility between you and the freight forwarder will depend on the type of incoterms you choose. Read our guidance on moving goods and using freight forwarders.

13. Inspection Certificate

A pre-shipment inspection (PSI), is required in certain countries. The certificate issued guarantees the specifications of the goods being shipped. The inspection is performed by a third party such as Intertec, SGS, Cotecna or Bureau Veritas. The required inspection agency is contracted by the country of destination.

14. Insurance Certificate

An insurance certificate is a document prepared by the exporter or freight forwarder to provide evidence that insurance against loss or damage has been obtained for the goods.

15. Pro forma Invoice

A pro forma invoice can act as a quotation and is prepared by the exporter before shipping the goods. It informs the buyer of the goods to be sent, their value, and other key specifications. Sometimes exporters say they are being paid by "Proforma". They mean payment in advance with their buyer using this document as a notification of the full amount to be paid.

16. Tariff

Tax or duty imposed on a product when it is imported into a country. When an exporter knows the tariff code for their product they can look up the import duty. This duty would usually be paid by the buyer/importer unless the exporter is selling on incoterms such as DDP where they include the duty in their selling price.

17. Tariff Code

A tariff, or commodity code, is a unique number that's assigned to every product type. The same code is used in all countries of the world so it is relatively easy to find out the import duty for your product.

Words and Expressions

consignment	n.	发送的货物，运送物；发送，投递；寄售，寄卖；委托，托付
Incoterms	n.	国际贸易术语，国际贸易术语解释通则（国际商会）

英文	词性	中文
shipment	n.	运输，运送，发货；运输的货物，装载的货物量
dispatch	v.	发送，派遣
tariff	n.	关税
bill of lading		提货单，提单
air waybill		空运提单（一种由承运人或其代理人签发的文件，证明货物已经收到并承诺将其运输到指定目的地）
certificate of conformity		合格证书（一种证明产品、服务或系统符合特定标准或规范的文件）
commercial invoice		商业发票，正式签证的贸易发票
consular invoice		领事发票（一种由出口国的领事机构签发的发票，用于证明货物的来源和价值，通常用于进口商所在国的海关清关）
customs declaration		报关单；申报关税，报关
customs invoice		报关发票（一种用于国际贸易的发票，包含货物的详细信息，如数量、价值、重量等，用于向海关申报进出口货物）
export licence		出口许可证（一种政府颁发的许可证，允许企业将特定商品或服务出口到其他国家）
export packing list		出口装箱单
freight forwarder		货运代理（一种为货物运输提供服务的公司或个人，负责安排货物从一个地点运输到另一个地点，包括处理相关文件、报关、保险等事务）
inspection certificate		检验证书（一种证明产品或设备已经过检验并符合相关标准和规定的文件）
insurance certificate		保险凭证，保单
pro forma invoice		形式发票（一种预先提供给买方的发票，通常在货物发货前提供，用于向买方提供关于货物的详细信息，如价格、数量、运输方式等）
tariff code		关税号码

Unit 16 Import and Export Practices

1. **International Chamber of Commerce (ICC) 国际商会**

   International Chamber of Commerce is the largest, most diverse business organization in the world. ICC represents 45 million companies in over 100 countries with broad business interests.

   ICC's networks of committees and experts represent the full range of business sectors. They also maintain contact with the United Nations, the World Trade Organization, and other intergovernmental agencies.

   The mission of ICC is to make business work for everyone, every day, everywhere by promoting open international trade and investment systems that foster peace, prosperity and opportunity for all.

   ICC's neutrality and independence is the key determinant of her ability to build trusted relationships with policymakers and international organizations, and is the hallmark of the products and services ICC provides to companies large and small to enable cross border commerce.

   ICC was founded in 1919 in the aftermath of the First World War, at a time when no world system of rules governed trade, investment, finance or commercial relations. The founders were a group of industrialists, financiers, and traders determined to replace fear and suspicion with a new spirit of hope and cooperation. Acting on their conviction that the private sector is best qualified to set global standards for business, they called themselves "Merchants of Peace".

   ICC emerged as an organization that would represent business everywhere. A century after our founding, ICC issued a Declaration on the Next Century of Global Business setting out a vision to shape the future of global business for the next century. Via the declaration, the whole world embraces ICC's renewed purpose to enable business worldwide to secure peace, prosperity and opportunity for all.

2. **certificate of origin (COO) 原产地证书**

   A certificate of origin (CO) is a document declaring in which country a commodity or good was manufactured. The certificate of origin contains information regarding the product, its destination, and the country of export. For example, a good may be marked "Made in the USA" or "Made in China".

   Required by many treaty agreements for cross-border trade, the CO is an important form because it can help determine whether certain goods are eligible for import, or whether goods are subject to duties.

   Customs officials expect the CO to be a separate document from the commercial invoice or packing list. Customs in these countries also expect it to be signed by the exporter, the signature notarized, and the document subsequently signed and stamped by a chamber of commerce. In some cases, the destination customs authority may request proof of review from a specific chamber of commerce. Chambers of commerce usually only certify that which is verifiable. However, if the chamber is presented with a declaration attesting to commercial details, the accuracy of which it cannot check, it must confine itself to stamping the document attesting to the position and the identity of the signatory.

There is no standardized certificate of origin (CO) form for global trade, but a CO, normally prepared by the exporter of goods, has at least the basic details about the product being shipped, a tariff code, the exporter and importer, and the country of origin. The exporter, with knowledge of the specific requirements of border control at the importing country, will document these details, get the CO notarized by a chamber of commerce, and submit the form with the shipment. Detail requirements depend on the type of goods being exported and where they are going.

Exercises

I Make verb phrases by linking those in Column A and Column B.

Column A	Column B
facilitate	statements
deliver	responsibilities
assume	transactions
define	goods
sign	risks

II Match the following words or terms with their definitions.

patent	conformity	dispatch	waybill	consign
forwarder	invoice	certificate	Incoterm	validate

1. _____ : the legal right to be the only one who can make, use, or sell an invention for a particular number of years

2. _____ : an expression from a list made by the International Chamber of Commerce that is used in the trade of goods from one country to

		another
3.	_____ :	the sending of someone or something to a destination or for a purpose
4.	_____ :	a document that shows the details of and instructions relating to goods that are being transported by a company
5.	_____ :	an official document that states that the information on it is true
6.	_____ :	a company that arranges for goods to be transported, especially to another country
7.	_____ :	a statement listing goods or services provided and their prices, used in business as a record of sale
8.	_____ :	to send goods to someone, usually the person who is buying them
9.	_____ :	to make something officially acceptable or approved, especially after examining it
10.	_____ :	compliance with standards, rules, or laws

III Reading comprehension: choose the best answer from the four choices.

1. According to the text, Incoterms usually define the following things except _____ .

    A. costs

    B. risks

    C. services

    D. obligations

2. The seller has to bear all costs and risks needed to bring the goods to the place of destination followed by _____ .

    A. "D"-terms

    B. "F"-terms

    C. "E"-term

    D. "C"-terms

3. Which statement about bill of lading is not true?

    A. It is a contract between the owner and the shipper.

    B. It proves ownership of the goods.

    C. A shipper's orders bill of lading is not negotiable.

    D. A straight bill of lading is not negotiable.

4. A commercial invoice provides the information needed to clear your goods through customs in the destination country. It should not provide _____ .

    A. measurement for each package

B. address of the shipper and seller
C. description of goods
D. delivery and payment terms

5. According to the text, which of the following statements is true?
   A. A tariff is not a unique number that's assigned to every product type.
   B. A customs declaration is needed in the UK for any goods that are being exported out of the country.
   C. A customs invoice provides evidence for the quantity of the goods.
   D. A consignment is an arrangement where an importer delivers goods to a distributor.

Part Two Case Study

DESPITE GROWING COMPETITION, CHINESE AND VIETNAMESE ECONOMIES ARE MORE OF COMPLEMENTARY NATURE: EXPERTS

By **Center for WTO and International Trade, Vietnam Chamber of Commerce and Industry**, 12/05/2022

As Vietnam, an emerging manufacturing hub in Southeast Asia, recorded a stellar performance in foreign trade in the first quarter, the news has aroused wide discussions about the country's eating into orders that would have been placed to China—frequently referred to as the "World's Factory".

It is acknowledged that Vietnam is profiting from a shift in global supply chains amid the pandemic and its competition with China and other manufacturing nations has forged in a number of industries, yet it should also be seen that the economies of China and Vietnam are largely complementary.

More noticeably, it remains unlikely that a large number of multinationals will shift all their assembly lines out of China where the supply network has matured over the past decades, business groups and industry observers told the Global Times.

Vietnam's export-import revenue in the first quarter of this year was estimated to be \$176.35 billion, up 14.37 percent year-on-year, of which \$88.58 billion was from exports, rising 12.9 percent on a yearly basis. In March alone, export value reached some \$34.06 billion, a jump of 45.5 percent month-on-month and 14.8 percent year-on-year, according to data from Vietnam's Ministry of Industry and Trade.

In 2021, manufacturing has accounted for 25 percent of Vietnam's economic output, and the country has become an important exporter of electronics, the volume of which has surpassed that of rice, coffee, and textile products.

Vietnam, as a leader in low-cost manufacturing and sourcing compared to other developing markets in the region, is expected to benefit greatly from the Regional Comprehensive Economic Partnership (RCEP), a mega regional free trade deal, said the World Bank.

Are Orders Shifting?

There have been some narratives hyped by some Western media surrounding multinationals seeking to extract their industrial chain or supply chain out of China, hyping the "investor flight" theory, due to the country's stringent anti-Covid-19 measures adopted in some major Chinese cities like Shanghai and Beijing to curb the rapid spread of Omicron variant.

Some orders that could have been placed to China have shifted to neighboring countries like Vietnam, Cambodia and Thailand where population structure is relatively young and labor is abundant and relatively inexpensive, aiding their power of building up exports.

According to an analysis report by CITIC Securities, the substitution effect of labor-intensive products represented by clothing, shoes and hats is more likely to occur, particularly in shipping those products to the US.

"We did have lost some orders, but we should be aware that it's a natural development of international industrial division of labor," Bai Ming, deputy director of the International Market Research Institute at the Chinese Academy of International Trade and Economic Cooperation, told the Global Times.

There are four stages in the international division of labor in the industrial chain: the first is the countries unable to enter the industrial chain, the second is the countries engaging in low-end manufacturing, the third is the countries trying to move into the high-end industrial manufacturing, while the fourth refers to dominance of the industrial chain, according to Bai.

"China is now at the third stage and striving to enter the fourth one, while Vietnamese factories are now mainly doing simple processing and assembling," he said.

"High-end industries now account for an increasing proportion of China's exports, and the order change will not have a significant impact on China's industrial power," Gu Xiaosong, dean of the ASEAN Research Institute of Hainan Tropical Ocean University, told the Global Times.

Complementary in Nature

Compared with the shifting orders, industrial transfer is deemed a bigger decision for the multinationals because the production cost is significant reduced. The shifting order from China to Vietnam usually do not involve the entire industry, but some specific links in the production process of the industry—mainly the links with low demand for the supply chain and high labor costs, experts said.

A worker with an electronics manufacturer based in South China's Guangdong Province told the Global Times that "some Chinese factories have also moved away from the Pearl River Delta region to Vietnam trying to explore business opportunities there by taking advantage of local cheap labor, but most of them had to come back due to Vietnam's lack of mature supply chains."

In contrast, China's southern manufacturing hub in the Delta has accumulated experiences for as many as 20-30 years in the ICT (Information and Communications Technology) and other related industries and the Delta has complete chain churning out the so-called upstream, middle and downstream components.

"The industrial chain between China and Vietnam is more of a complementary nature," Bai said.

China is Vietnam's largest trading partner, on which the Southeast Asian country relies for the sourcing of raw materials and equipment. Its imports from China rose 30 percent to reach $110 billion in 2021.

Vietnam's clothes and shoe factories are struggling to meet orders as supplies of raw materials from China are drying up amid the latter's fight against the pandemic, which has hurt the Southeast Asian nation's production and exports, the Bloomberg News reported on Friday, citing Pham Xuan Hong, chairman of the Ho Chi Minh City Garment, Textile Embroidery Knitting Association.

Questions for Discussion

1. Despite growing competition, how to make China's economy and Vietnam's economy complement each other?

2. There are four stages in the international division of labor in the industrial chain, what are they? Which stage is China in now?

Translation

1. Vietnam, as a leader in low-cost manufacturing and sourcing compared to other developing markets in the region, is expected to benefit greatly from the Regional Comprehensive Economic Partnership (RCEP), a mega regional free trade deal, said the World Bank.

2. According to an analysis report by CITIC Securities, the substitution effect of labor-intensive products represented by clothing, shoes and hats is more likely to occur, particularly in shipping those products to the US.

3. Compared with the shifting orders, industrial transfer is deemed a bigger decision for the multinationals because the production cost is significant reduced. The shifting order from China to Vietnam usually do not involve the entire industry, but some specific links in the production process of the industry—mainly the links with low demand for the supply chain and high labor costs, experts said.

4. Vietnam's clothes and shoe factories are struggling to meet orders as supplies of raw materials from China are drying up amid the latter's fight against the pandemic, which has hurt the Southeast Asian nation's production and exports.

Unit 17
Economic Integration

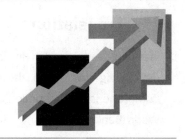

Introduction

Much international trade is practically taking place in a context where countries accord differential treatment to their trading partners. This treatment usually occurs by way of economic integration, where countries join together to create a larger economic unit with special relationships among the members. In the text, we discuss several different types of economic integration, present a framework for analyzing the welfare impacts of these special relationships, and examine recent integration efforts in the world economy. Given that integration efforts such as the North American Free Trade Agreement are becoming prominent in public debate, it is important that students of international economics have a basic understanding of the general trade and welfare effects of these agreements.

Part One Text

When countries form economic coalitions, their efforts represent a partial movement to free trade and a attempt by each participating country to obtain some of the benefits of a more open economy without sacrificing control over the goods and services that cross its borders and hence over its production and consumption structure. Countries entering special trade arrangements soon realize that the more they remove restrictions on the movement of goods and services between members of the group, the more domestic control of the economy is lost. Consequently, actions taken to integrate economies often take place in stages, and the first preferential agreement is potentially less threatening to the loss of control than the later stages. Four basic types of formal regional economic arrangements are usually distinguished.

Free-trade Area (FTA)

The most common integration scheme is referred to as a free-trade area (FTA), in which all members of the group remove tariffs on each other's products, while at the same time each member retains its independence in establishing trading policies with nonmembers. In other words, the members of a FTA can maintain individual tariffs and other trade barriers on the "outside world". This scheme is usually assumed to apply to all products between member countries, but it can clearly involve a mix of free trade in some products and preferential, but still protected, treatment in others. It needs to be noted that when each member country sets its own external tariff, nonmember countries may find it profitable to export a product to the member country with the lowest level of outside protection and then through it to other member countries whose protection levels against the outside world are higher. Without rules of origin by members regarding the source country of a product, there is nothing to preclude nonmember countries form using this transshipment strategy to escape some of the trade restrictions in the more highly protected member countries. The most prominent free-trade area for many years has been the European Free Trade Association (EFTA)

Customs Union

The second level of economic integration is a customs union. In this stage, all tariffs are removed between members and the group adopts a common external commercial policy toward nonmembers. Furthermore, the group acts as one body in the negotiation of all trade agreements with nonmembers. The customs union is thus a step closer toward economic integration than the FTA. An example of a customs union is that of Belgium, the Netherlands, and Luxembourg (Benelux), which was formed in 1947 and absorbed into the European Community in 1958.

Common Market

The third level of economic integration is referred to as a common market, in which all tariffs are removed between members, a common external trade policy is adopted for nonmembers, and all barriers to factor movements among the member countries are removed. The free movement of labor and capital between members represents a higher level of economic integration and, at the same time, a further reduction in national control of the individual economy, the Treaties of Rome in 1957 established a common market within the European Community (EC) on November1, 1993.

Economic Union

The most comprehensive of the four forms of economic integration is an economic union. It includes all features of a common market but also implies the unification of economic institutions and the coordination of economic policy throughout all member countries. While separate political entities are still present, an economic union generally establishes several supranational institutions whose decisions are binding upon all members. When an economic union adopts a common currency, it has become a monetary union as well. While this level of economic integration is often aspired to and has been ratified by the 15 members of the EU, member countries find it extraordinarily difficult to give up the domestic sovereignty the scheme requires.

Thus, there are several different forms of economic integration, and existing integration units exhibit a wide variety of differing characteristics.

Static Effects of Economic Integration

Economic integration implies differential treatment for member countries as opposed to nonmember countries. Since this type of integration can lead to shifts in the pattern of trade between members and nonmembers, the net impact on a participating country is, in general, ambiguous and must be judged on the basis of each individual country. While integration represents a movement to free trade on the part of member countries, at the same time it can lead to the diversion of trade from a lower-cost nonmember source (which still faces the external tariffs of the group) to a member country source (which is longer faces any tariffs). These two static effects of economic integration, meaning that they occur directly on the formation of the integration project, are called trade creation and trade diversion. These terms were coined by Jacob Viner (1950), who defined trade creation as taking place whenever economic integration leads to a shift in product origin from a domestic producer whose resource costs are higher to a member producer whose resource costs are lower. This shift represents a movement in the direction of the free-trade allocation of resources and thus is presumably beneficial for welfare. Trade diversion takes place whenever there is a shift in product origin form a nonmember producer whose resource costs are lower to a member country producer whose resource costs are higher. This shift represents a movement away from the free-trade allocation of resources and could reduce welfare. Since both trade creation and trade diversion are clearly possible with economic integration, we find ourselves in the world of second best because economic integration represents only a partial movement to free trade. Whether or not it produces a net benefit to participating countries is an empirical issue.

Dynamic Effects of Economic Integration

In addition to the static effect of economic integration, it is likely that the economic structure and performance of participating countries may evolve differently than if they had not integrated economically. The factors that cause this to come about are the dynamic effects of economic integration. For example, reducing trade barriers brings about a more competitive environment and possibly reduces the degree of monopoly power that was present prior to integration. In addition, access to larger union markets may allow economies of scale to be realized in certain export goods. These economies of scale may result internally to the exporting firm in a participating country as it becomes larger, or they may result from a lowering of costs of inputs due to economic changes external to the firm. In either case, they are triggered by market expansion brought about by membership in the union. The realization of economies of scale may also involve specialization on particular types of goods, and thus (as has been observed with the European Union) trade may increasingly become intra-industry trade rather than inter-industry trade.

It is also possible that integration will stimulate greater investment in the member countries from both internal and foreign sources. Investment can result from structural changes, internal and external economies, and the expected increases in income and demand. It is further argued that integration stimulates investment by reducing risk and uncertainty because of the large economic and geographic market now open to producers. Furthermore, foreigners may wish to invest in productive capacity in a member country in order to avoid being frozen out of the union by trade restrictions and high common external tariff.

Finally, economic integration at the level of the common market may lead to dynamic benefits from increased factor mobility. If both capital and labor have the increased ability to move form area of surplus to areas of scarcity, increased economic efficiency and correspondingly higher factor incomes in the integrated area will result.

Words and Expressions

coalition	n.	结合，联盟
scheme	n.	方案，计划
preclude	v.	排除，阻止
unification	n.	统一，一致，单一化
supranational	a.	超国家的
sovereignty	n.	主权，最高统治权，独立国
empirical	a.	以经验为根据的
dynamic	a.	活动的，动态的
monopoly	n.	独占，垄断

Notes

1. **economic integration   经济一体化**

   Economic integration is a term used to describe how different aspects between economies are integrated. The basics of this theory were written by the Hungarian Economist Béla Balassa in the 1960s. As economic integration increases, the barriers of trade between markets diminish. The most integrated economy today, between independent nations, is the European Union and its euro zone.

2. **North American Free Trade Agreement   北美自由贸易协定**

   The North American Free Trade Agreement is the trade bloc in North America created by the North American Free Trade Agreement (NAFTA) and its two supplements, the North American Agreement on Environmental Cooperation (NAAEC) and The North American Agreement on Labor Cooperation (NAALC), whose members are Canada, Mexico, and the United States. It came into effect on 1 January 1994.

3. **free trade area (FTA)   自由贸易区**

   A free trade area is a designated group of countries that have agreed to eliminate tariffs, quotas and preferences on most (if not all) goods between them. It can be considered the second stage of economic integration.

4. **European Free Trade Association (EFTA)   欧洲自由贸易联盟**

   The European Free Trade Association (EFTA) was established on May 3, 1960 as an alternative for European states that were not allowed, or did not wish, to join the

European Economic Community (now the European Community).

5. **customs union** 关税同盟

    A customs union is a free trade area with a common external tariff. The participant countries set up common external trade policy, but in some cases they use different import quotas. Common competition policy is also helpful to avoid competition deficiency.

6. **European Community (EC)** 欧洲共同体

    The European Community is an economic and political alliance designed to foster trade and cooperation among its member countries. It was originally founded on March 25, 1957 by the signing of the Treaty of Rome under the name of European Economic Community. The 'Economic' was removed from its name by the Maastricht treaty in 1992, which at the same time effectively made the European Community the first of three pillars of the European Union, called the Community (or Communities) Pillar.

7. **common market** 共同市场

    A common market is a customs union with common policies on product regulation, and freedom of movement of all the three factors of production (land, capital and labour) and of enterprise. The goal is that movement of capital, labour, goods, and services between the members is as easy as within them.

8. **the Treaties of Rome** 《罗马条约》

    The Treaties of Rome, signed by France, West Germany, Italy and Benelux (Belgium, the Netherlands and Luxembourg) on March 25, 1957, established the European Economic Community (EEC) and came into force on 1 January 1958. According to George C. McGhee, former US ambassador to West Germany, it was nurtured at Bilderberg meetings.

9. **trade creation** 贸易创造

    Trade creation is an economic term related to international economics in which trade is created by the formation of a customs union.

10. **trade diversion** 贸易转移

    Trade diversion is an economic term related to international economics in which trade is diverted from a more efficient exporter towards a less efficient one by the formation of a free trade agreement.

11. **economies of scale** 规模经济

    Economies of scale characterize a production process in which an increase in the scale of the firm causes a decrease in the long run average cost of each unit.

I Make verb phrases by linking those in Column A and Column B.

Column A	Column B
adopt	a term
coin	in stocks
remove	a commercial policy
integrate	restrictions
invest	economies

II Match the following words or terms with their definitions.

| agreement | term | labor | transshipment | customs union |
| broker | treaty | integration | restriction | negotiation |

1. _____: the bringing together of separate elements to create a whole unit
2. _____: an arrangement between parties regarding a course of action
3. _____: the shipment of goods to an intermediate destination, and then from there to yet another destination
4. _____: a form of alternative dispute resolution
5. _____: work of any type
6. _____: a formal agreement between two or more parties
7. _____: word or phrase that defines a thing, concept, or process
8. _____: an individual or firm which acts as an intermediary between a buyer and seller, usually charging a commission
9. _____: a free trade area with a common external tariff
10. _____: the act of limiting or condition of being limited

III Reading comprehension: choose the best answer from the four choices.

1. How many basic types of formal regional economic arrangements are mentioned in the text?
   A. 3.   B. 4.   C. 5.   D. 6.
2. The member of a FTA does not _____.
   A. remove tariffs on the other members' products
   B. remove tariffs on the nonmembers' products

C. maintain tariffs on the nonmembers' products
D. set its own external tariff
3. Which of the following descriptions of the Customs Union is not true?
   A. All tariffs are removed between members.
   B. The members adopt a common external commercial policy toward nonmembers.
   C. The European Free Trade Association is the most prominent customs union.
   D. The group acts as one body in the negotiation of all trade agreements with nonmembers.
4. Which of the following descriptions of the economic union is not true?
   A. It has all features of a common market.
   B. It implies the unification of economic institutions throughout all members.
   C. The member countries act as one political entity.
   D. It is also a monetary union when it adopts a common currency.
5. Which of the statements of economic integration is not true?
   A. Economic integration represents only a partial movement to free trade.
   B. Trade creation and trade diversion are two dynamic effects of economic integration.
   C. Economic integration will stimulate greater investment in the member countries from both internal and foreign sources.
   D. Economic integration at the level of the common market may lead to dynamic benefits from increased factor mobility.

Part Two Case Study

FINANCIAL CRISES SPREAD IN EUROPE

By **Carter Dougherty, Nelson Schwartz and Floyd Norris**
From *The New York Times*, October 5, 2008

European nations scrambled on Sunday night to prevent a growing credit crisis[①] from bringing down major banks and alarming savers as troubles in financial markets

---

① In the fall of 2008, the credit crunch, which had emerged a little more than a year before, ballooned into Wall Street's biggest crisis since the Great Depression. As hundreds of billions in mortgage-related investments went bad, mighty investment banks that once ruled high finance have crumbled or reinvented themselves as humdrum commercial banks. The nation's largest insurance company and largest savings and loan both were seized by the government. The channels of credit, the arteries of the global financial system, have been constricted, cutting off crucial funds to consumers and businesses small and large.
In response, the federal government adopted a $700 billion bailout plan meant to reassure the markets and get credit flowing again. But the crisis began to spread to Europe, where governments scrambled to prop up banks, broaden guarantees for deposits and agree on a coordinated response.

spread around the world, accelerating economic downturns on three continents.

The German government moved to guarantee all private savings accounts in the country on Sunday, hoping to reassure depositors who had grown nervous as efforts to bail out a large German lender and a major European financial company failed.

Late Sunday, it was disclosed that new bailouts had been arranged for both of those companies, Hypo Real Estate, the German lender, and Fortis, a large banking and insurance company based in Belgium but active across much of the Continent.

The spreading worries came days after the United States Congress approved a $700 billion bailout package① that officials had hoped would calm financial markets globally.

The moves came as federal regulators were trying to help resolve a merger fight in the United States that could make investors more uneasy. Court hearings were under way in New York on Sunday over competing efforts by Citigroup and Wells Fargo to acquire Wachovia, a large bank that nearly failed a week ago.

In Europe, meanwhile, the crisis appears to be the most serious one to face the Continent since a common currency, the euro, was created in 1999. Jean Pisani-Ferry, director of the Bruegel research group in Brussels, said Europe confronted "our first real financial crisis, and it's not just any crisis. It's a big one."

The European Central Bank has aggressively lent money to banks as the crisis has grown. It had resisted lowering interest rates, but signaled on Thursday that it might cut rates soon. The extra money, aimed at ensuring that banks would have adequate access to cash, has not reassured savers or investors, and European stock markets have performed even worse than the American markets.

In Iceland, government officials and banking chiefs were discussing a possible rescue plan for the country's commercial banks. In Berlin, Chancellor Angela Merkel and her finance minister, Peer Steinbrück, appeared before television cameras to promise that all bank deposits would be protected, although it was not clear whether legislation would be needed to make that promise good.

Mindful of the rising public anger at the use of public money to buttress the business of high-earning bankers, Mrs. Merkel promised a day of reckoning for them as well.

---

① On Sept. 19, 2008, Treasury Secretary Henry M. Paulson, Jr. proposed a sweeping bailout of financial institutions battered by bad mortgages and a loss of investor confidence. In Mr. Paulson's original proposal — called the Troubled Asset Relief Program — he asked Congress for $700 billion to use to buy up mortgage-backed securities whose value had dropped sharply or had become impossible to sell.

According to the Federal Reserve chairman, Ben S. Bernanke, who worked with Mr. Paulson to develop the plan, the government would pay "hold to maturity" prices-meaning a price based on some estimate of what the asset would be worth once the crisis of confidence had passed, not on what the asset holder could get by selling it today. By doing so, they said, the government would provide troubled firms with an infusion of capital, reducing doubts about their viability and thereby restoring investor confidence.

"We are also saying that those who engaged in irresponsible behavior will be held responsible," she said. "The government will ensure that. We owe it to taxpayers."

Stock markets fell sharply in early trading on Monday in Asia on growing fears about the health of European banks and the resilience of the global economy.

The Nikkei 225 index dropped 3.4 percent in Tokyo on Monday, the Kospi index in Seoul fell 3.7 percent and the Standard and Poor's/Australian Stock Exchange 200 index in Sydney declined 3.3 percent. The events in Berlin and Brussels underscored the failure of Europe's case-by-case approach to restoring confidence in the Continent's increasingly jittery banking sector. A European summit meeting Saturday did little to calm worries.

President Nicolas Sarkozy of France and his counterparts from Germany, Britain and Italy vowed to prevent a Lehman-like bankruptcy in Europe but they did not offer an American-style bailout package.

<u>The crisis has underlined the difficulty of taking concerted action in Europe because its economies are far more integrated than its governing structures.</u>

"We are not a political federation," Jean-Claude Trichet, the president of the European Central Bank, said. "We do not have a federal budget."

Last week, Ireland moved to guarantee both deposits and other liabilities at six major banks. There was grumbling in London and Berlin about the move giving those banks an unfair advantage. But Germany proposed its deposit guarantee Sunday after Britain raised its guarantee to £50,000, or almost $90,000, from £35,000.

Unlike in the United States, where deposits are fully guaranteed up to a limit of $250,000 — a figure that was raised from $100,000 last week — deposits in most European countries have been only partially guaranteed, sometimes by groups of banks rather than governments. In Germany, the first 90 percent of deposits up to 20,000 euros, or about $27,000, was guaranteed.

The Paris meeting produced a promise that European leaders would work together to halt the financial crisis and reassure nervous investors, but even before the meeting began it was becoming clear that two bailouts announced the week before had not succeeded and that a major Italian bank might be in trouble. That bank, Unicredit, announced plans on Sunday to raise as much as 6.6 billion euros, or $9 billion, in capital.

Fortis, which only a week ago received 11.2 billion euros from the governments of the Netherlands, Belgium and Luxembourg, was unable to continue its operations. On Friday, the Dutch government seized its operations in that country, and Sunday night the Belgian government helped to arrange for BNP-Paribas, the French bank, to take over what was left of the company.

In Berlin, the government arranged a week ago for major banks to lend 35 billion euros to Hypo, but that fell apart when the banks concluded that more money would be needed. Late Sunday, the government said a 50 billion euro package had been arranged, with the government and other banks participating.

The credit crisis began in the United States, a fact that has led European politicians to claim superiority for their country's financial systems, in contrast to what Silvio Berlusconi, Italy's prime minister, called the "speculative capitalism" of the United States. On Saturday, Gordon Brown, the British prime minister, said the crisis "has come from America," and Mr. Berlusconi bemoaned the lack of business ethics that had been exposed by the crisis.

Many of the European banks' problems have stemmed from bad loans in Europe, and Fortis got into trouble in part by borrowing money to make a major acquisition. But activities in the United States have played a role. Bankers said Sunday that the additional need for funds at Hypo came from newly discovered guarantees it had issued to back American municipal bonds that it had sold to investors.

The credit market worries came on top of heightening concerns about economic growth in Europe and the United States. Many economists think there are recessions in both areas, and one also appears to have started in Japan, where the Nikkei newspaper reported Monday that a poll of corporate executives found that 94 percent thought the country's economy was deteriorating.

"Unless there is a material easing of credit conditions," said Bob Elliott of Bridgewater Associates, an American money management firm, after the retail sales figures were announced, "it is unlikely that demand will turn around soon."

Almost unnoticed as the United States Congress approved a $700 billion bailout for banks last week, it also agreed to guarantee $25 billion in loans for America's troubled automakers. European automakers said Sunday they would seek similar aid from the European Commission.

Henry M. Paulson Jr., the United States Treasury secretary, hoped that approval of the American bailout, which will involve buying securities from banks at more than their current market value, would free up credit by making cash available for banks to lend and by reassuring participants in the credit markets.

But that did not happen last week. Instead, credit grew more expensive and harder to get as investors became more skittish about buying commercial paper, essentially short-term loans to companies. Rates on such loans rose so fast that some feared the market could essentially close, leaving it to already-stressed banks to provide short-term corporate loans.

Altria, the parent company of the cigarette maker Philip Morris, said lenders wanted it to delay its planned $10.3 billion acquisition of UST, another tobacco maker, until

2009, but promised it would complete the deal.

Europe's need to scramble is in part the legacy of a decision to establish the euro, which 15 countries now use, but not follow up with a parallel system of cross-border regulation and oversight of private banks.

"First we had economic integration, then we had monetary integration," said Sylvester Eijffinger, a member of the monetary expert panel advising the European parliament. "But we never developed the parallel political and regulatory integration that would allow us to face a crisis like the one we are facing today," he added.

In Brussels, Daniel Gros, director of the Center for European Policy Studies, agreed. "Maybe they will be shocked into thinking more strategically instead of running behind events," he said. "The later you come, the higher the bill."

While the European Central Bank has power over interest rates and broader monetary policy, it was never granted parallel oversight of private banks, leaving that task to dozens of regulators across the Continent.

This patchwork system includes national central banks in each of the euro-zone's 15 members and they still retain broad powers within their own borders, further complicating any regional approach to problem-solving.

The European economic landscape today bears little resemblance to the 1990s, when the groundwork for the euro was laid. Back then, Mr. Pisani-Ferry recalled, few banks in Europe had cross-border operations on a significant scale.

A wave of mergers over the last decade created giants like HSBC and Deutsche Bank, which straddle continents and have major American exposure.

"The European banking landscape was transformed fairly recently," Mr. Pisani-Ferry said. "When the euro was first introduced, the question of cross-border regulation didn't really arise."

Optimists say one potential long-term benefit from the current turmoil is that it often takes a crisis to propel European integration forward.

"Progress in Europe is usually the result of a crisis," Mr. Eijffinger said. "This could be one of those rare moments in EU history."

Questions for Discussion

1. Can you list the financial crises in the history? State their impacts.

2. The Financial Crisis described in the case, originated from the credit crunch in America in the fall of 2008, spread to the continents and struck Asia, Europe and even the whole world. Please briefly elaborate its proceedings and affects on EU.

3. From this case, you may probably conclude that the economic integration is something as of a "two-blade sword". By taking EU for example, what are the two blades of this sword in this case? And how do these two blades affect EU?

4. How to understand what Mr. Eijffinger said in the last paragraph of the article, i.e., "Progress in Europe is usually the result of a crisis," and "This could be one of those rare moments in EU history."?

Translation

1. The extra money, aimed at ensuring that banks would have adequate access to cash, has not reassured savers or investors, and European stock markets have performed even worse than the American markets.

2. The crisis has underlined the difficulty of taking concerted action in Europe because its economies are far more integrated than its governing structures.

3. The credit crisis began in the United States, a fact that has led European politicians to claim superiority for their country's financial systems, in contrast to what Silvio Berlusconi, Italy's prime minister, called the "speculative capitalism" of the United States.

4. Europe's need to scramble is in part the legacy of a decision to establish the euro, which 15 countries now use, but not follow up with a parallel system of cross-border regulation and oversight of private banks.

Unit 18
Investment and Multinational Corporation

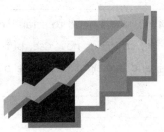

Introduction

Today the world economy is characterized by the international movement of factor inputs. The role of international capital flows (investment) is considered as a substitute for trade in capital-intensive products. The MNC (multinational corporation) plays a central part in this process. We are going to know what the most identifiable characteristics of MNC are.

Part One Text

Our attention so far has been on international flows of goods and services. However, some of the most dramatic changes in the world economy have been due to international flows of factors of production, including labor and capital. In the 1800s, European capital and labor (along with Africa and Asia labor) flowed to the United States and fostered its economic development. In the 1960s, the United States sent large amounts of investment capital to Canada and Western Europe; in the 1980s and 1990s, investment flowed from Japan to the United States. Today, works from southern Europe find employment in northern European factories, while Mexican workers migrate to the United States. The tearing down of the Berlin Wall in 1990 triggered a massive exodus of workers from East Germany to West Germany.

The economic forces underlying international movements in factors of production are virtually identical to those underlying international flows of goods and services. A nation in which labor is scarce can either import labor-intensive products or import labor itself; the same applies to capital. Thus, international trade in goods and services and lows of productive factors are substitutes for each other. One can not conduct a satisfactory study of international trade without also analyzing the international mobility of labor and capital (investment).

A. Foreign Direct Investment Versus Licensing

Once a firm choose foreign production as a method of supplying goods abroad, it must decide whether it is more efficient to establish a foreign production subsidiary or license the technology to a foreign firm to produce its goods.

In the United Kingdom. There are KFC establishments that are owned and run by local residents. The parent US organization merely provides its name and operating procedures in returns for royalty fees paid by the local establishments.

B. The Multinational Corporation

There is no single agreed-on definition of what constitutes a multinational corporation. But a close look at some representative MNCs suggests that these businesses have a number of identifiable features. Operating in many host countries, MNCs often conduct research and development (R&D) activities in addition to manufacturing, mining, extraction, and business-service operations. The multinational corporation cuts across national borders and is often directed from a company planning center that is distant from the host country. Both stock ownership and company management are typically multinational in character. A typical MNC has a high ratio of foreign sales to total sales, often 25 percent or more.

Parts of the manufacturing process can be located to low-cost countries, while R&D can be located in a region with specialized competencies with its costs spread across many markets. In the case of service firms, much of the value chain has to be generated locally: that is, there is little in the way of opportunity to centralize activities to low-cost locations. To a greater or larger degree, services have to be tailored for each client unlike, for example, pharmaceuticals, which can be mass-produced. Sharing advanced knowledge is also more problematic. In manufacturing companies it can be made available through patented technologies or unique products. In service companies it has to be transferred from country to country through learning processes.

C. Motives for Foreign Direct Investment

Nevertheless with the liberalization of recent years, the share of services in Foreign Direct Investments (FDI) has risen significantly particularly within telecommunications, utilities, investment banking, business consulting, accountancy and legal services. The major factors that influence decisions to undertake Foreign Direct Investment are: market demand, trade restrictions, investment regulations and labor productivity and costs.

Despite setbacks such as the Asia crisis of the late 1990s, the long-term flow of Foreign Direct Investment (FDI) is one of inexorable increase. The annual average FDI growth rate between 1986 and 2000 was 30 per cent or more for 65 countries including Denmark, Finland, China, Germany and Finland. Another 29 countries, including Austria, the Netherlands and Russia, had FDI growth rates of 20 – 29 per cent. For 1999 and 2000 over three-quarters of global FDI inflows went to the developed world partly because of intense cross-border mergers and acquisitions activity. The major recipients at the end of the 1990s were the USA and the European Union (EU), with Germany, the United Kingdom and the Benelux countries figuring particularly strongly. Among developing countries China (including Hong Kong) was by far the most important recipient: nearly 400 of the Fortune 500 firms have invested in China to date. Within these recipient countries subsidiaries tend to cluster geographically in and around areas with well-developed infrastructures including suppliers, skills and innovative capabilities. In the USA, California, New York, Texas, Illinois and New Jersey are the main magnets; in Japan it is Tokyo, and in China it is the coastal regions.

D. FDI Versus Licensing

An MNC, i.e. actively managed substantial Foreign Direct Investment made by firms that have a long-term commitment to operating internationally. We have thereby excluded several prevalent forms of internationalization such as licensing and contract manufacturing.

Once a firm choose foreign production as a method of supplying goods abroad, it must decide whether it is more efficient to establish a foreign production subsidiary or license the technology to a foreign firm to produce its goods. Although licensing is widely used in practice, it presupposes that local firms are capable of adapting their operations to the production process or technology of the parent organization.

In short, the decision to establish foreign operations through direct investment or licensing depends on the following factors: the extent to which capital is used in the production process, the size of the foreign market and the amount of fixed cost a business must bear when establishing an overseas facility.

E. Pros and Cons of MNCs

MNCs have a number of advantages over local companies. Their size provides them with the opportunity to achieve vast economies of scale in manufacturing and product

Unit 18 Investment and Multinational Corporation

development. Their global presence also exposes them to new ideas and opportunities regardless of where they occur. Moreover, their location in many countries can be used as a bargaining chip in obtaining favorable conditions from governments anxious to preserve inward investment and jobs. However, with all the advantages size confers, there are also the potential liabilities of slowness and bureaucracy. MNCs are not necessarily successful. Indeed, many MNCs are not particularly good at managing their foreign activities, particularly in regard to digesting acquisitions, and that strong core competencies do not guarantee international commercial success. Furthermore, the gap between the best-and worst-performing companies is growing. Over 40 years ago Hymer raised the question of why MNCs existed at all given that they are "playing away from home" both in national and cultural terms. Domestic companies have "the general advantage of better information about their country: its economy, its language, its laws and its politics" (1960/1976: 34). Certainly the liability of foreignness is particularly severe in the initial entry phase. An MNC will often have to compete head on with domestic companies that have a number of natural advantages.

Words and Expressions

substitute	n.	代用品,代替者,替代品
	v.	代替,替换,替代
exodus	n.	大批的离去
foster	v.	养育,抚育,培养,鼓励,抱(希望)
	n.	养育者,鼓励者
representative	n.	代表
	a.	典型的,有代表性
ratio	n.	比,比率,[财政]复本位制中金银的法定比价
endowment	n.	捐赠,捐赠的基金(或财产),天资,捐款
substantial	a.	坚固的,实质的,真实的,充实的
thereby	ad.	因此,从而,在那方面,在那附近
pharmaceutical	n.	药物
	a.	制药(学)上的
consulting	a.	商议的,顾问资格的,咨询的
setback	n.	顿挫,挫折,退步,逆流,(疾病的)复发
commitment	n.	委托事项,许诺,承担义务
facility	n.	容易,简易,灵巧,熟练,便利,敏捷,设备,工具

inward	ad.	向内，在内
	a.	向内的，内在的
liability	n.	责任，义务，倾向，债务，负债（与 assets 相对）
bureaucracy	n.	官僚，官僚作风，官僚机构
capital flow		资本流入
substitute for		代替……，替换……，取代……
foreign subsidiary		外国子（附属）公司
ascribe to		归于
pros and cons		赞成与反对，正反双方的理由

1. **the Berlin Wall　柏林墙**
   The Berlin Wall was known in the Soviet Union and in the German Democratic Republic as the "Anti-Fascist Protective Rampart," and was a separation barrier between West and East Germany. An iconic symbol of the Cold War, the wall divided East and West Berlin for 28 years, from the day construction began on August 13, 1961 until it was dismantled in 1989. When the East German government announced on November 9, 1989, after several weeks of civil unrest, that entering West Berlin would be permitted, crowds of East Germans climbed onto and crossed the wall, joined by West Germans on the other side in a cheerful atmosphere. Over the next few weeks, parts of the wall were chipped away by a euphoric public and by souvenir hunters; industrial equipment was later used to remove the rest of it. The fall of the Berlin wall paved the way for German reunification, which was formally concluded on October 3, 1990.

2. **KFC (Kentucky Fried Chicken)　肯德基**
   KFC Corporation, based in Louisville, Kentucky, is the world's most popular chicken restaurant chain. KFC has more than 11,000 restaurants in more than 80 countries and territories around the world.

3. **the Asia Financial Crisis of the late 1990s　20 世纪 90 年代末的亚洲金融危机**
   The Asian Financial Crisis was a period of economic unrest that started in July 1997 in Thailand and South Korea with the financial collapse of Kia, and affected currencies, stock markets, and other asset prices in several Asian countries, many considered Four Asian Tigers. It is also commonly referred to as the East Asian currency crisis or locally

as the IMF crisis although the latter is somewhat controversial. There is general consensus on the existence of a crisis and its consequences, but what is less clear are the causes of the crisis, its scope and resolution. Indonesia, South Korea and Thailand were the countries most affected by the crisis. Malaysia, Laos, the Philippines, and Hong Kong of China were also hit by the slump. China, Singapore and Vietnam were relatively unaffected. Japan was not affected much by this crisis but was going through its own long-term economic difficulties. However, all nations mentioned above saw their currencies dip significantly relative to the US dollar, though the harder hit nations saw extended currency losses. Out of all the countries affected, South Korea was hit hardest.

4. **European Union** 欧盟

The European Union (EU) is a union of twenty-seven independent states based on the European Communities and founded to enhance political, economic and social co-operation. Formerly known as European Community (EC) or European Economic Community (EEC, 欧洲经济共同体).

I Make verb phrases by linking those in Column A and Column B.

Column A	Column B
foster	favorable condition
establish	across many markets
spread	a foreign subsidiary
share	goods abroad
supply	its development
obtain	advanced knowledge

II Match the following words or terms with their definitions.

host countries	commitment	Foreign Direct Investment	investment
crisis	European Union	subsidiary	MNC
licensing	bureaucracy		

1. _____: a financial means for an economy such as a company to earn more money on its own money with relative safety

2. _____: a company from one country making a physical investment into building a factory in another country

3. _____: arrangement in which a local firm in the host country produces goods in accordance with another firm's specifications; as the goods are sold, the local firm can retain part of the earnings

4. _____: a nation in which representatives or organizations of another state are present because of government invitation and/or international agreement

5. _____: the countries pool their sovereignty in order to gain a strength and world influence none of them could have on its own

6. _____: a company whose voting stock is more than 50% controlled by another company, usually referred to as the parent company

7. _____: a form of organization in which officeholders have defined positions and (usually) titles

8. _____: a situation that has reached a critical phase

9. _____: a corporation or an enterprise that manages production establishments and/or delivers services in at least two countries

10. _____: thing or task one has promised to do, or undertake

III Reading comprehension: choose the best answer from the four choices.

1. Foreign Direct Investments has two forms: joint venture enterprise and enterprise with 100% foreign investment. In the following options, which is a disadvantage of the former?
   A. Opinions are divided on the management.
   B. The potential liabilities of slowness.
   C. Bigger risk.
   D. Some resistance from the people.

2. A big multinational corporation has a tendency to build an _____.
   A. international joint venture enterprise
   B. international cooperative enterprise
   C. exclusively foreign-owned enterprises
   D. equity joint venture

3. Though foreign direct investment is done in overseas enterprises, the disadvantage is that _____.
   A. construction cycle is much longer
   B. the local enterprises cannot use the overseas enterprises' technology

C. the local enterprises cannot use the overseas enterprises' marketing channel

D. it is easy to be hedged about with laws and difficulty of the host countries

4. Once a firm decide to establish foreign operations through direct investment or licensing it will not depend on _____.

   A. the extent to which capital is used in the production process

   B. the technology which is used in the production process

   C. the amount of fixed cost a business must bear when establishing an overseas facility

   D. the size of the foreign market

5. California, New York, Texas, Illinois and New Jersey in the USA, Tokyo in Japan, and the coastal regions in China have some similarities except _____.

   A. well-developed infrastructures

   B. large population

   C. suppliers, skills

   D. innovative capabilities

Part Two Case Study

US COMPANIES CHOOSE: NATIONAL MULTINATIONAL OR "A-NATIONAL"?

When Isaac Merritt Singer set up a branch of his sewing machine maker in Paris in 1855, he probably did not think he was blazing a trail US companies would still be following more than 150 years later. Singer's expansion in France turned the New York-based company into the first US multinational, pioneering a business model that would be adopted by other icons of American capitalism, from Ford to Standard Oil to General Electric.

But perhaps the most important legacy of Singer's daring move is that it worked: within six years of the French opening, foreign sales had exceeded US revenues. It is a lesson not lost on today's corporate leaders.

As the US economy is squeezed by a housing slump, credit turmoil and higher fuel prices, a gap has opened up between companies with large overseas operations and those focused on the domestic market. The second-quarter results season drawing to a close has provided the starkest evidence yet of this trend.

Over the past three months, blue-chips such as General Electric, the conglomerate, IBM, the technology giant, and UPS, the logistics group, have hitched a ride on a global economy growing faster than the US. By contrast, companies that depend on domestic consumers such as Wal-Mart, the retail bell-wether, and Home Depot, the do-it-yourself chain, have released disappointing results and gloomy predictions.

"US companies are in the midst of an unprecedented boom in global earnings," wrote Joseph Quinlan, chief market strategist for Bank of America, in a recent note to clients. "The second-quarter earnings season was a tale of two earnings: robust overseas earnings ... versus weak/soft domestic earnings".

This dichotomy has been reflected in US stock markets, particularly during the past few weeks as investors have run for cover from domestic woes. After monitoring more than 40 stock-picking techniques, Merrill Lynch analysts concluded that buying shares in S&P500 companies with the highest percentage of international sales was the second-best performing investment strategy this year.

But if foreign earnings have helped US multinationals stave off a fall in profitability, the question is whether the current reliance on the rest of the world is just a cyclical phase or the harbinger of a transformation in corporate America.

Could the importance of overseas markets destroy — as Sam Palmisano, IBM's chief executive, has argued — the old multinational model whereby companies decentralized manufacturing and sales operations but kept key functions such as the executive office, research and product design in the "home country"? And if so, are some US companies ready to become truly "transnational" by scattering their top executives around the world?

At first sight, there are significant cyclical forces behind the recent rise of US multinationals — forces, in other words, that could change in the near future.

First, the dollar has lost nearly a third of its value against America's largest trading partners over the past seven years, making it easier for US exporters to sell to the world and boosting the dollar value of overseas earnings.

Second, US multinationals have been boosted by global economic growth, which has largely been driven by emerging markets hungry for infrastructure and consumer goods — two of America Inc's strongest suits.

But macro-economic and trade factors are only part of the reason overseas profits of US companies are about to register a record 20th consecutive quarter of double-digit growth. US executives argue that they are reaping the benefits of decades of investment aimed at shifting their companies' centre of gravity away from the domestic market.

"This is not something that has just happened," says David Abney, chief operating officer of UPS, a company that, with its main rival FedEx, is both a chief beneficiary and key facilitator of global trade. "We first saw it coming 30 years ago and began redoubling our efforts after the fall of the Berlin Wall and the subsequent collapse of trade barriers around the world."

Building a business that spans time zones and countries, not to mention a myriad of customers, government, regulations and cultures, is neither easy nor quick. Alexander Cutler, chief executive of Eaton, the diversified manufacturer, recalls that when he took over in 2000, its overseas operations were struggling. "We had these foreign outposts that were supposed to defeat the cyclicality of the US business but we had soldiers dying on the ramparts every day," he recalls. After an extensive period of rebuilding, Eaton now derives nearly half of its revenues from outside the US.

For some experts, such radical transformations have been more common among US companies than their foreign rivals for two key reasons: corporate America's constant need to satisfy demanding investors and the presence of fewer regulatory and labour constraints in a country renowned for its free-market spirit.

But even if economic changes and internal revolutions at companies mean, in the words of Steve Mills, head of IBM's global software business, that "things cannot go back to the way they were", will more companies abandon national allegiance and become truly "a-national"?

"Big Blue" — as IBM is known — claims to be just that, with operations in more than 150 countries and key functions spread around the world. Its head of procurement, for example, is based in Shenzhen, China, half a world away from Mr. Palmisano's headquarters in Armonk, New York. "Ours is a boundary-less way of thinking," says Mr. Mills.

Halliburton, the oil services group run by Dick Cheney before he became US vice-president, recently followed the petrodollars trail and moved its chief executive from Houston to Dubai.

However, many US chief executives regard such moves as impractical, if not outright dangerous. They argue that being rooted in the US is not only an insurance policy in case the globalization tide turns, but also a way of maintaining order and focus in increasingly complex and disperse enterprises — of letting everybody know where the bucks stops and who is in charge.

Jeffrey Immelt, who heads GE, one of the most "global" companies in the US, recently distilled this view: "We're an American company but in order to be successful we've got to win in every corner of the world."

In other words, global aspirations tinged with national pride — which Singer would have understood — is just as recognizable today among US business leaders.

Questions for Discussion

1. The MNC (multinational corporation) plays a central part in the world. Do you think what is the multinational corporations' responsibilities?

2. "We're an American company but in order to be successful we've got to win in every corner of the world." How do you understand the sentence?

Translation

1. As the US economy is squeezed by a housing slump, credit turmoil and higher fuel prices, a gap has opened up between companies with large overseas operations and those focused on the domestic market.

2. This dichotomy has been reflected in US stock markets, particularly during the past few weeks as investors have run for cover from domestic woes.

3. But if foreign earnings have helped US multinationals stave off a fall in profitability, the question is whether the current reliance on the rest of the world is just a cyclical phase or the harbinger of a transformation in corporate America.

4. First, the dollar has lost nearly a third of its value against America's largest trading partners over the past seven years, making it easier for US exporters to sell to the world and boosting the dollar value of overseas earnings.

Unit 18 Investment and Multinational Corporation

5. For some experts, such radical transformations have been more common among US companies than their foreign rivals for two key reasons: corporate America's constant need to satisfy demanding investors and the presence of fewer regulatory and labour constraints in a country renowned for its free-market spirit.

Unit 19
International Financial Market

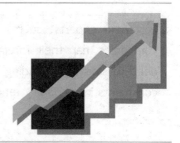

Introduction

A financial market is a market for the exchange of capital and credit, including the money markets and the capital markets. It serves six basic functions, briefly listed below.

➤ Borrowing and Lending: Financial markets permit the transfer of funds (purchasing power) from one agent to another for either investment or consumption purposes.

➤ Price Determination: Financial markets provide vehicles by which prices are set both for newly issued financial assets and for the existing stock of financial assets.

➤ Information Aggregation and Coordination: Financial markets act as collectors and aggregators of information about financial asset values and the flow of funds from lenders to borrowers.

➤ Risk Sharing: Financial markets allow a transfer of risk from those who undertake investments to those who provide funds for those investments.

➤ Liquidity: Financial markets provide the holders of financial assets with a chance to resell or liquidate these assets.

➤ Efficiency: Financial markets reduce transaction costs and information costs.

Part One Text

In attempting to characterize the way financial markets operate, one must consider both the various types of financial institutions that participate in such markets and the various ways in which these markets are structured.

Who Are the Major Players in Financial Markets?

By definition, financial institutions are institutions that participate in financial markets, i.e., in the creation and/or exchange of financial assets. At present in the United States, financial institutions can be roughly classified into the following four categories: brokers, dealers, investment banks, and financial intermediaries.

1. Brokers

A broker is a commissioned agent of a buyer (or seller) who facilitates trade by locating a seller (or buyer) to complete the desired transaction. A broker does not take a position in the assets he or she trades — that is, the broker does not maintain inventories in these assets. The profits of brokers are determined by the commissions they charge to the users of their services (either the buyers, the sellers, or both). Examples of brokers include real estate brokers and stock brokers.

2. Dealers

Like brokers, dealers facilitate trade by matching buyers with sellers of assets; they do not engage in asset transformation. Unlike brokers, however, a dealer can and does "take positions" (i.e., maintain inventories) in the assets he or she trades that permit the dealer to sell out of inventory rather than always having to locate sellers to match every offer to buy. Also, unlike brokers, dealers do not receive sales commissions. Rather, dealers make profits by buying assets at relatively low prices and reselling them at relatively high prices (buy low, sell high). The price at which a dealer offers to sell an asset (the "asked price") minus the price at which a dealer offers to buy an asset (the "bid price") is called the bid-ask spread and represents the dealer's profit margin on the asset exchange. Real-world examples of dealers include car dealers, dealers in US government bonds, and Nasdaq stock dealers.

3. Investment Banks

An investment bank assists in the initial sale of newly issued securities (i.e., in IPOs, Initial Public Offerings) by engaging in a number of different activities.
- Advice: Advising corporations on whether they should issue bonds or stock, and, for bond issues, on the particular types of payment schedules these securities should offer.
- Underwriting: Guaranteeing corporations a price on the securities they offer, either individually or by having several different investment banks form a

syndicate to underwrite the issue jointly.
- Sales Assistance: Assisting in the sale of these securities to the public.

Some of the best-known international investment banking firms are Morgan Stanley, Merrill Lynch, Salomon Brothers, First Boston Corporation, and Goldman Sachs.

4. Financial Intermediaries

Unlike brokers, dealers, and investment banks, financial intermediaries are financial institutions that engage in financial asset transformation. That is, financial intermediaries purchase one kind of financial asset from borrowers — generally some kind of long-term loan contract whose terms are adapted to the specific circumstances of the borrower (e.g., a mortgage) — and sell a different kind of financial asset to savers, generally some kind of relatively liquid claim against the financial intermediary (e.g., a deposit account). In addition, unlike brokers and dealers, financial intermediaries typically hold financial assets as part of an investment portfolio rather than as an inventory for resale. In addition to making profits on their investment portfolios, financial intermediaries make profits by charging relatively high interest rates to borrowers and paying relatively low interest rates to savers.

Types of financial intermediaries include: Depository Institutions (commercial banks, savings and loan associations, mutual savings banks, credit unions); Contractual Savings Institutions (life insurance companies, fire and casualty insurance companies, pension funds, government retirement funds); and Investment Intermediaries (finance companies, stock and bond mutual funds, money market mutual funds).

However, these four types of financial institutions are simplified idealized classifications, and many actual financial institutions in the fast-changing financial landscape today engage in activities that overlap two or more of these classifications, or even to some extent fall outside these classifications. A prime example is Merrill Lynch, which simultaneously acts as a broker, a dealer (taking positions in certain stocks and bonds it sells), a financial intermediary (e.g., through its provision of mutual funds and CMA checkable deposit accounts), and an investment banker.

What Types of Financial Market Structures Exist?

The costs of collecting and aggregating information determine, to a large extent, the types of financial market structures that emerge. These structures take four basic forms.
- Auction markets conducted through brokers.
- Over-the-counter (OTC) markets conducted through dealers.
- Organized exchanges, such as the New York Stock Exchange, which combine auction and OTC market features. Specifically, organized exchanges permit

buyers and sellers to trade with each other in a centralized location, like an auction. However, securities are traded on the floor of the exchange with the help of specialist traders who combine broker and dealer functions. The specialists broker trades but also stand ready to buy and sell stocks from personal inventories if buy and sell orders do not match up.

➢ Intermediation financial markets conducted through financial intermediaries.

Financial markets taking the first three forms are generally referred to as securities markets. Some financial markets combine features from more than one of these categories, so the categories constitute only rough guidelines.

1. Auction Markets

An auction market is some form of centralized facility (or clearing house) by which buyers and sellers, through their commissioned agents (brokers), execute trades in an open and competitive bidding process. The "centralized facility" is not necessarily a place where buyers and sellers physically meet. Rather, it is any institution that provides buyers and sellers with a centralized access to the bidding process. All of the needed information about offers to buy (bid prices) and offers to sell (asked prices) is centralized in one location which is readily accessible to all would-be buyers and sellers, e. g., through a computer network. No private exchanges between individual buyers and sellers are made outside of the centralized facility.

An auction market is typically a public market in the sense that it opens to all agents who wish to participate. Auction markets can either be call markets — such as art auctions — for which bid and asked prices are all posted at one time, or continuous markets — such as stock exchanges and real estate markets — for which bid and asked prices can be posted at any time the market is open and exchanges take place on a continual basis. Experimental economists have devoted a tremendous amount of attention in recent years to auction markets.

Many auction markets trade in relatively homogeneous assets (e. g., Treasury bills, notes, and bonds) to cut down on information costs. Alternatively, some auction markets (e. g., in second-hand jewelry, furniture, paintings etc.) allow would-be buyers to inspect the goods to be sold prior to the opening of the actual bidding process. This inspection can take the form of a warehouse tour, a catalog issued with pictures and descriptions of items to be sold, or (in televised auctions) a time during which assets are simply displayed one by one to viewers prior to bidding. Auction markets depend on participation for any one type of asset not being too "thin". The costs of collecting information about any one type of asset are sunk costs independent of the volume of trading in that asset. Consequently, auction markets depend on volume to spread these costs over a wide number of participants.

2. Over-the-Counter Markets

An over-the-counter market has no centralized mechanism or facility for trading. Instead, the market is a public market consisting of a number of dealers spread across a region, a country, or indeed the world, who make the market in some type of asset. That is, the dealers themselves post bid and asked prices for this asset and then stand ready to buy or sell units of this asset with anyone who chooses to trade at these posted prices. The dealers provide customers more flexibility in trading than brokers, because dealers can offset imbalances in the demand and supply of assets by trading out of their own accounts. Many well-known common stocks are traded over-the-counter in the United States through NASDAQ (National Association of Securities Dealers Automated Quotations).

3. Intermediation Financial Markets

An intermediation financial market is a financial market in which financial intermediaries help transfer funds from savers to borrowers by issuing certain types of financial assets to savers and receiving other types of financial assets from borrowers. The financial assets issued to savers are claims against the financial intermediaries, hence liabilities of the financial intermediaries, whereas the financial assets received from borrowers are claims against the borrowers, hence assets of the financial intermediaries.

Words and Expressions

aggregation	n.	聚合，总合，集合
liquidity	n.	流动性
broker	n.	掮客，经纪人
dealer	n.	经销商，交易员
offer	n.	报盘，报价
securities	n.	有价证券，证券
underwrite	v.	签名于下，给……保险
syndicate	n.	企业联合，辛迪加，财团
casualty	n.	灾祸，意外
pension	n.	养老金，退职金，津贴
real estate		房地产，房地产所有权
asked price		买方报价
bid price		出价，标价
bid-ask spread		买卖差价

1. stock 股票

   Stock is a type of security that signifies ownership in a corporation and represents a claim on part of the corporation's assets and earnings. There are two main types of stock: common and preferred. Common stock usually entitles the owner to vote at shareholders' meetings and to receive dividends. Preferred stock generally does not have voting rights, but has a higher claim on assets and earnings than the common shares.

2. financial assets 金融资产

   It is an asset that derives value because of a contractual claim. Stocks, bonds, bank deposits, and the like are all examples of financial assets.

3. investment banker 投资银行家,投资银行

   It is an individual or institution which acts as an underwriter or agent for corporations and municipalities issuing securities. Most also maintain broker/dealer operations, maintain markets for previously issued securities, and offer advisory services to investors.

4. inventory 存货,盘存

   It refers to the securities bought by a broker or dealer in order to resell them. For the period that the broker or dealer holds the securities in inventory, he/she is bearing the risk related to the securities, which may change in price.

5. NASDAQ (National Association of Securities Dealers Automated Quotations) 纳斯达克(全美证券交易商协会自动报价系统)

   It is a computerized system established by the NASD(全美证券交易商协会) to facilitate trading by providing broker/dealers with current bid and ask price quotes on over-the-counter stocks and some listed stocks. The Nasdaq does not have a physical trading floor that brings together buyers and sellers. Instead, all trading on the Nasdaq exchange is done over a network of computers and telephones. Also, the Nasdaq does not employ market specialists to buy unfilled orders.

6. initial public offering (IPO) 首次公开发行

   It refers to the first sale of stock by a private company to the public. IPOs are often issued by smaller, younger companies seeking capital to expand, but can also be done by large privately-owned companies looking to become publicly traded.

7. **Morgan Stanley (MS)** 摩根史坦利

   It is one of the largest and the most reputed investment banks headquartered in New York City.

8. **Merrill Lynch** 美林

   Merrill Lynch & Co., Inc., through its subsidiaries and affiliates, provides capital markets services, investment banking and advisory services, wealth management, asset management, insurance, banking and related products and services on a global basis. The firm's global headquarters is located in New York City, and it is one of the most recognizable names in financial services.

9. **Salomon Brothers** 所罗门兄弟

   Salomon Brothers was once a Wall Street investment bank founded in 1910. It remained a partnership until the early 1980s, when it was acquired by the commodity trading firm then known as Phibro Corporation. Eventually Salomon was acquired by Travelers Group in 1998, and following the latter´s merger with Citicorp Salomon became part of Citigroup.

10. **First Boston Corporation** 第一波士顿公司

    First Boston Corporation was a New York-based investment bank, founded in 1932 and acquired by Credit Suisse in 1988, when it became "CS First Boston". Globally referred to as Credit Suisse First Boston after 1996, the First Boston part of the name was phased out in 2006.

11. **Goldman Sachs** 高盛

    The Goldman Sachs Group, Inc., or simply Goldman Sachs (NYSE: GS) is one of the world's largest global investment banks. Goldman Sachs was founded in 1869, and is headquartered in the Lower Manhattan area of New York City at 85 Broad Street.

12. **over-the-counter (OTC)** 场外交易

    Over-the-counter trading is to trade financial instruments such as stocks, bonds, commodities or derivatives directly between two parties. It is the opposite of exchange trading which occurs on futures exchanges or stock exchange.

13. **New York Stock Exchange (NYSE)** 纽约证券交易所

    NYSE is a corporation, operated by a board of directors, responsible for listing securities, setting policies and supervising the stock exchange and its member activities. The NYSE also oversees the transfer of members' seats on the Exchange, judging whether a potential applicant is qualified to be a specialist.

Unit 19 International Financial Market

Exercises

I Make verb phrases by linking those in Column A and Column B.

Column A	Column B
charge	the assets
liquidate	a seller
locate	trade
engage	in asset transformation
facilitate	the commissions

II Match the following words or terms with their definitions.

bond	credit	auction	mortgage	dealer
casualty	pension	contract	savings	intermediary

1. _____ : a monetary amount that is added to an account balance
2. _____ : a third party who facilitates a deal between two other parties
3. _____ : an individual or entity which buys and sells products and holds an inventory
4. _____ : a loan in which property is used as security for the debt
5. _____ : a legally binding arrangement between parties
6. _____ : a public sale in which property or items of merchandise are sold to the highest bidder
7. _____ : liability or loss resulting from an accident
8. _____ : money saved; an amount of money saved
9. _____ : a debt instrument issued for a period of more than one year with the purpose of raising capital by borrowing
10. _____ : a sum of money paid regularly as a retirement benefit or by way of patronage

III Reading comprehension: choose the best answer from the four choices.

1. Which of the following is not a financial institution?
   A. Brokers. B. Dealers.
   C. Investment bankers. D. Organized exchanges.
2. According to the text, which of the descriptions of the dealers is not true?

A. Dealers do not engage in asset transformation.
B. Dealers maintain inventories in the assets they trade.
C. Dealers receive sales commissions.
D. Dealers make profits by asset exchange.

3. Which of the following statements of financial institutions is not true?
   A. Brokers make profits by charging commissions of their services.
   B. Financial intermediaries engage in financial asset transformation.
   C. Investment banks assist in the sale of newly issued securities to the public.
   D. Financial intermediaries hold financial assets as an inventory for resale.

4. Which of the statements of financial market structures is false?
   A. Auction markets, OTC markets, organized exchanges and intermediation financial markets are four basic forms of financial market structures.
   B. Organized exchanges combine auction and intermediation financial markets features.
   C. Auction markets, OTC markets and organized exchanges are referred to as securities markets.
   D. New York Stock Exchange is an organized exchange.

5. Which of the following statements is not true?
   A. A financial market is a market for the exchange of capital and credit.
   B. A financial market includes the money markets and the capital markets.
   C. Financial markets increase transaction costs and information costs.
   D. Financial markets provide the holders of financial assets with a chance to resell or liquidate these assets.

Part Two Case Study

FIRMS NOT READY FOR GLOBAL GROWTH

By **Pauline Skypala**
From *Financial Times*, Tuesday, July 17, 2007

Financial markets worldwide are set to grow dramatically, particularly in emerging markets, but few financial firms are in a position to capitalise on this growth.

The universal banks, such as Citigroup, Deutsche Bank, HSBC and JPMorgan, that operate in both retail and institutional markets worldwide, are widely seen as the most likely to succeed, given their global presence. But when considered on the basis of their capabilities in areas viewed as key drivers of shareholder value, they are outclassed by specialist competitors.

This is supported by financial analysis that shows specialists have enjoyed higher revenue growth and better margins than universal banks over the past five years. "Every type of specialist manager outperformed universal banks," said Suzanne Dence, managing consultant for the financial markets industry at the IBM Institute for Business Value, and co-author of an exhaustive new report on global financial markets.

The report, based on interviews with more than 800 senior financial markets executives and more than 100 of their corporate clients, predicts a doubling of worldwide investable assets to nearly $300,000 bn (€21,000 bn, 149,000 bn) by 2015, and a rise to $700,000 bn by 2025. But 60 per cent of this is expected to come from emerging markets, including South Korea, Mexico, Poland and Turkey, as well as China, India and Russia.

Brazil, one of the major emerging markets, is not on the list because it is not expected to develop a sophisticated financial sector. Growth in sophistication is one of the main determinants of investable asset size, the other being GDP per capita growth.

"The question is: will financial markets firms be looking in the right places? And will they be capable of capturing these more globally dispersed opportunities?" said Ms Dence.

Industry leaders would be firms that "successfully specialize around what clients value most and become fluid, adaptable, globally integrated enterprises".

The report found a disparity between what clients said they were willing to pay for and what providers thought they would value. For example, clients ranked the ability to provide a "one-stop-shop" and best-of-breed products at the bottom of their lists, "calling into question many of today's dominant business models".

This was a concern, said Ms Dence. One of the main reasons why globalization presents an opportunity is to broaden the client base. "If you don't understand your client base at the moment, how can you broaden it?"

She named Goldman Sachs and Barclays Global Investors as examples of firms likely to be successful in exploiting global opportunities. Goldman views risk as a strategic competitive advantage rather than as a tool and has been effective at delivering consistent client service throughout the world.

BGI grew up as a passive index player, but realised the need to assume risk to counteract margin compression on the passive side and is now one of the largest hedge fund managers.

"The key is to specialise in what clients will pay for, given your capabilities," said Ms Dence. Both firms also have a strong culture. "Culture is the number one barrier to an organisation's ability to profit from globalization, but also the number one enabler," she said.

Ms Dence also pointed to State Street's partnership with a university in China as an example of successful use of alliances to enter new markets, seen as an important way forward.

The industry in general was not ready for the partnering approach, said Ms Dence, and did not rank it as significant for global operating capability. Compared with other industries, financial firms have far fewer, far shallower and less successful alliances, largely because of their culture.

Get global. Get specialised. Or get out. Unexpected lessons in global financial markets.

 Questions for Discussion

1. Why are the universal banks which are widely seen as the most likely to capitalize on the growth of financial market actually outclassed by specialist competitors?

_____
_____

2. According to Dence's report, the clients and the banks have different opinions of what the clients would value. Whose opinion should be more respected and why?

_____
_____

3. From the examples of Goldman Sachs and BGI, what can the financial market firms learn about how to capture the opportunities presented by globalization?

_____
_____

4. In your own opinion, what opportunities or advantages can partnering approach bring to the financial firms for their global operating capability?

_____
_____
_____

 Translation

1. Growth in sophistication is one of the main determinants of investable asset size, the other being GDP per capita growth.

_____
_____

2. Industry leaders would be firms that "successfully specialise around what clients value most and become fluid, adaptable, globally integrated enterprises".

3. For example, clients ranked the ability to provide a "one-stop-shop" and best-of-breed products at the bottom of their lists, "calling into question many of today's dominant business models".

4. BGI grew up as a passive index player, but realised the need to assume risk to counteract margin compression on the passive side and is now one of the largest hedge fund managers.

Unit 20
Foreign Exchange Market

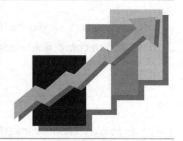

Introduction

The movement of financial assets and goods and services reflected in the balance of payments takes place between many different countries, each with its own domestic currency. Economic interaction can only occur in this instance if there is a specific link between currencies so that the value of a given transaction can be determined by both parties in their own respective currencies. This important link is the foreign exchange rate. This text examines how this link is established in the foreign exchange market and underlying economic factors that influence it. The principal components of the market are analyzed and various measures of the exchange rate discussed.

Part One Text

The foreign exchange rate is simply the price of one currency in terms of another (for example, US$/UK£ or, alternatively, UK£/US$). Not surprisingly, this price can be viewed as the result of the interaction of the forces of supply and demand for the foreign currency in any particular period of time. Although this price is fixed under some monetary system arrangements, if a country is to avoid continual BOP surpluses or deficits, the fixed exchange rate must be approximately that which would result from market determination of the exchange rate. We will therefore proceed to examine the foreign exchange rate assuming that it is the result of the normal market interaction of supply and demand. This market simultaneously determines hundreds of different exchange rates daily and facilitates the hundreds of thousands of international transactions that take place. This worldwide network of markets and institutions that handle the exchange of foreign currencies is known as the foreign exchange market. Within the foreign exchange market, current transactions for immediate delivery are carried out in the spot market and contracts to buy or sell currencies for future delivery are carried out in forward and futures markets.

Demand Side

Individuals participate in the foreign exchange market for a number of reasons. On the demand side, one of the principal reasons people desire foreign currencies is to purchase goods and services from another country or to send a gift or investment income payments abroad. For example, the desire to purchase a foreign automobile or to travel abroad produces a demand for the currency of the country in which these goods or services are produced. A second important reason to acquire foreign currency is to purchase financial assets in a particular country. The desire to open a foreign bank account, purchase foreign stocks or bonds, or acquire direct ownership of real capital would fall into this category. A third reason that individuals demand foreign exchange is to avoid losses or make profits that could arise through changes in the foreign exchange rate. Individuals who believe that the foreign currency is going to become more valuable in the future may wish to acquire that currency today at a low price in hopes of selling it tomorrow at a high price and thus make a quick profit. Such risk-taking activity is referred to as speculation in a foreign currency. Other individuals who have to pay for an imported item in the future may wish to acquire the needed foreign currency today, rather than risk the possibility that the foreign currency will become more valuable in the future and would increase the cost of the item in local currency. Activity undertaken to avoid the risk associated with changes in the exchange rate is referred to as hedging. The total demand for a foreign currency at any one point in time thus reflects these three underlying demands: the demand for foreign goods and services (and transfers and investment income payments abroad), the demand for foreign investment; and the demand based on risk-taking or risk-avoidance activity.

Supply Side

Participants on the supply side operate for similar reasons (reflecting credit items in the balance of payments). Foreign currency supply to the home country results firstly from foreigners purchasing home exports of goods and services or making unilateral transfers or investment income payments to the home country. For example, US exports of wheat and soybeans are a source of supply of foreign exchange. A second source arises from foreign investment in the home country. Foreign purchases of US government bonds, European purchases of US stocks and placement of bank deposits in the United States, and Japanese joint ventures in US, automobile or electronics plants are all examples of financial activity that provides a supply of foreign exchange to the United States. Finally, foreign speculation and hedging activities can provide yet a third source of supply. The total supply of foreign exchange in any time period consists of these three sources.

Now, let us discuss in a general way how foreign exchange market operates (See Figure 20-1). The foreign exchange market here is presented from the US perspective and, like any normal market, contains a downward-sloped demand curve and an upward-sloped supply curve. The price on the vertical axis is stated in terms of the domestic currency price of foreign currency, for example, $\$_{us}/franc_{swiss}$, and the horizontal axis measures the units of Swiss francs supplied and demanded at various prices (exchange rates). The intersection of the supply and demand curves determines simultaneously the equilibrium exchange rate and the equilibrium quantity supplied and demanded during a given period of time. An increase in the demand for Swiss francs on the part of the United States will cause the demand curve to shift out to D'_{Sfr} and the exchange rate to increase to e'. Note that the increase in the exchange rate means that it is taking more US currency to buy each Swiss franc. When this occurs, the US dollar is said to be depreciating against the Swiss franc. In similar fashion, an increase in the supply of Swiss francs (to S'_{Sfr}) causes the supply curve to the right and the exchange rate to fall to e''. In this case, the dollar cost of the Swiss franc is decreasing and the dollar is said to be appreciating. It is important to fix this terminology in your mind. Home currency depreciation or foreign currency appreciation takes place when there is an increase in the home currency price of the foreign currency (or, alternatively, a decrease in the foreign currency price of the home currency). The home currency is

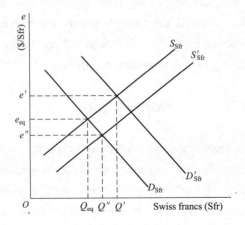

Figure 20-1 The basic foreign exchange market

thus becoming relatively less valuable. Home currency appreciation or foreign currency depreciation takes place when there is a decrease in the home currency price of foreign currency (or an increase in the foreign currency price of home currency). In this instance, the home currency is becoming relatively more valuable. Changes in the exchange rate take place in response to changes in the supply, and demand for foreign exchange at any given point in time.

The link between the balance of payments and the foreign exchange market can readily be shown using supply and demand. For purposes of this discussion, consider the supply and demand for foreign exchange as consisting of two components, one related to current account transactions and the other linked to the financial flows including the speculative and hedging activities (capital account transactions). In Figure 2, the demand and the supply of foreign exchange are each broken down in terms of these two components. Ignoring unilateral transfers, $D_{G\&S}$ and $S_{G\&S}$ portray the demand and supply of foreign exchange associated with the domestic and foreign demands for foreign and domestic goods and services, respectively. The demand and supply of foreign exchange associated with financial transactions are then added to each of the curves, creating a total demand and a total supply of foreign exchange. If the financial desire for foreign exchange is assumed to take place primarily for reasons such as expected profits, expected rates of return, and so forth (that is, for reasons independent of the exchange rate), the total curves are drawn a fixed distance from the $D_{G\&S}$ and $S_{G\&S}$ curves. If the exchange rate influences these financial flows, then the relationship between the goods and services curves and the total curves is more complex. For ease of discussion however, we proceed with the curves as drawn in Figure 20-2.

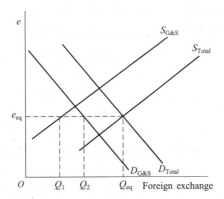

Figure 20-2　The foreign exchange market and the balance of payments

The equilibrium exchange rate is now seen to be determined by the intersection of the D_{Total} and the S_{Total} curves.

Words and Expressions

alternatively	ad.	二者择一地,作为选择地
deficit	n.	赤字
futures	n.	期货
speculation	n.	投机
unilateral	a.	单边的
axis	n.	轴

Notes

1. **spot exchange rate** 即期汇率,现货兑换率

   The spot exchange rate refers to the current exchange rate. The forward exchange rate refers to an exchange rate that is quoted and traded today but for delivery and payment on a specific future date.

2. **balance of payments (BOP)** 国际收支差额,国际收支平衡表

   The balance of payments measures the payments that flow between any individual country and all other countries. It is used to summarize all international economic transactions for that country during a specific time period, usually a year. The BOP is determined by the country's exports and imports of goods, services, and financial capital, as well as financial transfers. It reflects all payments and liabilities to foreigners (debits) and all payments and obligations received from foreigners (credits). Balance of payments is one of the major indicators of a country's status in international trade, with net capital outflow.

3. **foreign exchange market** 外汇市场

   The foreign exchange (currency, forex or FX) market exists wherever one currency is traded for another. It is by far the largest financial market in the world, and includes trading between large banks, central banks, currency speculators, multinational corporations, governments, and other financial markets and institutions.

4. **spot market** 现货市场

   The spot market or cash market is a commodities or securities market in which goods are sold for cash and delivered immediately. Contracts bought and sold on these markets are immediately effective. Spot markets can operate wherever the infrastructure exists to conduct the transaction. The Spot market for most securities exists primarily on the internet.

5. **hedging** 对冲，套购保值

   In finance, a hedge is an investment that is taken out specifically to reduce or cancel out the risk in another investment. Hedging is a strategy designed to minimize exposure to an unwanted business risk, while still allowing the business to profit from an investment activity.

6. **currency depreciation** 货币贬值，通货贬值

   Currency depreciation is the loss of value of a country's currency with respect to one or more foreign reference currencies, typically in a floating exchange rate system. It is most often used for the unofficial increase of the exchange rate due to market forces, though sometimes it appears interchangeably with devaluation.

7. **currency appreciation** 货币升值，通货升值

   Currency appreciation means that the given currency has become more valuable with respect to another currency.

I Make verb phrases by linking those in Column A and Column B.

Column A	Column B
open	in the foreign exchange market
purchase	foreign currency
participate	an account
avoid	BOP deficit
acquire	goods and services

II Match the following words or terms with their definitions.

appreciation	fund	speculation	deposit	delivery
deficit	depreciation	hedging	exchange	futures

1. _____: a situation in which liabilities exceed assets, expenditures exceed income, imports exceed exports, or losses exceed profits

2. _____: voluntary transfer of title or possession from one party to another

3. _____: taking large risks, especially with respect to trying to predict the future

4. _____: money transferred into a customer's account at a financial institution

5. _____: the increase in value of an asset

6. _____: a decline in the value of a given currency in comparison with other currencies

7. _____: to give in return for something received; trade

8. _____: commodities or stocks bought or sold upon agreement of delivery in time to come

9. _____: cash, securities, or other assets designated for a specified purpose

10. _____: an investment or strategy designed to reduce or cancel out the risk in another investment, or to minimize exposure to an unwanted business risk

III Reading comprehension: choose the best answer from the four choices.

1. If the EUR/USD exchange rate is 1.3, then 10 EUR = _____ USD.
   A. 10   B. 13   C. 7.7   D. 1.3

2. Individuals do not desire foreign currency when they _____.
   A. want to purchase a foreign automobile
   B. plan to travel abroad
   C. desire to purchase foreign stocks
   D. believe the foreign currency is going to become less valuable in the future

3. Which of the following is not the source of the supply of foreign exchange?
   A. Foreigners purchasing of home exports of goods and services.
   B. Foreigners making unilateral transfers to the foreign country.
   C. Foreign investment in the home country.
   D. Foreign speculation and hedging activities.

4. Which of the following statements is not true?
   A. Home currency depreciation takes place when there is an increase in the home currency price of the foreign currency.
   B. Foreign currency appreciation takes place when there is a decrease in the home currency price of the foreign currency.
   C. Home currency appreciation takes place when there is a decrease in the home

currency price of foreign currency.

D. Foreign currency depreciation takes place when there is an increase in the foreign currency price of home currency.

Part Two Case Study

THE LESSONS ASIANS LEARNT FROM THEIR FINANCIAL CRISIS

By **Martin Wolf**
From *Financial Times*, Wednesday, May 30, 2007

The Asian financial crisis of 10 years ago taught two contrasting lessons: the one the majority of western economists thought the Asians should learn; and the one Asians did learn.

The western economists concluded that emerging economies should adopt flexible exchange rates and modern, well-regulated and competitive financial markets. The Asians decided to choose competitive exchange rates, export-led growth and huge accumulations of foreign currency reserves. The question is whether the Asians need to change their choice. The answer, I believe, is "yes".

When downward pressure on the Thai baht started 10 years ago, nobody expected what followed - its devaluation in early July. That seemingly small event generated a financial tsunami that engulfed most of east Asia and overwhelmed Indonesia, Malaysia, the Philippines, South Korea and Thailand. Exchange rates collapsed, financial systems went bankrupt, governments teetered on the edge of default and economies succumbed to deep recessions. Officials from the International Monetary Fund raced from one crisis-hit country to the next. In its last movements, the crisis went global, overwhelming Russia in August 1998 and Brazil in early 1999.

As surprising as the onset of the Asian crisis has been its aftermath. With the important, but geographically limited, exceptions of Argentina and Turkey in 2001, the crises of 1997 – 1998 have so far been the last in the long series of financial crises that afflicted emerging economies in the 1980s and 1990s. Today, the desire of outside investors to put their money in these economies is overwhelming, as is shown in the strength of their financial markets, the low spreads on external borrowing and the size of the private capital inflow: in 2006, for example, net private capital flow to emerging economies was $256 bn. The IMF is now almost entirely out of business.

What explains this new stability? As Nouriel Roubini of New York University's Stern

School of Business argues, the Asians did not learn the lessons most western economists thought they should. This is not to deny that there have been substantial structural improvements in Asian economies, notably in the capitalization and regulation of financial systems. But this is not the heart of the matter. The big event has been elsewhere: the great mistake, Asian policymakers concluded, was not pegged, but overvalued, exchange rates. That error was what had brought the humiliating dictation by IMF officials operating under the thumb of the US Treasury.

"Never again" became the watchword. Never again has been the result. Now the east Asian emerging economies are mostly creditor nations. Moreover, much of their accumulation of external assets is in official hands (see chart). By February of this year, the foreign currency reserves of east and south Asian countries had reached \$3,280 bn, up by \$2,490 bn since the beginning of 1999. China's reserves alone reached \$1,160 bn, up by \$1,010 bn over the same period. While a substantial accumulation of reserves seemed a justified (if expensive) form of insurance in the aftermath of the crisis, today's levels look excessive. In most east Asian economies the ratio of reserves to short-term foreign currency debt is four or five to one.

The scale of the reserve accumulation demonstrates the obvious: these countries have refused to adopt the freely floating exchange rates many outside economists recommended. They have, instead, chosen to keep their exchange rates down. This, in turn, has generated current account surpluses. Sustaining such surpluses requires a stable excess of savings over domestic investment. <u>One instrument they have used has been sterilization of the monetary consequences of reserve accumulations, to prevent the normal expansion of money and credit, overheating, inflation and so loss of external competitiveness.</u>

If a substantial part of the world economy is generating huge current account surpluses, somebody else has to run offsetting deficits. That conclusion became still more potent when oil prices soared, since this shifted income to countries that painful experience has taught not to spend their additional revenue quickly. In a world of fluctuating currencies, however, accumulating large quantities of net foreign liabilities is easiest for countries able to borrow freely in their own currencies. The reason is simple: only such countries can borrow without risking significant currency mismatches inside their financial systems. <u>It is no accident then that the US has emerged as the world's chief deficit country — its "borrower of last resort".</u> It alone is able to be a vast net borrower without risking the health of its financial system.

So is what some economists have called "Bretton Woods Two" — a fixed exchange rate system anchored on the US dollar — both the answer to financial instability in emerging market economies and a basis for sustainable export-led growth?

Mr. Roubini argues that it is not. The policy generates ultimately unsterilizable increases in foreign currency reserves. This causes excess monetary growth, domestic asset price bubbles, overheating, inflation and the loss in competitiveness that governments had tried to prevent by suppressing the rises in nominal exchange rates. It distorts domestic financial systems, by pushing interest rates below equilibrium levels. It generates a waste of resources in accumulation of low-yielding foreign currency assets exposed to the likelihood of huge capital losses. It makes Asian economies excessively dependent on demand from outside the region. It exacerbates US protectionism. Finally, it compels US monetary authorities to sustain easy monetary policy, in order to offset the leakage from domestic demand caused by the huge current account deficits.

The post-crisis policy system has proved more durable than many (including myself) expected. At its heart, however, is China. Though not affected directly by the crisis, it was one of the countries that learnt its lessons in the Asian way. Today's result is a dynamic behemoth accumulating foreign currency reserves at a rate of $50 bn a month in the first quarter of the year and expected by the IMF to generate a current account surplus of 10 per cent of gross domestic product this year. I do not believe these astonishing trends are desirable or sustainable. Why that is so and what to do about it I intend to discuss next week.

Questions for Discussion

1. Why should the Asians change their choice of competitive exchange rates, export-led growth and huge accumulations of foreign currency reserves?

   _____
   _____
   _____

2. The Asian countries chose to low down their exchange rates and accumulated substantial foreign currency reserves after the crisis, but today the levels of the reserves seem excessive. So, what consequences would the excessive reserve accumulation bring about?

   _____
   _____
   _____

3. If the "Bretton Woods Two" is adopted to maintain financial stability and sustainable export-led growth of the Asian countries, will it work? And why?

   _____
   _____

4. From the passage, what lessons do you think China should learn from the Asian financial crisis?

Translation

1. Exchange rates collapsed, financial systems went bankrupt, governments teetered on the edge of default and economies succumbed to deep recessions.

2. Today, the desire of outside investors to put their money in these economies is overwhelming, as is shown in the strength of their financial markets, the low spreads on external borrowing and the size of the private capital inflow: in 2006, for example, net private capital flow to emerging economies was $256 bn.

3. One instrument they have used has been sterilisation of the monetary consequences of reserve accumulations, to prevent the normal expansion of money and credit, overheating, inflation and so loss of external competitiveness.

4. It is no accident then that the US has emerged as the world's chief deficit country — its "borrower of last resort".

References

[1] COULTHARD M. An introduction to discourse analysis. Longman, 1977.
[2] DENNIS R A, ALFRED J F, Jr. International economics. 3rd ed. New York: McGraw-Hill, 1998.
[3] DOLAN E G, LINDSEY D. Macroeconomics. Orlando: The Dryden Press, 1991.
[4] FLESHER B M, EDWARD J R, THOMAS J K. Principles of macroeconomics. Simom & Schuster Higher Education Publishing Group, 1989.
[5] FRANK R H, BEN S B. Principles of macroeconomics. 2nd ed. Beijing: Tsinghua University Press, 2003.
[6] FLYNN S M. Economics for dummies. New York: Wiley Publishing Inc., 2005.
[7] MANKIW N G. Principles of macroeconomics. Orlando: Harcourt College Publishers, 2001.
[8] MCCONNELL C R, STANLEY L B. Economics. 17th ed. New York: McGraw-Hill/Irwin, 2006.
[9] SOWELL T. Basic economics: a common sense guide to the economy. 3rd ed. New York: Basic Books, 2007.
[10] SWALES M. Genre analysis: English in academic and research setting. London: Cambridge University Press, 1990.
[11] 陈威, 赵凌. 世纪商务英语综合教程. 大连: 大连理工大学出版社, 2004.
[12] 帅建林. 国际贸易实务. 北京: 对外经济贸易大学出版社, 2007.